BEHIND
THE SIGNS

BEHIND THE SIGNS

A JOURNEY THROUGH HOMELESSNESS

Kirk Toncray

iUniverse, Inc.
Bloomington

BEHIND THE SIGNS
A Journey through Homelessness

iUniverse books may be ordered through booksellers or by contacting:

iUniverse
1663 Liberty Drive
Bloomington, IN 47403
www.iuniverse.com
1-800-Authors (1-800-288-4677)

Because of the dynamic nature of the Internet, any web addresses or links contained in this book may have changed since publication and may no longer be valid. The views expressed in this work are solely those of the author and do not necessarily reflect the views of the publisher, and the publisher hereby disclaims any responsibility for them.

Any people depicted in stock imagery provided by Thinkstock are models, and such images are being used for illustrative purposes only.
Certain stock imagery © Thinkstock.

ISBN: 978-1-4759-5456-2 (sc)
ISBN: 978-1-4759-5457-9 (hc)
ISBN: 978-1-4759-5455-5 (ebk)

Library of Congress Control Number: 2012919119

Printed in the United States of America

iUniverse rev. date: 10/19/2012

CONTENTS

DEDICATION

In honorable memory for those who suffered the difficult journey with me during the most challenging and memorable part of my life:

(In respective order of their times of departure from this earth)

Billy
John
Linda Lou
Nimrod
Dusty
Danny
Beth

Rest in peace my friends.

PREFACE

Being raised in a Christian home, I learned at a very young age not to judge others by the way they looked, smelled, or how much money a person had. I went through my high school years without suffering or facing many of the hardships others were feeling. Never having to deal with any sort of poverty was a blessing that was, and still is taken for granted by many. Trying to figure out where my next meal was going to come from or where I was going to sleep from one night to the next just wasn't even a thought that crossed my mind.

During my high school days, I was well-liked and didn't really pay much attention to some of the less fortunate students and really had no idea how difficult it was for their families to carry on during the beginning of a struggling economy. After graduation, I entered the workforce and spent a few years working in the woods, even though my heart was always in the mechanical field. I worked hard and spent as much money as I pleased without the burden of any major responsibilities or needing to save anything for the future.

I fell in love with a girl that attended the same school that I did and in October of nineteen-eighty-five, we became husband and wife. I continued working in the woods but never lost my desire to become a Diesel Mechanic. Since the timber industry had fallen off, mostly due to environmental issues, I was partially without employment. I spent the days that I would normally be working, venturing out to find an entry level job that had potential to evolve me into becoming a Diesel Mechanic.

In early nineteen-eighty-seven, I landed a job washing heavy equipment at a construction equipment rental yard where after some time, persistence, and dedication eventually evolved me into the position of Lead Heavy Equipment Mechanic and a few years later, Service Manager. The income was good and I climbed right up the ladder of success without looking back. I never knew of the many hardships others were facing because I didn't need to know and it really didn't matter much to me.

Being married at a very young age, my wife and I were setting our lives up with two wonderful children, a home, and nice vehicles; not to mention a fairly decent individual retirement account and plans for an even more fulfilling lifestyle before the age of thirty.

All of that changed in nineteen-ninety-eight when I suddenly found myself in a divorce where I was left with basically nothing except my clothes, tools, and a disabled pickup truck. Things slipped downhill even further from there as I had already severely broken my leg at a new job and then, right after the divorce, I developed a seizure disorder taking me out of the mechanical field completely

With everything falling down all around me, I had no clue as to what the future would hold for me. This sudden awareness of not knowing which way to turn was all new to me and I was in a predicament that was tugging and dragging me straight to the bottom. I didn't realize that the challenges others had faced in their lives was the same challenge I was approaching in my own life.

I spent the next few years living with my parents and others as I tried to figure out what I would do with the rest of my life. I really didn't want to be a burden on anyone and since the doctors had placed major restrictions on what I could and could not do, my hands were tied as far as employment goes. I took courses in college to brush up on my computer skills, attended Vocational Rehabilitation through the state, and tried various jobs, only to have my paychecks slashed in half for child support garnishment.

Not knowing what the future might bring and having no guidance as to where I might end up in life was something that most persons will hopefully never experience. I was going through a major change and didn't know which way to turn. The largest part of the next decade I spent many days and nights learning about life in a way I never would have contemplated before.

I always thought of homeless persons as nothing more than lazy people who had no goals or drive to move forward in life. I looked at them not with compassion but with self-righteous disrespect, and a feeling of authority. Trying to understand what the homeless persons in today's society actually go through just to survive was something that just never occurred to me. When the majority of people today speculate and wonder why these people supposedly choose to be that way, the real reasons all too often get overlooked, mostly due to the lack of actual knowledge of the homeless.

There are plenty of stereotypes that follow the homeless but there's no blanket explanation as to why there are those who still suffer on a daily basis. Most people have a certain way of viewing the homeless which includes drugs; alcohol; smoking; child abuse; criminal activity, and any number of other categorizations that may or may not fit. When it comes to those groupings, we need to dissect each person's life separately and ask one simple question. Which came first, the chicken or the egg?

This book explains in magnificent detail the reasons for becoming homeless and not being able to pull away from that lifestyle for each individual in this true story. It also shows how you may get so caught up in their life that sometimes you might feel angry at the way homeless persons were treated by others. On the other hand, you may find places within this story that will bring tears to your eyes or even laugh at some of the absolutely hilarious situations that arose.

I never envisioned in the wildest reaches of my imagination that *I* would ever end up in a situation that would leave *me* homeless. I always thought; *me, one of the most respected construction equipment mechanics in the area winding up on the streets and holding a sign? No way!* It did happen and now, looking back after the long journey has ended, God has provided me with the skills and knowledge to tell others about it.

Although it is commonly believed that homeless persons exist primarily in large cities and communities laced with poverty, the Behind the Signs storyline took place on the outskirts of a midsize town in the Pacific Northwest. Many of the episodes in this true story occurred just outside city limits on private property owned by a large timber management company.

CHAPTER 1

THE ROCK

Someone had already pulled the bus stop signal cord as the bus veered over to the station on the east edge of town. I readied my things and proceeded towards the rear-side door located towards the middle of the articulated people hauler. As I stepped off the bus I saw the two same guys at the same place as I had talked with on and off for the last couple of months. I approached them and made some small talk as I usually would do, just to be friendly. I remembered their names from speaking to them in the past. The first guy I spoke too was Danny.

"Hey, guys, how's it going?" I asked.

"Hey, how's it going Kirk?" Danny replied.

"Just fine, thanks," I responded. "I just got out of one of my computer classes up at the college."

John had nothing to say at the time, he was more interested in rolling a cigarette than participating in small talk. Since I had some money in my pocket, I decided to buy a round of beers for the three of us. They were both happy to accept my generous offer. The other man, John, was the first to jump up and grab his sign that read, "CAN YOU PLEASE SPARE SOME CHANGE? THANK YOU AND GOD BLESS" and stashed it behind a mission newspaper drop box.

The three of us made small talk as we left 'The Rock' and headed towards the mini-mart. I plucked out two of their favorite brand and one of my favorite and set them on the counter. I paid for the three beers and held the door open for the two of them.

We walked over to the nearby fence line, kind of out of sight from the general public, and proceeded with the beer and the bullshit session. John was quiet as usual as Danny and I conversed about different things we had accomplished, and the usual other bullshit. John kicked in a few words but he was anxious to get back on the rock before someone else showed up to take their spot.

There were four rocks sitting along the entry way to a small shopping center that included Albertsons Supermarket, a haircut place, and other small businesses. The small entryway was sandwiched between the bus station and a McDonald's restaurant. The first rock, heading out of the lot, was John's favorite because of the drive-thru at McDonald's. As people were driving out with a load full of kids screaming from the back seat, the last thing the driver wants to do is fumble around trying to stash the change in a pocket while trying to pass out happy meals and drive all at the same time. Needless to say, many people will just hand out the money to the first person that jumps up. That would mainly be John since he would usually sit on the first rock. Danny usually sat down on the second rock so if John missed a 'hit' then Danny could grab it. That way it wouldn't get missed. The other two rocks were up for grabs for anyone who wanted to fly sign there.

They seemed to have fun there too. There were a lot of things that happened both in the parking lot and on the streets because of the busy interchange from the freeway to Main Street and the busy shopping center. Also, there was a lot of joking there as well, John was a quiet prankster.

One day while I stood there bullshitting the two of them, Danny stood up with a dumbfounded look on his face and started walking towards McDonald's while John sang a drawn out tune, "Pee—Pee—Pee, Pee, Pee,—You ain't gonna make it!" Danny turned around to flip John off while we studied a wet spot on the front of his jeans.

It wasn't funny that Danny couldn't make it to the toilet; after all, he was not a young man. What was funny though was how John knew what was going to happen. He had obviously witnessed that before.

I didn't spend much time with them on the rock at that time because I usually was dressed for one of my weekly club meetings that I attended. I felt that hanging around those two holding their sign, while I'm there in dress slacks and dress shoes, with a nice coat covering my upper half might put a damper on their profits.

I knew that the two flying that sign every day on the rock were both homeless and living together in a tent somewhere but I didn't know where and it wasn't any of my business to ask. They were on the dirty side, of course, and this I could understand. They both were always friendly and I often wondered what their previous lives held. Danny talked several times of the filbert orchard that he used to own that included several acres. He had several tractors, specialized harvest equipment, plus two large farm trucks. He also had a nice Diesel pickup truck, and a three bedroom house. He said something about losing it all to someone but never mentioned who or why.

I left them that day knowing I would see them another day and perhaps many more times to come. As I rode the bus towards my parent's house where I was staying, I couldn't help but wonder why they were in that situation and what exactly happened to put them there. *Time will tell,* I thought, but somehow I couldn't help but feel a bit compassionate for them.

There were no standing rules on the rock except for common sense. Anyone who came along and had the desire to sit down could do so. All the proceeds were split up as to however many people were there. Everyone was included until he or she left, although a slight break to go use the restroom, make a beer run, or to make change was an exception. Usually there were no new faces on the rock, just the regulars; Danny, John, Billy, Linda Lou, Skippy, and Randy; most of the time it was in that order. Usually everyone respected each other's time on the rock as to not allow more than three people there at once, although every now and then the rock would draw a crowd and no one would stop and hand out anything. I figured that most people thought it must have been some kind of party or something along those lines.

All in all, most days went about the same as far as I could tell but I only saw from the outside; not from doing but from seeing. However, later on I discovered a lot more about the people on the rock flying a sign, what happened to put them there and what their previous lives were like.

CHAPTER 2

PROGRESSION

Staying with my parents was both comfortable and uncomfortable at the same time. There never was a problem of going without food, clothing, and a warm bed; although remembering how I had already designed and built my own lifestyle, before an abrupt and unexpected divorce, left me with a feeling of living someone else's lifestyle. It just wasn't appealing to me. After all, I was a grown man who had worked hard all my life to make myself who I thought I was.

There were times I had to find a way to get out for a while and unwind. One way I achieved this was to go for long walks which included hiking into territory I had never been before. Going on these excursions included a small amount of supplies. I took my Panasonic headset radio, a can of sardines, and a couple of beers.

One typical morning while getting dressed I got a wild hair up my ass to take a bus ride down to the rock to visit the good old boys there, and then proceed to the mini-mart before heading up on an old log truck haul road. I didn't expect to be gone all that long, just long enough to unwind and spend a little time by myself.

Hardly anyone ever walked up in this area because of the locked gate at the bottom of the road and the lack of people even knowing how far that road actually went. I had hiked this area many times and it always relaxed me. I would listen to my radio and have a couple of beers without interruption from anyone.

While totally ignoring the forecast that I had heard on the radio, I ventured onward and proceeded to get myself in one hell of a mess. The forecast was for freezing rain and lows in the mid to upper twenties. With day-old snow already on the ground, continuing my journey turned out to be a not-so-wise choice.

As the weather turned bad, I continued onward against my better judgment. When the rain began to freeze as soon as it hit the ground, I took shelter at an abandon homeless camp about thirty yards uphill from the main road and completely out of sight. The camp hadn't been occupied for several months, possibly longer. I carefully unzipped the partially leaned over tent to see what I could scrounge up for a nasty night if I were forced to stay because of the weather.

After taking a quick look inside the tent, I decided to walk down and check the condition of the road. Climbing down the trail towards the road was slow and steady although I made it without falling on my ass. The freezing rain had covered the road with a half-inch sheet of ice. I knew there was very little chance of getting down that hill and to the bus stop without falling and possibly injuring myself so I went back to the camp and made arrangements for the night.

Inside the tent I found a three wick candle, a single wick candle, and a lighter. Those items would be my heat and some light for the long, cold night. To arrange the blankets, I chose the cleanest ones of the bunch and put them towards the position where I would be sleeping.

I sat up in the old, leaned-over tent and listened to my headset for several hours until it was time for sleep. During the radio broadcasts I made sure that I paid close attention to the weather report. It didn't sound good and I knew it was going to be a real hassle to get out of there when morning came and I would probably stick it out until the afternoon. That way maybe the ice would have melted off.

Morning came along so I crawled out and took a long, warm pee while looking around. It was cold and icy at the campsite. I wondered what the road down the hill would be like but first things first. I cracked open the can of sardines that I carried up with me. It wasn't really all that tasty but it was energy anyway.

Down the trail I went towards the road with fir boughs painfully slapping me on my cold face. The road was covered with ice and nearly impossible to walk on. I decided to walk off to the side to gain traction from the frozen grass and weeds. Steady and slowly, I finally made it to the gate. I crossed it and walked carefully down the sidewalk towards the bus stop. Once I was there, I stepped on the next bus and headed towards downtown.

It felt good to sit down on the seat inside the warm bus and I enjoyed it the whole trip. I thought about what I was going to tell my parents because I knew that they were worried sick about me. With the weather the way it was, and knowing I wasn't prepared for it, made things really rough for them.

Once I arrived downtown I walked to a phone booth and called my mom. She was panic-stricken. My parents had been left worried sick not knowing where I was or even if I was dead or alive. They were not really aware of my survival skills, doing whatever you have to stay warm and alive, so naturally they were pretty upset with me.

My mom came and took me to their house. Not much was said on the trip home except that they were out of their minds, worried. They had called the hospital and the police. They didn't know who else to contact. There was no way of knowing where I was, so they were not happy with me at all.

I was approached by them that evening and a brief conversation began. Dad told me, "We were so worried about you that we just don't know what to do anymore. We can't handle the stress of not knowing where you are or if you are even dead or alive. I have called the mission and I think it would be wise if you stayed there from now on. We just are at wits end and can't deal with it anymore. You do understand where I'm coming from, don't you?"

"Yes, I do understand," I answered. "I'll get some bags ready to go."

"We don't like doing this but it's just not fair to your mother and me."

"I realize this. I'll be ready in a few minutes," I spoke to my dad in a low voice.

"You don't have to go right now, you can get ready and I'll take you over there in the morning," my dad offered.

The next morning, my dad drove me across town to the mission. I had never been to an establishment like this before so I didn't have a clue what to expect. It was an experience I will never forget. I had never been anyplace quite like it, not even while in custody for being unable to pay child support. After standing in line for Chapel, followed by supper, it was then time to shower with fifty other naked guys, seven at a time. After that unusual event we all got dressed for the night in rags that they called pajamas and went to our designated bunk beds. Not wanting to be there at all was the only thing on my mind as I lie there in bed after the shower experience. I attempted to sleep although it was nearly impossible due to the thunderous snoring and nasty smelling gasses erupting from God only knows whose filthy ass.

The next morning at five-thirty on the nose, out that gate I went never to return except for going back to retrieve my belongings. I decided right then and there I would rather live in the woods, cold and wet, but there was no way in hell I was going back to that place, period!

CHAPTER 3

OFFICIALLY HOMELESS

B eing out in the elements is no picnic by any means. Simply staying warm sometimes you face unexpected challenges no matter how prepared you think you are. A few nights of snow and freezing rain proved my theory.

One evening while hiking to the campsite area I had a queasy feeling deep inside me that something wasn't right. I continued to the campsite when I immediately noticed the tent was on the ground and cut to shreds. Pissed off, of course, I headed back down the hill just in case the assholes that performed the task were still in the area. I didn't see anyone around so I walked back to see what was salvageable from the mess.

As I dug through the remains I concluded that nothing was missing, the tent was just totally ruined. There was nothing really of value there but what was there was useful. There were just some old blankets and sleeping bags as well as candles and other items of no interest to anyone who had a roof over their head at night.

It was getting late so I figured I'd better find another place to spend the night. The only place that came to mind, that would be easy to find in the dark, was behind the fence where everyone went to drain down a cold one every now and then. Behind the fence there was a row of bushes so I came up with an idea. I studied the situation and concluded that I could easily fit unnoticed between the bushes and the fence.

I needed something to lie on and cover me so I went on a cardboard hunt. I walked behind the supermarket and found just what I needed. I scored one large box, kind of thick, and one that was thinner but larger to use as a cover. I carried the cardboard over to the makeshift sleeping area and proceeded to make a bed. My pillow consisted of an oval shaped river rock about eight inches long and five inches in diameter. It was the perfect size. It wasn't soft, it was a rock of course, but at least it was some elevation for my head.

After I had everything in place I went for a walk around the area. After that I walked over to McDonald's to warm up and use their facilities one last time before returning to my new found comfort zone for what would be a night of cold, wet sleep.

The rain drops on the cardboard kept a constant enough rhythm to put me to sleep. I was exhausted anyway so sleep came relatively easily. When my bladder wakened me that it was time to pee, I rolled out from under the cardboard to discover that I was sleeping under a white blanket of snow. I finished my business and crawled back underneath and fell back asleep. I woke up again at daylight and figured the best thing to do would be pick up all the cardboard and place it back in the recycle bin before things got busy. After that I walked over to the mini-mart for a cup of hot coffee, taking as long as possible to warm up as much as I could.

I then jumped on the bus and headed across town to donate plasma. After I stepped off the bus I walked over to the McDonald's by the plasma center. I used their restroom then ordered a McMuffin and water before walking across the street to the plasma donation center. Inside the center it is always warm and comfortable with a DVD playing for the people to enjoy as they wait for a bed to donate their plasma. Usually there is some kind of conversation in the back of the room, if you want to join in, but I only paid attention to the movies.

After I received my cash for donating, I jumped on the bus and headed back towards the rock. On the bus was a familiar face of someone I had seen on the rock but had never talked to. We exchanged glances a few times before he slid onto the empty seat beside me. He was a somewhat handsome man in his early sixties with gray hair and a neatly groomed gray beard. He stuck out his hand and looked at me with piercing deep blue eyes said, "I see you all the time. I'm Billy the kid, and yours?"

"My name is Kirk. I'm known as Captain Kirk," I answered.

He smiled and chuckled a bit so the conversation was on for the remainder of the trip. We talked of the people who were riding the bus that day, and swapped stories of what each of us had experienced on the bus before. The speaker system on the bus then abruptly announced in a computer voice: *Fifty-fourth and main*, which was my stop, so I jumped up and stepped off the bus.

Interestingly enough, Billy got off the bus at the same place I did. There was a little store near the stop that I shopped at every now and then. I walked in and bought myself some nachos with jalapenos and my favorite beverage. Billy purchased his favorite beverage and out the door we went. We walked down an alley commonly known as 'the field' and continued our conversation. He came across as a gentle man with manners and good morals. I liked him from the beginning, and had a hunch that we would become good friends.

After talking with Billy for a while I discovered he too didn't have any place to live except for out in the elements. I did not yet know what his reason was or why exactly he was in that situation. I wanted to know although I knew I shouldn't pry. After all, we had just officially met not more than an hour or so before.

My list of friends that are homeless was growing but of which ones could I really trust was an issue that would come only with time. Which ones really meant well, and didn't just say they did, was another issue that only time would tell. Who would stab me in the back or steal from me when I am not looking? Those are questions that would be answered in time. After all, when you are homeless, sometimes it is dog eat dog and I was learning that lesson fast.

I knew I could trust Billy and I could probably trust John but I knew very little about him since he didn't talk much. I knew his honesty was there but he chose not to speak enough to really understand his morals. With Danny, I really had to pay close attention not to believe everything he said. So that left me with one for sure, Billy, and maybe John.

It was a whole new ball game for me. I was unsure of where I would sleep from night to night, and there was no guarantee that someone wouldn't harm me in the middle of the night while I did sleep. I was indeed officially homeless and a little frightened.

CHAPTER 4

BILLY THE KID

As time went on, Billy and I became very good friends, just as I suspected we would. I began to really trust him like I felt I couldn't trust the others that I was hanging around. Also he could make me laugh and I could make him laugh or cry. Billy the kid quickly became very special to me and me to him.

I didn't mean to ever make him cry but later I discovered that he had a soft spot. Her name was Josie. All I had to do would mention a lost love and Billy was howling like a coyote stuck in a trap. There was only a couple ways of pulling him out of it. One was to tell him to shut up and quit whining, or sing to him.

Billy always told me I had an excellent voice. It started when he coaxed me into singing for him one day. The only song that came to mind was an old country tune that I knew by heart from a compact disk that I once owned. When the beer would kick in and he would start that crybaby stuff, other people would walk off and leave. Not me, I would start to sing that song and it would change his attitude completely.

I knew Billy wasn't lying to me just by the way he acted when I spoke about my marriage that ended and the pain that never seems to leave. He understood that pain. That meant something to me. He related with it so much that I could tell that he had been hurt, deeply hurt.

Billy was not a big man; in fact, he was kind of a wimp. But when he got enough beer in his belly he would say, "I'm Billy the Kid and don't you forget it," as he looked you in the eyes and added, "I'll kick your ass!"

Knowing good and well that Billy didn't have it in him physically or mentally to do anything like that, most everybody just ignored him. When he would say those things, you had to remember he that had a heart of gold and belly full of beer. The beer would talk but his true nature prevented him to act. That's a good thing because depending on the other person, Billy would probably get his ass kicked.

It was sort of humorous though when the beer would make him indestructible in his own mind. One warm afternoon on the rock it was John, Billy and I sitting on the rock flying sign. Billy started that 'ass kicking' jargon with John. Little quiet John had enough of it, told Billy to shut the hell up, and popped him a good one up side the noggin. Billy took it well though. He stood up and asked if I would join him in a cold one over by the fence. That was a quick and easy remedy to that problem.

One of Billy's biggest problems was his assumption that nobody liked him, when in fact pretty much everyone loved him. One person who really liked him, and as a matter of fact had a crush on him, was Linda Lou. The two of them became quite an item off and on.

Billy and I went through some good times and some tough times together. One difficult time in particular was winter and we had nowhere to sleep other than between the fence and the bushes. It was extremely cold so Billy went searching for cardboard and came back with some prime stuff as far as cardboard goes. We spread the cardboard and sat up talking for a while until it was time to get some sleep. Billy looked at me and said, "Son, you know I'm not a faggot but I think we need to share each other's body warmth tonight." I had no objection to that, so we scooted closer together and covered up with cardboard and slept for about four hours. When we woke up, we went walking around to get the blood moving and waited for the sun to come up.

After walking around for a while, we went over to McDonald's to use the restroom and put our change together for two cups of coffee. Billy was old enough to get the senior discount so we just had enough for the warm liquid to assist in warming up our innards. After we purchased the coffee, we sat at the bus station and planned the day. It didn't take much to conclude that the day would most likely consist of flying sign.

Billy, Danny, John, and I were on the rock when the conversation came up about this little skinny gal that had an apartment nearby, and maybe she would let us come over and take a shower and warm up. Billy said she was a good person that has seen some rough times and that I would get along with her just fine. "Well that's all fine and dandy," I told them, "but I'm not going to invite myself into some stranger's home."

Come to find out, we didn't have to invite ourselves. Here came that skinny little gal walking towards Albertsons supermarket. Billy stood up and looked while I took a peek at her.

Danny said, "Hey Beth, this is Kirk." He introduced the two of us and another friendship began.

CHAPTER 5

THE BETHOLIZER

Danny, Billy, John, and I followed Beth to her apartment. We carried groceries for not only ourselves but some to leave some for Beth and her two sons. Beth had something cooking that smelled really appetizing; she was fixing lasagna. That caught my attention right away. I hoped she would share some with us. In return we would, of course, replace all ingredients and then some.

I surveyed Beth's kitchen and bathroom facilities and found them to be fairly clean. They were used of course, but clean. She didn't know she was going to be entertaining company therefore she didn't have time to tidy up the place. She popped in a video cassette and we ate dinner while we watched a movie. It was a good time had by all and anyone who wanted to shower could do so.

Beth turned out to be one on the more significant people around at the time. She appeared to be a little on the mouthy side but that was alright. It wasn't anything I'd never witnessed before. She seemed like a good person and her two sons were well behaved.

With all these new people in my life, I never realized how much of a friend Beth would become to me. She had her stories like everyone else but there was something in her that I found in Billy. She had gone through some really rough times and managed to get through them in one piece, even while raising two boys as a single parent.

She was born on Andrew's Air Force base and lived most of her childhood being an Air Force brat. That took its toll on her childhood as she was bounced all over the U.S. from base to base. She attended Catholic schools and never really settled down until her family moved to Pennsylvania. Then her mother and father got divorced and Beth later settled in Oregon and married one of the biggest jerks I believe has ever walked on this planet.

After knowing what he had done, I couldn't help but find a little bit of pity for her. On the other hand, I also found a little admiration. I ordinarily wouldn't believe some of the stories she told me but she spoke with so much emotion and detail that they had to be true. The stories were either true or she was one hell of a good liar. One story she told Billy and I, as we were taking a break from the rock, was how her husband fired a rifle at her and her two sons. She said she placed herself in between that monster and the kids. Did it sound heroic? Of course it did. Was it even remotely believable? Not really, that is until I spoke with one of her sons about the incident. After talking with her son, I couldn't believe she would even jeopardize her children being around that asshole. When the subject was brought up again, Billy took her hand and told her, "Don't worry sweetie, if he ever comes around you again, me and Kirk will take turns kicking his ass!"

I had to laugh at Billy when he told Beth that. I looked at him and said, "Thanks for including me, Billy!"

"Well son, you don't want to see this little darling get hurt do you?" he asked.

Billy knew damn good and well I would step in on any situation that even remotely resembled a creep attacking someone as small and unprotected as Beth seemed to be. In the back of Beth's mind, she knew it too. Once Beth and I got to know each other, we both knew that we would be friends for a long, long time.

CHAPTER 6

HELL WEEK

Now that Billy and I were spending so much time together, Linda Lou became a little jealous. She wanted to spend all of her time with Billy and wasn't getting what she wanted. In return, she decided to hang around with a guy named Randy even though he drove her nuts.

Randy was a different kind of character. Probably the most obvious reason why he seemed so unusual is that he shit his pants on a regular basis. Therefore, he was appropriately nick-named, *Poopy-Pants*. If his diet would have consisted of such things as solid food he probably wouldn't have that problem. Instead, his diet consisted mainly of cigarettes and beer.

Randy and Linda spent a lot of time together even though Linda and Billy had a little something going. No one wanted to see Billy get hurt by Linda being with Randy; it was sort of a two-timing affair on her part. Even Beth didn't care much for the idea of the threesome. It appeared as if whoever spent the most time with Linda was labeled the winner for the day.

Linda and Poopy-Pants spent most of their nights sleeping in a field near the shopping center. This was before the state punched a new road through that lengthened the freeway. The grass was tall enough so that they were mostly out of sight from passersby.

One evening Danny and I were bullshitting and the subject of Randy, Linda Lou, and Billy came up. Danny had already premeditated a plan that was sure to make life a little uncomfortable for Linda and Randy. He filled me in saying, "You know Kirk, we should do something to those two while they are asleep over in that field."

"What do you have in mind?" I asked.

"You know how Linda is about her hair?"

"Yes I do; she is always running that damn brush through it."

"Well, ya want to lube it up for her?"

I thought about it for a while, and my brain was definitely in high gear. I told Danny, "Yeah, I'm capable of pulling off a stunt like that."

Linda was always particular about her hair. She had an alright body for her age, not so pretty in the face, but her hair was always nearly perfect. It was bleach blonde right down to the black roots.

That night when everything was quiet I walked into the store, as per Danny's idea, and purchased a large bottle of cooking oil. The generic store brand had a bigger hole in the top for a faster pour, so I opted for it. I left my coat in small clump of bushes about thirty feet away and snuck up on Linda and Randy. After making sure they were sound asleep, I gently took the lid off and began pouring the oil all over Randy's hair first. I knew he wouldn't wake up. Then it was Linda's turn. I slowly poured the slick oil on her blonde hair until she started to move. I quickly propped the jug up on a rock that was near her head and listened to the oil make a *glut-glut* noise as it saturated her near perfect hair.

Linda sat up like there was a fire in her pants and shouted, "What the hell . . ." as I quietly stepped to the bushes, grabbed my coat, and then ran like a raped ape towards a fence and then crouched down behind some bushes.

I stood up behind the fence peeking through a small hole while laughing my ass off. Linda was rubbing her head with her hands and cussing up a storm. It was dark so I couldn't see exactly what was happening but I was sure it was one hell of a mess. Randy didn't seem to get really excited about the ordeal, he just rolled a cigarette and lit it.

I went to my sleeping area and cracked a beer while laughing at what I had accomplished. I really didn't know how that would affect a breakup between Billy and Linda, but it sure was funny. I lay down and went to sleep making sure my head was covered by the cardboard that I used as a blanket.

The next morning Linda and Randy were up and walking around at just about daylight. Linda looked like a drowned rat. As for Randy, he just slicked his hair back as if he just came from the barber shop and looking like some old-timers do when they use that hair oil that has that smells weird. Linda looked at me like someone had just tragically died and kept repeating in a most serious voice, "IT WON'T COME OUT! IT WON'T COME OUT!"

Trying to maintain a straight face at that moment was like trying to keep a straight face in school when someone cuts a fart. It was nearly impossible; especially when I was the guilty party and must ask, "Linda, what-happened-to-your-hair?" I don't know how I managed to not bust a gut laughing right in her face. She mumbled and looked around while Randy came forward and explained how someone had dumped oil on them while they slept.

"Where did that happened?" I asked like I didn't know.

"Over there by that tree in the field," he stated as he rolled himself another smoke. As he dug around for his lighter he grumbled, "Linda has been in the bathroom at Albertsons for a half an hour trying to wash it out."

I had to turn around and chuckle, I simply couldn't hold it any longer. I knew that if I caved and started laughing, they would know that I was the guilty one who created that mess.

An hour later Billy showed up and I saw John and Danny walking across the parking lot to start their day. Billy was sympathetic to Linda's hair problem. He didn't know it was me that pulled that ornery little stunt off, and if luck held, he wouldn't find out either. Danny knew of course, and so did John a few minutes later when Danny told him what happened.

I walked by the rock where John was sitting when he started chuckling and said, "Kirk, You didn't!" It was more of a comment than a question.

"Afraid so," I replied as I kept walking and leaving him laughing hysterically.

That was the first time I ever saw John belly laugh. I knew that he had been a little crafty in his past too. He had told me of a few things he had pulled off. They were harmless things, of course, but still ornery things all the same.

It was getting towards noon and then here came Beth. She wasn't sloshed so she wasn't the Betholizer yet. She too wanted to know what happened to Linda's hair as she gazed at her from a distance. I had to be the person to explain, "Somebody dumped cooking oil all over Linda and Poopy-Pants." She gave me a glare strait in the eyes that would penetrate solid rock.

I asked, "Why are you looking at me like that?"

"Nothing," she quickly answered.

She read me like a book, knowing damned good and well that I was the culprit. She didn't know me all that well but she knew me well enough to know that I was totally capable of pulling off that kind of a silly stunt.

The day went on with everyone taking turns flying sign and wondering what else might come up. Later that evening the wondering stopped when Danny overheard Linda, Billy, and Randy saying how they would spend the night in the outhouse behind the shopping center. He, of course, informed me of their ingenious plan.

There was a Mexican restaurant moving in and the contractors had a portable toilet put there as they worked remodeling the place. That was the only port-a-pisser around that I could think of, so that had to be the one. My wheels were spinning and so were Danny's.

The plastic structure was a typical one seat unit with a pisser mounted on one side wall and a roll of toilet paper closely hanging on the other. It was a self-contained unit with that blue smelly gunk in the tank which is located under the seat, and a small vent chimney poking out the top. There's not a lot of room in those things for one person, let alone three. Their plans were to all three pile in there and keep out of the elements while they slept for the night. I laughed uncontrollably as I pictured that in my mind.

While considering what the three of them planned to do that night, I had to figure out some way of making their make-shift motel stay a little less delightful. A Careful study of the toilet facility uncovered something that I could make use of. Each one of those port-a-pissers has a bracket on the front to install a padlock if the owner/renter felt the need to lock it up at night. Well I decided to make use of that little bracket with the three of them in there. I told Danny of my little plan and he wanted to be a part of that one.

Daylight was going away fast and as darkness settled in, and ironically so did the three of them. They actually planned to spend the night all cramped up in that shitter. Billy was carrying a paper bag which no doubt had some beers in it for the three of them. I knew that sooner or later they would have to step out and let one at a time take a piss, so to kill time I walked around looking for something suitable to use as a lock. I found a piece of welding rod along the side of the road. *This is perfect*, I thought as I moseyed back to the scene of the soon to be comedy show.

As I watched and listened from distance, my theory proved to be correct. They were taking turns using the toilet for what it was designed for. The beer went through them so they all took turns inside relieving their bladders and then packed back in there for the night.

I walked by flashlight up to Danny and John's camp to let Danny know it was time. As I approached their tent I whispered, "Don't shoot, it's me, Kirk. Hey Danny; lock and load. It's show-time."

Danny unzipped their tent, passed me a beer and ordered, "Here, drink that while I get my boots on!"

I cracked the beer open and asked John if he wanted to come along. Smiling and kind of laughing from the previous incident with the oil, he answered, "No; that's alright. I'm sure I'll hear all about it. I don't want to be *no* part of it when Linda Lou comes unglued when she finds out who's doing this shit to her; especially after messing up her hair!" He was laughing as he was explaining his excuse for not participating.

Danny crawled out of the tent, grabbed his cane and down the hill we went. John called out from the tent, "You two boys be careful now!" He was chuckling the whole time. I know he was enjoying what we were about to do. It was all for the sake of splitting up Billy and Linda. It was basically harmless to anyone and entertaining as hell.

Danny and I watched and waited while listening to the three of them rustle around and talk amongst themselves. Apparently, one of them had to go piss again or something, and they needed to open the door of the shitter. That's when the fun began. After they tried to open the door several times, they finally realized that they were locked in. I don't know whose decision it was, or if Linda made the decision herself, but she kicked that door with all of her strength to the point where the door almost came off of its hinges. The door swung open revealing the three of them tightly squeezed together on the shitter side by side. I folded over laughing, with my hand over my mouth, trying not to let out even the slightest noise.

The next day Billy approached me to go somewhere and shoot the breeze for a while. As we walked he mentioned that someone had locked them in the portable outhouse the night before. Playing stupid of course, I responded, "Why would anyone do something like that?" It wasn't just something to say, it really was a question. Billy didn't take it as a question, therefore did not know what the answer would or could be.

It didn't stop there. The next night it started all over again. This time Danny stuck around. He didn't go to camp with John and then come back. We waited and waited for the three of them to enter their private, little, green motel for another night of talking and eventually arguing. Linda would get so pissed off at Poopy-Pants just for simply talking that the yelling would then begin. Danny and I both knew it would be a while before they calmed down and things would get quiet enough for us to sneak up and imprison them again inside the little, green, portable toilet facility.

We walked over to the mini-mart and grabbed a couple of beers and took them up towards Danny and John's camp. We could hear John up there a little farther up the hill, so we talked back and forth about what we were about to do. John yelled, "What are ya going to do if they catch you?"

"They aren't going to catch us, we will be totally quiet," I yelled back.

We finished our beers and down the hill we went. Me and Danny with his cane were ready for another adventure at the scene of the soon to be comedy show.

I already had acquired an appropriate locking device, so it should have been short and sweet. All we had to do was just slip the wire through the two lined up holes, give it a twist and then slip away and wait for them to commence their piss break activity. We quietly walked up to the outhouse and I carefully slid the wire through the holes, twisted it, and put my finger to my lips showing Danny to be extra quiet.

I began quietly walking towards the fence when I heard this loud wrap three times. I turned around and there went Danny hobbling with his cane toward a garbage dumpster just as fast as he could hobble. I ran to the fence and hid thinking, *Danny, you stupid dumb ass!*

Danny had wrapped the side of the plastic shithouse so hard with his cane that it made an echo. That door came flying open with one big thunderous crash and out came Linda Lou staring at Danny as he tried to take cover behind a dumpster.

She yelled, "Danny! I see you! Danny, you little bastard! I know where you sleep!"

She was not happy at all, and Danny was most definitely busted. No one saw me because I was hidden. Danny headed back to camp; the fun was over for the night. No more locking them in, they were on to us. It was all over.

The next day nothing was said about the actions that took place except when Beth showed up and I filled her in. She told me that I was mischievous. I gave her an innocent look, such as to articulate, *who, me?*

That night it was the same old thing to begin with but with entirely different outcome. I had totally nothing to do with this one; I was simply minding my own business watching the three of them sardine themselves back inside the green latrine while I sucked down a beer. Then I heard them inside arguing again. I couldn't hear Billy but I heard Randy, and most definitely Linda. It was her and Randy going at it again, and this time it was loud. I decided to make myself scarce and moved farther away. Then I saw a police cruiser pull up to the tiny conference room with both spotlights blazing a stream of light upon it. Then another black and white showed up right behind the first. The officer in the front cracked through the loudspeaker, "You, in the outhouse, open the door and come out slowly!" This was better than the movies and I didn't have to pay to get in.

I could only imagine what went through those two cops' minds when three grown adults, two men and one woman, came filtering out of that tiny outhouse one by one. It was quite a show but had to restrain any laughter, or be visible; otherwise I would be questioned by the police.

The police took all their identification and ran them through the computer. No one had outstanding warrants although Linda Lou and Randy did get a free ride to the drunk tank to dry out that night. Billy acted cool enough that he didn't get to go. Later I came out of the woodwork and talked with Billy about the nights events. I thought: *How much fun could one possibly have at someone else's expense?*

That question was quickly answered the next day. Linda and Poopy Pants returned from the drunk tank all sobered up. Linda had some money so the two of them commenced to hammer down the beer. By noon the temperature was climbing into an uncomfortable level so about five of us gathered under a tree located by the shopping center.

Randy passed out from a combination of heat and beer. I kept looking over at him since he was lying down right beside where I was sitting. "No, I shouldn't," I told the group as I grabbed my permanent marker from my shirt pocket.

"Well, I talked myself into it," I said to them as the cap came off of the marker.

Checking to make sure he was unconscious, I lightly tapped Randy's face a couple times. He was out so the festivities began. It started out with a simple eyebrow job but quickly evolved into a mustache and beard job as well. Everyone was laughing as I put the marker away. About five minutes later I turned and told the group, "What the hell. He's still out of it. If I'm going to do it, I might as well just do it right."

Right then I commenced the raccoon face. I painted the under eyes and wrapped them clear around the side of his head. After I finished all the detailing, I capped my marker and placed it back in my shirt pocket.

We all laughed and laughed but the funniest part came when he woke up, asked if anyone needed anything from the store, then proceeded across the parking lot. There he went, into the store, decorated I mean really decorated and not having a clue about what he looked like. He waltzed right into Albertsons like nobody's business. I almost felt sorry for the poor guy. When he returned, we could see that he had tried to wipe it off but you could still see the remnants from my artwork. He wasn't terribly upset about it though; he just wanted another beer.

CHAPTER 7

MOUNTAIN VACATION

The bus station beside the rock was a convenient place to meet up with people, retreat from a downpour, or just hang out for a moment and shoot the bull. You never knew who might show up there. Some people were regular walkers just doing their exercise walks, others were total strangers who you may or may not ever see again.

One guy in particular that came along lived in a homeless camp deep in the old growth Douglas Fir trees about thirty miles up the river, beyond any town and just before the mountain pass. His name was Matt and he always had some time to spare at the station before catching the only bus that ran up the river.

Matt and I had talked off and on for a few weeks. I found out that he often took the bus from up the river to the other side of town and flew sign there. He talked about the serenity he appreciated at his camp and invited me up to stay for a while.

He told me, "You look like you could use a little break. Do you want to come up to my camp for a while and get away from here for a while? I warn you though; the mosquitoes are huge up there."

"That sounds like fun. The mosquitoes won't bother me all that much," I replied.

That evening I told everyone that I'm headed to the forest for a while to get away. Beth wasn't happy about that but there wasn't much she could do about it. She didn't have anyone around that she knew once she left her apartment. The next day was just like any other with the exception of me having all my gear packed up and ready to go. When the bus stopped at the station, I jumped on and sat across from Matt.

We chatted all the way up there while I was enjoying the spectacular sights God had crafted on this planet. The bus stopped at the last little grocery store and gas station before turning around and heading back to town so I gathered my gear and followed Matt off the bus and into the store.

Inside the store we each purchased a small amount of supplies; ice, beer, and snacks, and placed them in our backpacks and started walking on a road that lead us into the old growth forest. Matt grabbed a fir bough and told me, "Remember this spot. It's the entrance to the trail."

I kicked a stick sideways up the embankment and stored its image in my brain. The trail was not visible from the road and not easy to follow even while walking on it. It was a steep trail with many cutbacks and required climbing over a few fallen old growth logs that went down from various storms throughout the last two-hundred years or so.

Once at the camp, I realized that I was in total isolation. It was awesome to be able to enjoy the astonishing seclusion and beauty that most people will only see in pictures or on television. There were no automobile sounds, no yelling, just the sounds of nature. It was pure nature at its best.

I made a comment on the cleanliness of the camp to Matt. His response was, "Thanks, and that's the way it will stay."

"Of course," I agreed, "You bring it in, and you take it out! I always practice that rule."

He nodded his head and we started to get my things set up, just me, Matt, and some of the biggest blood suckers I had ever seen. He had forewarned me about the mosquitoes but those things were absolutely huge!

Later that evening after we had some cold-cut sandwiches and chips, we sat down to chat and have a couple of beers. Since there were no fires allowed, that was a given, the only lighting we had was battery powered. I of course had my trusty Mini Maglite with me. Matt had a couple flashlights and a Coleman battery powered fluorescent light to illuminate the camp and unfortunately attract more mosquitoes until bedtime.

He talked about taking turns going to town to fly sign in his territory. I thought that would be a good idea, I had never tried it across town. We agreed that we would both go one day so he could show me where to go and the best way to operate that particular spot, and then we would take turns. One would go to town and the other would stay back and watch the camp, do some cleaning, walk to the store or whatever.

When it was time for bed Matt walked inside his gigantic tent while I crawled into mine. His tent was nicknamed *The Motel* and rightfully so. The thing was huge. It was an eight man tent meaning four could sleep comfortably with a generous amount of supplies. My tent was a one man pup-tent, meaning one man that didn't move inside it. It kept the bugs down though, and during the day it kept the critters out while no one was around.

When the lights were all extinguished for the night, it was dark, really dark. Any light that might penetrate the huge old growth trees was immediately absorbed by smaller cedar trees that manage to survive from sunlight left behind from the limbs of the massive three-hundred foot tall fir trees. When I had to crawl out in the middle of the night for an unwelcome piss break I had to turn on my Mini Maglite. There was no natural night vision whatsoever that would help. It was totally black inside the deep forest.

The next morning my alarm sounded on my wristwatch so I rolled out of my tiny domain for a breath of cool, crisp mountain air as I crept of into the brush for morning rituals. I decided to make a really quick job of it as I watched and felt the stings from the yellow jackets swarming around my legs as my lowered trousers brushed the top of their nest. I set a new record for speed wiping and very shortly after that I ran back to camp and finished fastening my trousers and then grabbed a glob of hand sanitizer that we had hanging from a tree.

After Matt crawled out and took care of his business, we gathered our things that we would take to town. Then we placed all food items inside his huge tent so the critters wouldn't feast on them. He then made sure his tent was secure, as did I with my tiny tent. I didn't want any surprises when I went crawling in there that night.

We scurried down the trail to the road and made it to the bus stop about four minutes early. We moved right along considering the terrain we had to traverse. He had this trip timed fairly well considering it was about a fifteen minute walk from camp to the road, even though it wasn't entirely daylight yet. It was just light enough to see the trail except for minor details one could trip and bust his ass on fairly easily.

About an hour and fifteen minutes later, we were in town at the main bus station. From there it was about five city blocks to walk. What a difference from where I just came from it was. The difference went from one extreme to the other. Within an hour, I experienced quiet peaceful nature; no people, cars, businesses, or smog, right into total chaos.

We made it to our destination so it was time to start flying sign. Matt informed me that it was a pretty hot intersection, meaning the people who traveled there daily were fairly well off. I had to agree with him judging by the amount of Volvos, Mercedes, and Hummers that I had noticed. I thought to myself, *We might just do pretty well here!*

Matt showed me the ropes so he took the west side of the four way intersection, and I took the east. In three hours or so Matt came over and asked how I did. I answered, "Not too bad, probably about thirty bucks."

He said, "Great, let's go get something to eat then head back on the early bus; we have nearly a hundred bucks together."

I couldn't believe it. I thought my thirty bucks was awesome. This place was hot, really hot. Although it didn't hurt matters much that a lot of that money came from his *regulars* that he gathered hits from frequently.

Not really caring much for eating in town, especially in that town, I had to buck up and follow Matt to his favorite grab-and-go food outfit. It wasn't too bad, some kind of burrito with several kinds of meat, (including fish), a few beans, several kinds of unidentified hippie vegetables, and weird tasting sauce. All of this somewhat strange variety was wrapped up in a brown tortilla shell. I could have done better for almost five bucks, but what the hell; I didn't want to offend Matt.

We stepped off the bus at the east station at five after one and low and behold, there was the Betholizer. She hardly talked to either of us but we didn't have much time anyway. We had enough time to walk to the mini-mart, purchase a couple cold ones, and drain them down before heading across the street to the local department store for supplies. We needed batteries, biodegradable toilet paper, more hand sanitizer, and another tarp to cover my tent just in case it would rain heavily.

We hopped on the outbound bus towards the forest and conversed with several people that utilized that route frequently. The beer went right through Matt and he leaned over to my ear to inform me that he had to piss. I was perfectly fine for the entire trip until he shared that little bit of information with me and then I had to piss as well. We still had a good twenty minutes to go. Luckily a fellow sitting near the front told the driver that he needed a restroom. The veteran driver knew of a place to stop, apparently as he had done so many times in the past, so relief was in sight.

We were then back on the road and to the final stop. We dismounted the bus and went inside the store to buy some beer, hot chicken and jo-jo potatoes. We ate that, threw our garbage away, and then headed for camp.

When we arrived there, a guy dressed in jeans, a tank top, and a baseball cap was sitting on a stump. Matt immediately recognized him and introduced us. His name was Bob. He looked at me, sort of bewildered like he knew me. He asked, "You ever lived in Lowell?"

Now he looked familiar to me. After exchanging last names I couldn't believe it. Of all places, out here in God's country was a man I went to school with twenty five, maybe thirty years before.

"For crying out loud! What the hell are you doing up here?" I asked as I handed him a cold one.

"I come to see Matt. I just got divorced and needed to get away for a while."

"I can relate to that, I've been there and done that. It isn't any fun," I responded.

He had a small tent with him, so now there were three of us in this nice, quiet get away. We bullshitted the afternoon away until we ran out of beer. It was supper time anyway, so we all got together and headed to the store for more chicken and jo-jos. They had been under the heat lamp for a while and they were a bit on the chewy side. We bought some more ice and stopped to fill up our water jugs we had stashed in the bushes. We filled them with fresh water right from the river. Crisp, cold, and clean natural water was something a person just cannot get in town.

Up the trail all three of us went. I perch my ass on a stump as Matt helped Bob set up his tent. We laughed and joked until wee hours of the night before turning in. Matt was going to town in the morning so he asked me to set my clock again. I informed him that it is always set at four-thirty so there was no need to worry.

We all said our goodnights so I slipped my Sony Walkman headphones over my ears to listen in on a late night radio show. It was a nationwide country music radio broadcast that I enjoyed. I listened until I almost fell asleep, so I turned it off, rolled up my headphones and went to sleep. My alarm had not gone off when I awoke; it was my bladder that decided it was time for me to crawl out. The morning light was just starting to peep through the trees. It was cool but comfortable with my jacket on.

Matt and Bob rolled out of their tents at the same time. Matt was finishing lacing up his boots while Bob was digging for some mountain money. "In that bag on the other side of the tree is where we keep the ass paper," I told him. He grabbed it and headed for the brush.

Matt ventured off to town leaving Bob and I behind. We made the best of it talking about the people we knew mutually. We cleaned up around camp and then we went for a walk further into the woods just to check out the scenery. We spotted a couple deer and lots of chipmunks. We also caught a glimpse of a very large bird but the trees blocked the view enough that we couldn't tell what it was. It could have been an eagle although an osprey is a more likely guess.

We reached a deep canyon and just started to head back when we both heard a loud swooshing sound as we witnessed two fighter jets heading west flying in the canyon. We both were in awe as these spectacular aircraft specimens weaved their way through the canyon probably on a training exercise. It was an impressive sight to see up in the middle of the U.S. National Forest.

Later that afternoon Matt came up the trail carrying his backpack and some beer. We each cracked a beer as we swapped stories about the day. I told Matt about the pair of silver wings we saw cruise the canyon and he told us that we were going to have a visitor tomorrow. Matt ran into the Betholizer and she wanted to come up there. Since it was my turn to go to town the next day, it would be me to show Beth the way to the camp. There went the men's retreat, and so much for the vacation. I figured it would be shot to hell as soon as she arrived.

I decided then and there that I would show Beth the way and then that was it. I was going back down to stay. The whole purpose was to get away from her for a while. Even though we were friends, I just needed to be away from her.

The next morning I went to town and flew sign across town before heading to the rock to meet up with Beth. She was flying sign on the rock so that made it even easier. I joined her informing her, "If we are to go up the river, you'd best be prepared. The clock is ticking to catch the bus that's heading up there."

We went and gathered all her things up then ventured over to the mini-mart to grab a couple brews. We went and drained them as the clock ticked away. "This is the last bus up today; we don't want to miss it," I told her as she belched and rolled a cigarette. "Better stop at McDonald's and piss before the ride," I instructed her further. She stepped inside and took care of business. Just as she came out, the bus had stopped so we climbed aboard.

The ride up was somewhat quiet because I didn't want to tell her yet that I wasn't staying past that night. My full intentions were to get up early and head to town first thing the next morning. She had no clue as to my intentions and it was to stay that way.

We traversed up the trail to the camp at a slower pace than I am used to. When you went somewhere with Beth, travel was slow. We finally made it up to camp. I introduced her to Bob and we all bullshitted while trying to wave the mosquitoes away from us as best as we could. Beth was to stay in Matt's tent. There was more than enough room for the two of them and their gear.

We continued to shoot the bull when Bob discovered that we were out of beer. I reminded everyone that we hadn't had supper yet. I offered my services to head down to the store to get some burritos and beer if someone would keep me company. I was hoping for Bob or even Matt, but Beth chimed in expressing her desire to poke her way down to the store with me.

As we crossed a log on the trail I told her, "Better get a move on. Darkness is about forty-five minutes away!"

"Where's your Maglite?" She asked.

"Where's yours?" I asked.

Appearing startled, she answered with another question, "Don't you have a flashlight with you?"

I wanted to really pry on that one but I left alone and explained, "Yes, of course I have my Maglite with me. When don't I have it?" I picked up the pace some more forcing her to beet cheeks a bit.

We made it back to camp just before dusk. Talk about cutting it close. In woods that dark, one little flashlight just doesn't quite do it for two people, especially when you are in totally unfamiliar territory. Every one ate supper as the florescent Coleman lamp shed ample light for a continuing bullshit session. Even Beth got involved in the conversation.

When it was time for everyone to hit the hay, I was the last one in. Matt had the big light so I relied on my Mini-Maglite for the night once more. I put my head phones on and listened to my music as Beth and Matt talked. That was all right by me, I just needed to double check my alarm and off to sleep I would go.

CHAPTER 8

BACK TO JAIL

Morning came a little faster than I would have liked it to but I had to get up and get ready before Beth had a chance to find out what my plans were. As far as she knew, I was coming back. She wouldn't know any different until I was taking my first step away from camp. When she did say something to me I told her that I planned to stay in town for a while. I walked down the trail, got on the bus and to town I went.

After I arrived in town, I got re-established and went out to fly sign on a daily basis. I visited with Billy, Linda Lou, and the others but did as I pleased without anyone tagging along and getting in the way of things that I wanted to do.

A few days had passed when I saw Matt and Beth together waiting to change busses at the station. They were paired up pretty good from what I could tell. That was the general thought of everyone around that saw those two together. I talked with them as they waited for their bus and even went to have a brew with them. They seemed content, good for them and everyone else.

Everything was alright until one morning Matt came to town to fly sign and more importantly to tell me that Beth was missing. The two of them had a falling out and she took off. She had been missing for two days. Immediately I knew I must act. She can barely take care of herself in town around people, let alone in the forest by herself without any direction whatsoever. She had no tent, no sleeping bag, and no supplies. Matt filled me in on the areas that he searched without any signs of her.

The best thing I could come up with is to call the sheriff search and rescue team. I walked over to the mini-mart and used the telephone to call, and then went inside and bought a beer. On the phone they asked where to meet me so I could give a better description of her and her last known location.

I walked over to the fence line to drink my brew before they showed up. Just as I finished here they came. *I cut that pretty close*, I thought, as the deputy exited the green Ford Crown Victoria with blue and red lights stashed in the grille. I asked myself: W*hy does the search and rescue team send a cruiser out to ask detailed questions for a rescue project?*

The officer called me by name and asked for identification. We then proceeded asking for a detailed description of the now missing Beth and a general location of where she might be. I gave the deputy a detailed, hand-drawn map of the area where the camp was located including the canyon south of the camp. I explained to him that her physical ability wouldn't allow her to wander off in that direction and that she probably was within a half to three quarters of a mile from the campsite as the crow flies.

The deputy asked if she had any food or water with her. I told him I did not think so, but there is a small stream about three hundred yards east of the camp. The deputy wrote down all the information then got on the radio inside the Crown Vic.

A few minutes later he returned, looked at me and said, "Now for problem number two. You have a warrant out for your arrest." Right then I knew why he showed up in a cruiser instead of a Dodge Durango. I also knew that it was that pesky child support thing biting at me again. That was one of the many kind departing gifts my wife blessed me with as she divorced me.

"It's the child support thing again isn't it?" I asked the officer.

"Contempt of court, so that could be. I don't have details, just the arrest warrant protocol."

I was calm and collected as I asked, "Could we step over to the other side of your vehicle so I'm kind of out of sight when you put the cuffs on me? A lot of people know me around here."

"Sure, I don't have a problem with that," the officer replied.

He emptied my pockets and patted me down but did not cuff me.

"Watch your head," he said as I climbed into the hard plastic back seat.

Off to jail we went at fifty-five miles per hour into nowhere. He could tell that I was of no threat and that I was not a criminal. He even kept the sliding Plexiglas window open and asked, "Is that enough cold air for you?" as he re-directed the air conditioning vents and let it blast on high.

"Just fine," I replied.

We exited the freeway and stopped about three blocks away from the jail where he informed me, "I have to put these on you before we go in or I'll get in trouble." I slowly put my hands behind my back as he applied the cuffs to my wrists, somewhat loosely.

I spent two days and one night in jail before being transferred to the Community Corrections Center which is a low security work release facility where people spend their time in plain clothes and go to work at normal jobs but must spend their spare time at the facility. Social passes were issued to the inmates for two to four hours to spend as they please with an approved sponsor. In my case, it was my dad. I went to work at a hose manufacturing facility that makes air hoses for wholesale customers.

On one of my social passes I wrote down the store that I need to go to get deodorant and batteries for my radio and Mini Maglite before heading to my parent's house. In front of the store, right beside the phone booth, where I was to make my check in call, stood Billy and Linda. I couldn't believe it. Billy called out; "Son!" as he stretched is arms out welcoming me into them for a big hug. Then it was Linda's turn for a hug. We talked briefly as I explained that I only had a couple more weeks and I would be out and free. It was really nice to see them. It had been about four months.

I went to my parents' house and visited while eating pizza until it was time to head back to the Center. I didn't have much time left there but those days seemed like weeks.

My big day finally came. I had everything packed and ready to go before I left for work on graveyard shift. That was the slowest shift I had ever worked. I hopped off the bus, grabbed my stuff and headed to the office. I signed the necessary papers and told the deputy at the desk, "Next time I see you it will be on better terms; probably at Costco or someplace."

"Okay, Kirk, you behave yourself," she said with a smile.

"Remember, I wasn't here for what I had done, I was here for what I didn't do," I explained as I walked out the door leaving her laughing.

I dropped my things off at a house where I had previously planned out and paid money in advance for a room to stay at. Then I jumped on the bus to go see the town and people I haven't seen for a little over four months. I hopped off the bus and saw some familiar faces on the rock. I proceeded over to the mini-mart where I received a lot of guff as soon as I walked in. "Hey, Here's the jailbird!" Kathy screamed while grinning from ear to ear. I didn't say much except for small talk as I purchased the first beer I'd had in over four months. I stepped out thinking: *This is really going to taste good.*

I walked over to the fence to indulge when Skippy went bouncing by informing me that Linda Lou was over at the rock. I finished my beer and walked on over. Linda's eyes were on me as she jogged forward and took me in her arms. She was trembling as she looked at me with her eyes full of tears and groaned with a wavering voice, "Billy is dead!"

CHAPTER 9

GOODBYE BILLY

Hearing that Billy was no longer here with us on this earth was devastating to many people. It didn't matter if they were homeless and on the streets, or just knew Billy, it was a real blow to many people. His death came as quite a shock to me. I even had a special song to sing for him after I was released from the Community Corrections Center. Billy did not get to hear that song in the flesh but he did get to hear it in spirit later. He always enjoyed hearing me sing.

I sat Linda down on a curb by the bus station and gently asked what happened. It still had not sunk in so I didn't need to compose myself yet. Linda explained how Billy walked to the store down Main Street a ways and bought some beer for everybody. On his return trip he was crossing Main Street. He made it to the turning lane and had to wait for traffic before continuing. He was standing alone as a four wheel drive Ford Explorer entered the turn lane early at a fast rate of speed and took him out.

Linda was near the scene, and I found out later that Beth was at the scene. Beth was beginning to perform CPR on Billy when the paramedics arrived. She could not do mouth to mouth because part of Billy's head was missing and his nose and mouth were filled with blood. He was pronounced dead upon arrival to the hospital. He was already gone as the Explorer came to a full stop; his heart just didn't know when to stop beating. The only comforts we had to focus on are one; he was in a better place, and two; he didn't know what hit him; he just knew what was about to hit him.

As Linda and I sat there for a moment in silence, I suggested we go and place some flowers at the sight where his mortal life ended and his life in Heaven began. Linda composed herself by blowing her nose, wiping her eyes, and running a brush through her hair. We walked over to the floral department inside Albertsons and picked through the flowers. We both decided on two of the same kind of flowers all neatly arranged in wicker baskets. I paid for them and we walked to the sight where Billy the Kid's life was tragically cut short by a man that shouldn't have even been driving due to a medical condition.

We placed the flowers beside a power pole at the location where someone had already had begun a memorial display. There was a poster with Billy's full name, his nick name, place of birth, and a heartwarming poem written just for him. I told Linda, "Let's go celebrate Billy's life, I have got money."

Linda agreed and I sang Billy's favorite song as we waited for the bus. When the lyrics of the sad song came to a heart melting chorus, Linda went to pieces. I had to wave the approaching bus on by so Linda could wipe the streams of tears from her eyes. She still had watering eyes when the next bus came but we boarded anyway. I paid for two day passes and we took our seats.

We headed across town and stopped at a mini-mart for some beer and munchies. "What kind of beer do you want?" I asked as Linda was digging through the chips.

"Let's get Billy's favorite," she replied.

I bought the same for myself on Billy's behalf. After all, we were to celebrate his life. I paid for the items and we walked out the door and down the sidewalk of the somewhat lonesome feeling road.

I rented a room at a nearby motel, non-smoking. Linda was kind enough to agree that she go outside to smoke. We were getting organized and cracking a brew at the same time when Linda spoke up, "I don't give a shit what people will think when they find out we went to a motel together!"

"They can take a high flying screw at a fast rolling donut for all I care," I told her.

"That's right, they all can kiss my ass," she said confidently.

"There is nothing going on here except two friends visiting after a dear friend's death. Let them think what they want to think. Maybe this will give them something to talk about."

"I can hear Danny now spouting off about how you probably got into my pants and John telling him to shut the hell up," she said.

"Well, we know better, and that's all that counts, let them have their fun. You want some pizza?" I quickly asked to change the subject.

I grabbed the phone book to find a pizza parlor close-by when Linda spoke up and yelled, "No anchovies!"

I gave her a look and asked, "What kind do you want? I was going to ask you anyway. I'm not inconsiderate, let's get what we want."

"Canadian bacon and pineapple," she returned.

I gave her another sour look and explained to her how I felt about her order. I dialed the number as Linda hit the bathroom to shower and wash her damn hair.

"Meat does not go with fruit you know but if that's what you want, I'll order us a half Hawaiian and half combination," I told her.

I clicked on the tube and started channel surfing. *The Three Stooges* appeared and I immediately thought of Skippy, Danny and John all lined up like birds on a wire at the rock. I really think the only ones out of the bunch that really gave a damn about Billy's departure was myself, Linda, John, and of course, Beth.

The pizza arrived just about the time Linda came out of the bathroom all dressed and still running that brush through her hair. It must have been a hobby or something. I paid for the pizza and gave the heavily pimpled delivery kid a fairly generous tip. We sat down and ate pizza and talked about experiences with

Billy; good, bad, funny, and sad. We laughed and cried for hours when Linda notified me that we were almost out of beer.

"Well, I'm buyin' if you're flyin'," I told her.

I gave her ten bucks as she left for the mini-mart and then I jumped in the shower. In the shower I sang while cussing those little bars of soap and trying to build up lather with that shampoo that smells like a sanitizer that a janitor would use in a doctor's office. I got clean anyway and was dressed and sitting backwards in a chair when Linda came through the door.

Linda explained to me with a surprised look, "Man, beer is expensive down there. That took that whole ten bucks!"

I looked in the bags and counted them. "You got six beers in there, three for you and three for me. That comes to about seven fifty back at the mini-mart where we usually shop," I explained.

Linda gave me a rolled eye look as she confessed in a low tone of voice, "Well, I had some change so I went ahead and bought a box of tobacco." She really felt guilty about it.

I told her, "Linda, you know me better than that. Do you really think I'm going to be upset about something as trivial as that? You need anything else, just ask me. If I can help I will!"

"Well since you put it that way, I could use some better shampoo. That shit in there is murder on my hair."

I should have seen that one coming; Linda and her damn hair.

We stayed up until about one in the morning drinking beer and talking. We were both about half tilted when I told Linda, "I'd better hit the pisser and get to bed before I have to resort to crawling. That beer is going to my head." She laughed at me as I stumbled to the bathroom to pee, then stumbled back and flopped on the bed. I told her, "You stay on your side and I'll stay on mine."

"I'm used to sleeping on the ground, I'll sleep on the floor," she quickly replied.

"Nonsense," I responded. "I'll take the floor and you sleep on the bed if for some reason you don't trust me."

She acted hurt when she said, "I'm sorry. It's not that I don't trust you, I trust you more than man on Earth. I'm just used to sleeping on the ground, that's all."

I was in no condition to argue so I tossed her a pillow and leaned back to sleep. We both were exhausted. It had been a lot to choke down hearing about Billy's death.

At about four in the morning I woke up and heard Linda crying. I turned on the light and made the dull-witted mistake of getting up before letting my eyes adjust. That, plus the remnants from the beer still flowing in my blood, sent me into battle with a chair. The chair won that battle as I ended up on my ass near Linda's feet. I crawled closer to her having a few words with the chair at the same time. She was sitting up laughing at me but with tears still in her eyes from crying. She was actually enjoying the show, at my expense of course.

"You alright?" She asked while easing into a full throttle laugh.

"Yeah, I'm alright. Nothing one more beer won't fix; it's almost time to get up anyway," I said.

I reached up and grabbed one of those flimsy plastic glasses that are supplied in motels and poured Linda some of the last beer and I guzzled the rest.

"I deserve this by golly. I was the one who ended up on the floor," I joked at Linda.

Linda was still chuckling when she decided she wanted a cigarette. She called it a "cigarettie." She attempted to roll one and failed. She blared out the F bomb so I told her, "Give it to me, I'll roll you one."

Now for a guy, who has never smoked in his life, much less rolled a cigarette, it proved to be much more of a challenge than I had first anticipated. It probably wouldn't have been so bad except all the beer I had consumed on top of everything else. I managed to roll one though. It was about a nasty looking thing but she said, "Thank you son," as she put on her coat and walked outside to smoke.

The day had already gotten off to kind of a weird start, or was it a weird end of yesterday? I wasn't quite sure. The days and nights seemed to intertwine for about a week or so. It was indeed the next day when I decided to splurge for another night so I wandered on down to the office and paid the gal at the desk. I went back upstairs and told Linda, "I'm not going to spend the whole day drunk, just the last part of it. Let's go to Target and do some shopping. I'm sure you need some socks or something, plus you wanted to get some decent shampoo and the walk will do us both good."

She agreed so we ate some left over pizza and drank some complimentary coffee.

Just as we were about to leave there was a knock at the door and someone saying, "Woom sewvice, woom sewvice."

"Great timing," I mumbled.

I opened the door for a smallish Hispanic lady with a cart containing all the necessary items to make our stay a little more clean and comfortable. She was a pleasant looking young lady so I had to watch my language and my temper.

"Dandy," I mumbled.

I plopped my ass into the chair and turned the television back on. "I wonder how long this is going to take now," I grumbled at low enough voice that there was no way for her to hear me.

The little lady started in the bathroom and scrubbed and polished like the place had never been cleaned before. She worked her way out towards the bed, so I kindly got up from the chair and stood in the corner. As she stripped the bed, Linda watched her every move since she had done this kind of work in the past. The little lady was having a hard time making the bed, probably because Linda was breathing down her neck. Then Linda grabbed the sheet and fluffed it up, laid it down, and performed the hospital corner thing perfectly. She was showing off basically, although it did seem like the little Hispanic lady was taking mental notes.

With the addition of a few clean cheap plastic cups all sealed in a plastic bag, and a flimsy plastic bowl, I guess for ice, and then she was off and running to the next room. Not till I slipped her a five spot though. I thought that was fair for the humiliation she must have gone through with Linda starring at her like a hawk. The poor lady was probably used to working alone.

Off to Target we went. It was a little further than I recalled so Linda talked me into stopping at a little store for a couple of brews. We went inside and bought a couple beers then walked out, both of us looking around. We were in a different part of town then, sort of out of our element.

"Now we have to find a place to drink them without Johnny Law sneaking up on us," I told Linda.

I spotted a couple trees with no buildings close by, so we walked back there. I warned Linda, "Make it quick girl! Drain it right down. We aren't in our neck of the woods anymore."

We finished our beers, and then found a garbage can to stick our empties in and walked on. Naturally, fifty steps further Linda informs me, "I gotta go pee."

"We're almost to the mall, just hold on for a minute," I said.

The look on her face, with her lips all puckered, was almost scary when she firmly told me, "I gotta go NOW!"

"Perfect!" I said to nobody. "Where the hell does a grown woman drop her drawers and piss in the middle of town?"

She said, "Wait here!"

I did.

We were almost to Target and once inside we should be alright. There were restrooms, a food court, and all of our shopping places were all right there in one convenient location.

I went to the men's room and took a big bathroom break just for good measure before heading out into the store for shampoo. I didn't want to get a big bottle because that'd be a bitch to carry around. Luckily Linda showed up with a package of panties and some socks. She found a small tube of some kind of shampoo that smelled like vanilla.

"Yuk, I hate vanilla smelling stuff," I told her.

"Why? What's the matter with it? I don't think there is anything wrong with it," she said.

"That shampoo reminds me of those tacky air fresheners people hang on their rear view mirrors. When the sun hits them for a while, it makes me want to bend over and puke. Oh well, it's just shampoo. I only gotta use it maybe once," I told her.

As we left the mall we stopped by the movie theater to see what was playing at the cheap seats. "This theatre, tickets are only a buck for the first show," I mentioned.

"I'm really not in the mood for a movie. Besides, we have cable back in the room. For another thing, we don't have any beer to take in with us," she informed me.

"Wow, now that's a for-sure way to get introduced to the security guards, then probably the cops," I told her.

We then headed on back toward the motel but first we had to stop at the little store and then visit those trees again. After that we went to that little mini-mart. It was closer to the motel so we wouldn't have to carry the sack full of beer very far. "Might as well get a bunch, we drink all this ain't neither one of us gonna make it to the store and back in one piece," I told her.

We loaded up with beer and more snacks and walked back to the motel room with both of us carrying more than enough to keep us there for the rest of the day and the night.

I slid the key card through the electronic lock and inside we went. I grabbed that stupid little plastic bowl and went to get some ice while Linda jumped in the shower. She couldn't wait to get some decent shampoo foaming up in her damn hair. What a hobby; Linda and her damn hair.

I returned with the ice and started channel surfing. We found a movie to watch as we consumed great quantities of beer. Linda developed a pretty good buzz and started crying about Billy. Well, that was kind of what we were there for. A celebration of life must include some sorrows as well as all the good times everyone had with Billy the Kid.

I pulled Linda out of her sorrow and right into a belly laugh when I reminded her about the beer that Billy dropped under the tree. She was there when it happened but I told her anyway. Billy had made a beer run and passed them out to everyone who placed an order. As he pulled his beer out of the bag he dropped it. It landed sideways on a small rock, puncturing a hole in the side of the can. It was spewing brew six inches away. I have never seen anyone move so quickly as he reached down, grabbed that can and sucked on the side of it where the beer was spewing from. He then moved his thumb up to cover the hole as he popped the can open moving the can upward all in one swift move. It was quite impressive for a guy in his early sixties. That did the trick for Linda, the laughs and jokes were on then.

That story moved right into another story that's kind of like that one. I told her that time it took place on the rock. John, Billy, and I were all sitting there in that order. John was messing around with his radio trying to get his favorite program tuned in when a lady in a mini-van pulled up with the window down and a hand stuck out. Billy had just cracked a beer and had no time to hide it. The lady was there with her hand out the window. Billy stood up to get the hit, grabbed it, and dropped his beer under her van as she was coasting away. The rear tire smashed his virgin beer flat. The lady must have saw it happen in her mirror, because she backed up, apologized, and gave him a dollar more to get him another beer! Only Billy could get a rise like that out of a total stranger.

Later that evening, I told Linda that we had better order something to eat. Well, she didn't want pizza again; I didn't blame her for that, but what else could we eat? She suggested Chinese food. I searched through the yellow pages and found a place that delivered. I ordered sweet and sour pork, stir-fry, and the usual stuff. When the knock came, I opened the door and paid the young lady for the food and gave her a tip. We sat down and ate the Chinese stuff, then cracked a beer and began talking again while watching a movie.

We were both tired and full of chow so Linda jumped in the bathroom. It would be an hour or so as she fluffed and puffed her damn hair before I could take a shower with that ever so fine smelling, vanilla scented shampoo. With that out of the way I lay down in bed with the remote control while Linda positioned herself on the floor. I didn't even offer her the bed that time.

Morning came quickly it seemed. Linda was in the bathroom when I woke up. She was already dressed when I finally crawled out of bed. She had a beer cracked while she brushed her damn hair. There was still one beer left but I didn't want it. It was seven in the morning, and that can lead to having a totally worthless day. We had to leave in a couple hours, so I hit the toilet for the morning ritual, cleaned up a bit and headed down stairs for a cup of complimentary coffee. When I returned to the room Linda was done with her damn hair and was getting her things arranged for our departure. That's when she came clean to me.

Linda told me, "I need to tell you something. Last night after we ate dinner I spotted a fifty dollar bill lying next to the phone on the night stand. I took it and put it in my purse. I cannot stand it anymore. I'm really, really sorry. I don't know why I did that. Here you go; I hope you can forgive me."

I hesitated a moment and thought about what I could say that would keep things neutral. I replied, "Well, you did come clean with me and told me about it. Let's just forget it. We have both been through a lot lately. Is that a deal?" I stuck my hand out for a shake. She shook my hand and then gave me a hug.

"I'm really sorry, son," she repeated.

She finished both beers and I could tell she was getting a pretty good buzz on. As she walked toward the bathroom, I told her, "Go piss now before we get on the bus, and make sure you have all your stuff. I'm going to the office and turn in the key card. I'll meet you down there." I returned just as Linda came out the door.

"Let's see what kind of bullshit those clowns come up with when we show up at the rock and they find out we went to a motel together. You know Linda; we could really play this up. Do you want me to push it?" I asked her as we headed down the stairs.

"Hell yes. Let's do it up right," she boldly answered.

CHAPTER 10

TEAMING WITH BETH

Linda and I hopped off the bus at the stop near McDonald's. Naturally she had to go piss. I told her where she could find me, on the rock. I moved onto the rock where sat John, Danny, and Beth respectively. That wasn't much of a surprise. I had Linda's approval to go ahead with the mind games so the games began.

"Hey guys, and uh, gal. Sorry Beth. What's up?" I spoke my introduction as Linda was still in the McDonald's restroom.

"Well," Danny spoke. "Where you two love birds been?"

He struck first so then it was my turn. I replied, "Oh Linda and I took a little vacation over to a motel. Whew! I am exhausted. I need to get some sleep. You get a few brews in her and she goes wild. I even ended up on the floor." I really poured it on. Like cats watching a bird, I had all of their attention guided towards me then.

I wasn't lying to them; I did end up on the floor after I tried traversing over that chair. But they didn't know that. I had full tendencies to really play it up when Danny started snickering at John. The Betholizer didn't even look at me but somehow I think she knew I was toying with those two clowns.

Then Skippy, *Jumpin' Jack*, came along just about the time Linda came out of McDonald's. He looked at us and stated, "Hi kids! Have fun?" Linda couldn't have buttered it up better when she told him, "It was incredible. We had so much fun!"

I had to leave. I had to leave right then or risk blowing the whole thing. I had to laugh so badly I was just about to explode when I said, "I'm going over to grab a cold one. It's about time."

I was still laughing as I walked over to the mini-mart when suddenly I could sense someone behind me. I turned and there was Beth and Linda. Now I know Linda wanted another beer and Beth probably wanted one too. But more importantly Beth wanted details. Both these gals knew how I was with women. They knew I was a pretty tough nut to crack. Beth was not dealing with the curiosity very well and that maybe Linda had gotten to me. *It's working,* I thought as we walked into the mini-mart.

We sat our beers on the counter. Beth held onto hers but I told her, "This one's on me."

She had some money but I paid for it anyway. I wanted to see just how long it took before she broke down and just asked if Linda and I made the bed bounce. It didn't take very long. A couple pulls off her beer and she couldn't wait anymore. "So, you two are a pair now that Billy's gone . . ." she inquired. Linda and I looked at each other with a shit eating grin and Linda answered, "No, you should know better than that, Kirk was a total gentleman. The only thing that happened is we got blitzed and talked about Billy. Nothing more than that! I even slept on the floor."

"Don't tell those three yahoos though; we want to see just how far those three dumb-asses will run with this," I added.

Beth acted relieved as if maybe she thought Linda and I really did have something going. I do think she was worried that Linda and I had actually become closer than just friends. She should have halted those notions as Linda and I went back way before Beth was even in the picture. It was kind of funny, and it went like a snowball downhill with the three dip-shits on the rock.

A little later I snuck up behind the three of them and listened in. I was propped up beside a mission drop box listening very word they said. When I heard Skippy say, "I didn't see any hickies on either one of em though!"

I popped out in front and looked at them and said, "You are just about the sorriest bunch of assholes this side of the Snake River. I've heard gossip before, but you idiots take the cake!"

John just looked towards the oncoming cars but Danny and Skippy just gave me that—deer in the headlight—look. It was priceless. They were busted and they knew it. John didn't say anything; I think he wanted to just stay out of it at that point.

As Beth approached the rock things got pretty quiet. She wanted to go and talk to me about what happened to her during my stay at the Community Corrections Center. She had gotten evicted from her apartment. That took me by surprise knowing that she was a fairly quiet, decent tenant that always paid her rent. She was on section-eight through the government so she received a discount anyway. I wanted some details so I outright asked for them. "How did you do to get booted out? Was it something your kid's did, or your beloved boyfriend?" She answered me with a very disgusted look, "I let a couple in my apartment that were homeless and while they were there and they both went into the bathroom. While they were in there they smoked some dope and set my bathroom on fire!"

"Why the hell were they doing dope in your house?" I asked her in total surprise.

"I didn't know they were doing dope! I wouldn't even have let them in my apartment if I would have known that," she explained.

"So now you are out on the streets?"

"Not really, I still have my car at the apartments but I let some kids borrow it and they blew the motor."

"It's an engine, not motor. Why did you let a bunch of kids take it, you had to know they would run the piss out of it?"

"It was a poor decision on my part, that's for sure," she answered.

Then I was thinking; she has no place to stay, not for very long anyway, and she is not particularly strong. She isn't well prepared for staying outside at the tail end of winter. It gets pretty cold at night, so I asked, "How long will you be able to sleep in your car on that property?"

I don't know, as long as I can get away with it I suppose," she answered.

That evening after she flew sign and made some money she asked if I would accompany her to her car. I figured what the hell. If it rained, which it did, at least it would be some sort of cover. Besides it would be safer for her with me there. Her car was an old beater of a Toyota, barley worth its weight in scrap metal, but it still had a roof and four wheels. Someone had even broken the driver side window out so all it had for protection from the elements was a piece of plastic taped in its place. It wasn't very secure to say the least.

I told her I would be happy to accompany her that night so we could shoot the shit and have a couple brews. After all; if I got sick of her I always had my Sony Walkman radio to tune her out.

I didn't get to talk to her about Billy until that night. We reminisced about him for a good couple of hours. She went to his viewing before they shipped his body to California and then to New Mexico for the burial. Beth swore she saw Billy grin at her while he was in his coffin. She became quite emotional about that.

"Why did he get shipped out of state, clear down to New Mexico?" I asked.

"There is a lot of money in his family, and they want him buried near them," she answered.

"Why was Billy on the streets if his family is so rich?"

She didn't know, and I figured I'd probably never know either. Beth told me that Billy's cousin owned a nationwide trucking company based in New Mexico. Remembering Billy's last name put the pieces of the puzzle all together.

"Yeah," I told Beth, "I know which trucking company you are talking about; it's a monster."

We chatted and drank our beers until it was time to sleep. Beth had several blankets in the car so we both stayed fairly warm. There were some trees behind us for a makeshift pisser when needed. No one could see in there; very few people ever walked by there anyway. It was as good of place as any to drain the bladder.

When morning came I climbed out of the little car, stretched, and took a look around. It was pretty quiet. I was kind of hungry so I asked Beth, "Do want some biscuits and gravy from little market across the street?"

"No thanks, but I'll take a beer," she responded.

I headed to the store as I mumbled in a low voice, "Wonderful. All ninety pounds of her will be sloshed before eight o'clock."

When I returned to the car, she was smoking a cancer stick while patiently waiting for her beer. I propped my ass up on a broken down street sweeper that had been parked there for a month or so and proceeded to drink my coffee and eat my biscuits and gravy with jalapenos on the side. I knew I would pay for that later on in the day.

Beth drained her brew and threw the can in her car then we headed toward the rock for another day of fun and excitement. We were there before anyone else so Beth grabbed her sign and propped her skinny little ass on the first rock. I told her, "I'll be over at the bus station watching and reading the paper." There was no reply from her so I walked on over. Just as I sat down to read I heard a familiar voice say, "Hey buddy! I haven't seen you around for a while. You had any more of them seizures?"

"Oh, hi Al," I replied. "No, I haven't been around for a few months now. I'm back now though."

"I got some tape for you but I haven't seen you but I got it at my house," he added.

Al was a bit different than most. His clock just wasn't wound up all the way. He was one heck of a nice guy, he just was a little on the slow side. Al always he had this thing for tape. I don't know where he got all of it, or even what I ever said to him about tape but he always kept me supplied with a variety of the stuff whether I needed it or not. Mostly not, but I always took it anyway just to give him his jollies.

After Al jumped on the bus, I saw Beth get her little ass off the rock and look over at me. That meant on of two things. One; she had to piss, or two; it was time for a beer run. This time it was both. That fooled me. We walked over to the mini-mart and she used the restroom while I grabbed a couple of beers. It was still kind of early but it was something to do. I told her we should go to the fence line and not bring attention to ourselves with open beers on the rock. Even though they would be hidden, it still wouldn't be a good idea. She agreed so off we went towards the fence.

We stood over by the fence and chit-chatted for a while as we wondered when we would see Danny and John come on down. I finished my brew and began teasing Beth about how she's so slow at even drinking a beer and that it gets really annoying. She said in her own defense, "I don't want to throw it up! Do you want me to throw it up?"

"No," I answered. "I just don't want to stand here for too long, you know how that nasty old fart over yonder can be. You know . . . Nasty Neighbor!"

She laughed at that, and the old fart then had a nick name. That name stuck too; it wasn't very long until everyone around knew who *Nasty Neighbor* was and where he lived.

She finally finished and we both headed over to the rock. Just about the time we sat our buns down on the hard surfaces I saw Danny and John headed out of Albertsons. John had his backpack, of course, and no doubt it contained a six pack of pounders of whatever was on sale.

Beth got a hit as I was looking the other direction. I counted it indiscreetly; it was all change, but it totaled out to be over three bucks worth. We had kind of a standing rule on the rock. *Don't count your money when cars are coming by.* If somebody were to see that you already had money, they would be less apt to kick out.

As the two approached the rock I went ahead and jumped up and Beth followed suit. John sat down on his usual rock and Danny sat next to him. Beth took a place on the third rock so I took a walk to kill time and get some exercise. When I returned about an hour later, the three of them hadn't done jack shit. It was almost lunch time so nobody wanted to leave except Beth; she wanted another beer. I knew that she was going to be pretty well lit by the end of the day and my prediction was correct.

We walked back to the mini-mart and mustered up two more. We stood there and bullshitted with the workers for a while and then we went on our way.

"You need to put something in your stomach besides beer. You didn't even eat any biscuits and gravy this morning," I told her.

"Beth will eat when Beth wants to eat," she snapped back.

I knew that when she started referring to herself in the third person sense that one more beer and she would become the all too well known, *The Betholizer*. I was right; after that beer was gone she hopped in the bushes along the fence line and took a piss. That was *not* a very smart move. People do walk by there occasionally. It is kind of a short cut from some homes to the bus station or the shopping center. She didn't care though. The Betholizer was back. The show was just beginning.

We made it back to the rock and Beth took her place. I walked over to McDonald's and used the facilities then ordered a four piece McNuggets with Ranch dressing. I was going to save a couple for The Betholizer but I figured that would piss her off so I ate all of them. Sometimes when she would put a few beers in her belly without anything else, she could really put on an attitude.

While I was in McDonald's, a few more hits came out the windows and, of course, the money was divided amongst the three of them. Jumpin' Jack showed up just as John was acquiring the money so he figured he should be involved. John told him no before the Betholizer could even respond. Lord only knows what she was prepared to say to him; I'm sure it wouldn't have been very nice.

Linda Lou hopped off of the bus and came over to visit and fly for a while. As we talked, Linda mentioned that she needed a place to stay for the night. Beth, of course, invited her to stay the night in the little car with us. I didn't know how that was going to work out but the plan was already in progress so it wouldn't have made any difference what I was thinking.

It was about dark, and getting cold, when I told Beth that if we're going to stay in that car with her that we had better get going. I wanted to stop at that little market and get some nachos for supper. She told me that she wanted another beer before we left. I told her we can get some at the little store near her car. She insisted that she must have a beer and a cigarette before we leave. Against my better judgment, away we went to the mini-mart. Beth bought her one but I didn't want one at that moment; I just had a funny feeling that it was just better if I didn't drink anymore at the time.

We went back to the fence line and Beth started consuming her beer. It was then dark as we set out towards her car. We were about a hundred and fifty yards from our destination when Beth's legs were suddenly acting like rubber. She was sloshed. I am glad I didn't buy any groceries or anything because I had to carry her the rest of the way to her car. Linda was behind us a ways, so she was of no help. Thank God it was dark because anyone driving by would no doubt wonder why I was carrying her. There were no cops that I saw either; a cop would no doubt stop and ask what the problem was. I wasn't drunk but Beth was fricken hammered.

We made it back to the car and I helped her into her seat. I then walked over to the little market and picked up a few things including a box of tobacco that she had asked for. I asked for two packs of matches and they charged me ten cents for them. I thought: *How cheap. They get these things for free!* I kept my mouth shut though and just grabbed the bag of goodies and headed back to the car.

I had my Maglite turned on and noticed a chalk mark on the left rear tire of Beth's Toyota. I crawled inside the car and told her, "We'd better move this thing first thing in the morning; the cops have marked it."

"I don't know how we are going to move it; it doesn't run," she said.

"I'll push it, dummy," I responded.

That would be a given to most people but I had to remember that she couldn't even walk, let alone think rationally. I popped open a can of smoked oysters offering some to Beth. She refused, of course. She still hadn't eaten anything all day and I figured she probably wouldn't. That is exactly why she was so unhealthy and thin. It was like carrying a bail of grass hay getting her to the car. She wasn't very heavy at all. I took a few stops to rest but I didn't have to take very many.

I cracked a beer as I enjoyed the smoked oysters and a grab-bag of chips. Beth grabbed a *Snickers* bar from the sack of goodies that was frozen from the store. She bit into that thing and immediately broke a cap off of one of her front teeth. She yelled a few sharp obscenities then said, "Great! I just lost a cap off my tooth!"

"You need to start eating a little healthier. You'll end up like poopy-pants with no teeth at all," I told her. I knew that wasn't going to go over very well.

"Beth will eat when Beth wants to eat," the Betholizer attacked.

I just ignored her for a few minutes. It was difficult to say anything to her when she got that way. I knew she was still pissed off about losing her apartment, but I didn't do it. I was in custody at the work release center. I needed to tell her about the chalk mark that I discovered though, and that would just add to her already pissed off attitude.

"You know, you're on borrowed time staying in this car. Now that the cops are onto you, and they've marked your tire. It's a sure thing that we're not going to be here much longer. You're going to be out in the elements *for real* here pretty quick; you'd better start eating some real food! I ain't kidding Beth; you'll die without proper nutrition out there," I explained to her. That sunk in as about as far as a balloon on peanut butter.

Linda Lou showed up so the three of us got to gabbing. Eventually it was just the women talking amongst themselves. It didn't really bother me too much; I was kind of used to talking to myself anyway. Sometimes, I was the only one who would listen to me.

I listened to my Walkman for a while to catch the weather report. It was calling for cold with lows in the mid-twenties. It was going to be cold inside that little Toyota but even colder outside. I told everyone goodnight then reclined the seat and went to sleep.

At five o'clock my wristwatch started beeping at me telling me it was time to crawl out and take that first morning yeller piss before heading over to the market for a cup of hot coffee. It was still dark as I opened the door and Beth woke up from the noise.

"I better go too or I'll just have to get up in a while and go anyway," she said.

"It's already working on six and I'm going to the store to get some coffee," I told her.

When she found out that I was going to the store, she reached in her pocket and pulled out a couple of bucks and then asked, "Here, get me a beer, would ya?"

"Get me one too," Linda mumbled out as she woke up.

They must not have been awake yet, or still hammered from the night before. I busted their bubble when I told them, "It's not even six yet. They won't sell it until seven. Besides, we have to push this thing down the road a bit before things start picking up. Get over there and piss. I'll be back in a couple minutes. Do you want some coffee?"

Beth answered, "Yeah, I guess so. That will at least warm me up."

Off I went to the store while looking over my shoulder wondering where Linda went to. It was definitely cold that morning; I thought it probably had dipped into the teens where we were located.

I sipped the coffee on the way back to the car. It was hot, but not as good as I had hoped it would be. I had to consider that it wasn't a fancy coffee shop or a restaurant; it was just a little mom and pop store. When I got back to the car I asked Beth, "Where did Linda Lou run off to? Did she head out already or just go take a piss?"

"I don't know. She just took off somewhere," Beth answered.

"Where do you want me to push your car to?" I asked.

"Just down the street a ways. Just as long as it is still not right here and the chalk mark isn't showing."

Those were my thoughts as well. I took one more sip of coffee then put it down on the sidewalk and told her to steer. She got inside so I turned and put my back to the rear of the car and started pushing. I could tell it was cold and the car had been there for a while. It was a little more difficult to push than I expected. Once I got it moving though there was no stopping. I kept pushing until she yelled, "Stop!" I did, and was damn happy about it.

With that little chore out of the way, it was time to get the hell out of Dodge before someone walked by and made trouble. I grabbed my coffee, that was now just kind of warm, and told Beth, "Let's go, it's daylight now." With that said we took off and headed for the rock to find out what kind of interesting event might come our way.

Beth made her way into McDonald's, which had just opened, to use the restroom and clean up a bit. I went to grab her sign that we had stashed under the newspaper box only to find that it was gone. Somebody knew where she had stashed it and took it away. That could only be Danny, John, or Skippy. We ruled out John knowing that he isn't that type of person. Danny, well . . . Would Jumpin' Jack? Yes, he would do that. He was the most logical choice especially since sometimes he would stay down there into wee hours of the night. It didn't matter at the time though; we just had to make a new sign. When Beth came out, we went to find another piece of cardboard.

We walked over to the cardboard box behind the mini-mart and started digging through to find the perfect piece. I came up with one that was just right. I already had my marker in my hand to start with the artwork when Beth asked, "What time is it?" I knew damn good and well she was hoping it was after seven so she could get a beer. I informed her that we had a few minutes to go before it was legal. I completed the sign but I knew she was not about to go back to the rock without a beer in her belly.

Into the mini-mart we went. I used the restroom just to kill a few minutes more than anything. When I came out, Beth had a couple of brews sat out on the counter sort of off to the side. *Happy-go-lucky Sarah* was working the morning shift. She was the store manager at the time. She was a new mom, and she just gleamed with joy every time that I saw her. She just always came across as a happy lady. She was proud of her baby that wished she didn't have to work, although she had to work just to make ends meet. When the clock ticked seven, she used the little hand-held bar code reader and rang up our total. I hesitated, knowing Beth had money. I had money too but I figured it is about time that she sprung for the brew. I really didn't want one at that moment, but it would kill time so I wouldn't have to go fly the rock by myself. Out the door we went to visit the fence line before going out to fly sign on that cool, brisk morning.

We flew for a couple hours, trading restroom breaks, when Danny and John showed up. The weather was getting pretty nice so we decided to go for a walk and let those two have the rock by themselves for a while. We had done fairly well, probably about eight bucks all together. We went back over to the mini-mart and purchased a couple more beers. I walked to Burger King and got a whopper Jr. I cut it in half and gave Beth half. She didn't eat all of it but she at least ate some of it.

When we finished, we headed back to the rock only to find another guy there. I sort of knew him, so did Beth and the others. He is kind of a different sort of fellow that gets meaner than hell when he gets a few beers in him. Well, he had a few in him and was starting to get mouthy.

John flat-out told him, "You need to shut the hell up if you're going to hang around here! Either shut your fricken mouth or you need to leave!"

That was a mutual feeling with everyone there. Shortly after that, Danny and John left, leaving Beth and I there alone with that mouthy asshole. I told Beth that I was going for a walk, and that she could either join me or stay there. She decided to stay; she would do better with fewer people there anyway.

When I returned, Beth informed me that that clown had punched her in the chest leaving a bruise. We talked about it for a few minutes, and then we called the cops.

"Call us cop callers if they want," I told Beth.

"I don't care what anyone thinks; he punched an innocent woman," Beth said.

"Did you happen to notice how the coward waited until all the guys were gone and then punched you? What an asshole," I stated.

The cops arrived, took a report, and then told us, "If you see him again just give us a call."

"Okay. Thank you, officers," I told them.

"He probably won't come around now," Beth told me.

"I hope not. We don't need his type around here. If he does, I *will* call the police just like they said to."

"Good for you and me. He had no right to do that," she said.

We flew sign for a while longer, talking about the event while we flew. We went over to the mini-mart and bought a couple more brews and walked up in the trees behind Burger King. Beth lifted up her shirt part way, exposing a fairly large bruise on her chest.

"Well, that's assault evidence right there. That's enough to put his ass away. There was no reason for him to act like an asshole like that. You know he isn't welcome there anymore, John won't put up with that kind of shit either," I told her.

We both thought it was all over until that night. We finished out the day flying sign over on the rock, and we filled John in on what happened. He chuckled at Beth and said, "No, I don't want to see it!" Then everyone knew of that asshole and his little stunt that he pulled off while all of the guys weren't there.

We all laughed about John's remark, all three wondering what people would think if Beth lifted up her shirt in front of us guys like that one stupid bitch, Ronda, did about a year before. You just never knew what you just might run into out there. We talked about that episode for a while, and then Beth and I packed it up and headed for the car. What we thought was over with that asshole, had indeed just begun.

CHAPTER 11

A NIGHT OF TURMOIL

I looked things over as we arrived at the car and found nothing unusual. Beth went ahead and rolled herself a smoke as I cleared out some garbage from inside the car. Then we walked over to the little market to pick up some beer, beef jerky, and, of course, a Snicker's bar for Beth. We came back to the car and were bullshitting away when here he came; that same ornery ding-bat that punched Beth was at it again. I was still not fully recovered from the seizure I had experienced a few days before but I launched out of the car anyway. I told him, "You'd better leave! The cops already know about you punching her. You and I have already had words before, so just walk away before things get real rough for you!"

"Cop caller are ya huh? Chicken shit," he yelled!

"You're the one on the verge of going to jail so it would be best on your part to just get the hell out of here and leave us alone," I said while approaching him rather quickly.

I got up in his face knowing he was a coward, and looked at him right-square in the eyes. I could tell at that point that he really didn't want to fight; he was just interested in being a total prick.

In the meantime Beth had already slipped by that prick and was at the little market on the phone with the police. Apparently, they knew that clown by name, and they also informed us that he was a trouble maker. About a minute later the cops came down the street, dark. They used no headlamps or anything. The jerk had already vanished before the police officers arrived.

One cruiser came down the street, and one came from the other direction. They stopped and took down more information and then one officer told us, "If he comes back, give us a call."

He gave us a speech about sleeping in a car within city limits and that it's against city ordinance but he let us by with it after Beth explained to them that it was only temporary. They had bigger fish to fry than to boot us out of the little Toyota at that time anyway.

We shook it off as the cops drove away and sat back down in the car to talk and drink our beer with our eyes wide open. I had a gut feeling that this wasn't the end for that asshole, and it wasn't. Just about the time we were both beginning to laugh and carry on a conversation, the ass end of the little car started bouncing up and down. The jerk was jumping on the rear bumper.

I looked at Beth and spoke loudly, "He's Back. Some people just never learn!"

"We had better go call the cops; they said to call them," she told me.

We both got out and made a b-line for the phone booth. The traffic going up and down Main Street proved ample light for Beth to dial the phone and enough light to make everything visible around us. The guy would have to have been a total fool to pull anything off there, but then again I wouldn't put anything past that creep.

"9-1-1 what is your emergency?" the lady asked.

Beth was shaking like a cat shitting peach pits.

"I called earlier and . . ."

She was interrupted by the dispatcher, "Is this Beth?"

"Yes. He's back!" Beth responded.

"The police are on the way. Stay where you are. Is your friend with you?"

"Yes," Beth replied, "he's right here."

The dispatcher told Beth the police should be there anytime as two black and whites pulled into the parking lot. One stayed with us, and one went up the street. We walked back to the car. The officers searched the area but didn't find him. One officer told us he would be up the road with his lights off for a while watching through his binoculars. That left some relief for us. We sat in the car for about forty-five minutes or so until the officer came down the road in his cruiser, stopped, and told us that he must move on that he couldn't stay any longer. We thanked him and he drove away.

We both knew darn good and well that the cops were going to come by and check throughout the night so we decided to chug a beer, go piss and get some rest. I walked up beside the tree and stood while Beth relieved herself, just in case that nut-head was hiding out somewhere near.

We got back in the car, both of us looking around, and straitened things out for the night. I told Beth that I was going to listen to the weather report. It turned out to be another cold night but we both still managed to go to sleep with one eye open.

I don't know what the problem with that guy was; I think that maybe he just got into the whiskey and went crazy or something. He had no right to hit Beth, but it did show his true colors, hitting a woman of her size.

I woke up at about two in the morning and wiped the windows so I could see out. I didn't hear or see anything so I tried to go back to sleep. I turned my radio on and listened to my favorite country station, and then as soon as my eyelids were heavy again I turned it off and fell back asleep.

CHAPTER 12

GOODBYE CAR

As usual, my alarm sounded when it was time to get up and get moving. The first thing that came to mind was to check and see if that asshole was hanging around. I didn't see anything to worry about so I took a piss and went to get Beth's ass up. She was already awake and ready to hop out as I walked up to the car. At least that night she wasn't totally gassed when all of that shit was going on, especially when we were speaking to the police.

I walked over to the store and bought one large and one small coffee then went back to the car. I sipped on the coffee while Beth got herself ready to go. Five or six minutes passed before she finally was ready to head towards the rock. The morning air was cold and brisk so we picked up the pace to get the blood flowing. When we arrived at the parking lot at the bus station Beth remembered that we stashed the sign in the bushes instead of under the mission box. We backtracked and retrieved the sign; naturally, I threw a fit about backtracking, and then we went to the rock.

Beth wasn't ready to sit her little ass down on that cold hard rock right then, and quite frankly, I wasn't all that crazy about it myself. Beth commented, "This wouldn't be so bad if I had a beer in me."

"Yeah, that would be alright," I replied. "At least it would take our minds off the cold. We still have about thirty minutes before we can buy it though."

We waited another twenty minutes and didn't get a single hit. I told Beth, "Let's go. We might as well walk slowly over to the mini-mart. We aren't doing any good here at the moment; all we are getting is cold."

She agreed so a slow walk to the mini-mart it was. Inside the small convenience store it was nice and warm. We bullshitted with Sarah for a while; she said it was kind of slow there that morning too. It was close to seven so Sarah unlocked the beer cooler. I grabbed a couple and headed towards the counter remembering that I forgot my jerky back at the car. I grabbed a bag of sunflower seeds instead of the jerky which was way overpriced. Sarah bagged our beverages and took my money so then off we went.

"I don't know about you but I'm into standing in the sunshine," I told Beth.

"I'm with you on that one," she responded.

We walked over behind the Burger King and cracked open our beers in the warm sunlight. It would get warmer later in the day, but right then it was down-right cold. Once the beer was gone, we headed back to the rock to continue flying sign.

Danny and John showed up a little later, as usual and took their normal spots. Beth and I just stood up and let them have the spots. The two of them were only there about five minutes when a guy in a white Chevy four wheel drive yelled out, "Hey! You want some cans?" John yelled, "Yeah." I went over first and took a look and then went hunting for a couple shopping carts. I thought two would be enough but it ended up being three carts full, stacked to the hilt.

Danny and Beth stayed behind to fly while John and I carted the cans into Albertsons to cash them in. They were always pretty good about taking them even if you went over the can limit. We were in there for about an hour and walked out with almost forty dollars. That wasn't too bad for an hour's work; it had to be split four ways. But it still was ten bucks each. No one complained about that!

I told Beth I was going over to Taco Time to get a couple of tacos. She said that sounded good and decided to follow. I thought to myself, "This might not be too bad of a day. Beth is going to eat and we already made some decent money."

We ordered our tacos and I didn't waste any time. I dumped a bunch of hot sauce on mine, stuffed them in between my jaws, and wolfed them down. I was finished with my meal while Beth was still putting pepper, salt, and mild sauce on hers. I commented on how she could be so damn slow, although out of politeness I stayed at the table and waited for her to finish eating.

We both figured we might as well wash those down so we hopped on over to the mini-mart and bought a couple more beers. This time we headed over to the tree beside the shopping center and sat down. It was somewhat secluded but we could still see everything. We finished drinking our beers and then headed over to the rock to finish out the day there.

Back to the car we went for another night's rest, so we thought. As we rounded the corner I looked up the street and exclaimed, "Uh-Oh. Your car is gone!"

Just like that, the decent day was shot to hell. Now the car, the blankets, and the beef jerky, were all gone. We then were at ground zero with nothing to sleep in.

"Well Beth," I said with a shrug, "Looks like it's going to be a cardboard night."

She started to cry while wondering what we were going to do. I told her, "Well, it was good while it lasted. Dammit! That idiot making a big scene and forcing us to get the cops involved didn't help matters, you know!"

"I know. That's no doubt why it got towed. I'm probably not going to get it back either," she said in a sad tone.

"Well, the cold hard truth is that it is not really worth retrieving," I softly told her.

"Yes, I know that. It's just, well, it was my car," she mumbled and sniffled.

We sat down on the curb to think for a while. After a few minutes I told her, "Well we better get going and find a spot for the night. We need to hunt down some good cardboard to keep warm and dry as possible, just in case it rains."

Beth got up as did I and we walked over to the tree. I told her, "We'll bed down over close to those bushes out of sight. We will wait till dark to do so, and we'll also be up and gone before daylight."

She agreed with a sad look. After all, she lost her car, blankets, clothes and some paperwork. I just lost some beef jerky and two pair of pants. Both of us were really bummed out that the car got towed away. It wasn't much, but it did have a roof, and it was enclosed and kept us out of the weather. I got a wild idea up inside me that Beth would probably go for. We could go and buy a bottle of high-powered wine.

I walked over to Albertsons and bought a bottle. Beth hadn't had much experience with wine, let alone this stuff. I came back with the bottle as Beth finished off another beer. If we were going to be cold, we were going to at least feel warm on the inside.

I twisted the cap off and took myself a man-size pull. It was as sweet as strawberry punch. After I let that gulp slide down to my belly, Beth had herself a relatively large swig as well.

I warned her, "Go easy on it Beth or you'll be over in the bushes on your hands and knees watching multi-colored stuff spew from your mouth *and* your nose!"

"This stuff tastes pretty good," she said.

"Yes it does, but it is also almost eighteen percent alcohol," I informed her.

"Wow! That's twice as much as strong beer."

"Yep, and if you keep chugging it like that you *will* taste it again; I guarantee it. The second time around it's not quite so tasty!"

She laughed and took another long pull. I pretty much knew she would sleep well that night, even though she was out in the open and lost her car. When strong wine like that stuff hits the bottom, sleep comes fairly easily.

CHAPTER 13

Beth Gets Sick

The night was going to be a long one since we had no shelter other than a few pieces of cardboard. We both had one to lie on and another piece to throw over the top of us. It would keep the frost from being directly on us but if it were to rain, we would just get wet. Some of the rain would run off of the cardboard, but there would be no escaping it completely.

Beth hacked and coughed all through the night. It wasn't the usual smoker's cough that I'd hear her do every day; this was a raspy cough coming from deep in her lungs. She calmed down a bit towards morning but that might have been just because I didn't notice it as much from finally being asleep.

She started coughing again when we woke up and it was getting worse. She wasn't used to being in the cold, and the last thing she needed then was to get sick. The weather was bitter and it could turn to cold, miserable rain at any moment without warning. Since we had absolutely no shelter to sleep under, it was definitely not the time to get sick.

I asked her, "Do you feel alright? You sound terrible."

"I feel a little weak, but it's just a cold. It'll pass," she answered.

"If it doesn't get any better by tomorrow night, I think you should get checked out by a doctor. You don't sound good at all."

"I'm not going to the hospital," she firmly told me.

"You will if you don't get any better; I don't care how pissed-off you get at me."

"I don't call the paramedics every time you have a seizure," she hastily said.

"That's different Beth! I don't need to go to the hospital unless I injure myself, or don't come out of the seizure. You know that; my doctor even said so," I explained.

"I'm not going to the hospital!"

I firmly told her, "You will if you get bad enough, you stubborn bitch!"

She was quiet for a while after that remark; she knew that I could be more hard-headed than she could ever think about being. Sometimes that worked to my advantage with her. It didn't always work, but that was usually when she was The Betholizer.

We got around and brushed the dirt from our clothing. We were both freezing our asses off so we went over to McDonald's and warmed up for a while before heading over to the rock to fly our sign.

To our surprise, we racked up almost fifteen dollars in about ten minutes. One lady smiled and wished us well while giving us a five dollar bill and some change that added to the rapid increase to our funds. We decided to walk over to the mini-mart, and then go over and sit in the sunshine for a while.

It felt good to have the sun in our faces although I could tell that Beth wasn't doing well at all. The color was gone from her face and she was coughing up a storm. I knew that it would only get worse; it was just a matter of time.

The empty cans were placed behind a bush to retrieve later but the paper sack I threw in the garbage on the way back over to the rock. When we reached the rock nobody had shown up yet so we sat down to fly sign again.

After about an hour of sitting there, Beth told me she had to use the restroom and then she wanted to go sit in the sun for a while again. She asked, "Would you walk over to the mini-mart and get us a couple beers and just meet me over by the fence?"

"Yeah, I guess so. Are you sure you're feeling alright?" I inquired.

"I just don't feel good. I have no energy. Maybe a beer will help."

"Well, I doubt that, but if that's what you want, I'll be back in a flash."

I left without saying another word and quickly walked to the mini-mart. I made the trip as swift as I could, not knowing how sick Beth actually was.

I returned to the fence to find Beth between the fence and some bushes asleep. I knelt down and felt her forehead only to find she was burning up with fever. I made the decision then and there that she needed medical attention right away.

I woke her up and told her, "I'm going to make a phone call, hang tight."

"I'm not going to the hospital!" she screamed.

"You are burning up with fever, dammit!" I screamed back.

She attempted to get up then bent over and puked. I stayed with her until she was done vomiting and then I made sure she was sitting up in a good position. I ran over to the phone booth and dialed 9-1-1. I then ran back to her to find her nearly unconscious again. I aroused her attention by saying, "Sit up Beth, they will be here in a minute."

"I told you not to call them. I'm not going! Why can't you understand that?" she asked me.

"Hate me tomorrow. I don't give a rat's ass if you don't ever talk to me again! You are going to the hospital," I firmly told her.

Just as I finished those words, I saw the fire truck and the ambulance coming across the parking lot with the lights on. There were no sirens, only the flashing strobe lights were alerting busy traffic.

"Here they are, Beth. Let's see what *they* have to say about you," I told her.

The paramedics from the fire truck were the first ones to her. One of the paramedics just happened to be a guy in which I grew up with. Naturally, he was the one who talked to me about Beth's situation. I heard Beth in the background arguing to the other paramedics about going with them.

"Listen lady, you are running a temperature of a hundred-two and a half. I suggest you stop being difficult and go with us to the hospital," one of them argued back.

I couldn't hear her response, it was kind of muffled. They asked me how much she had to drink. I told them she had some but not a great deal. At that time they were loading her into the ambulance.

I put one leg up on the rear of the ambulance and told her, "I'll be there in a few minutes Beth, okay?" She tried to answer but the paramedics were busy plugging her nose with oxygen tubes. They closed the ambulance doors and off she went to the hospital. They didn't have the lights on; they just delivered her to the hospital where she needed to be.

As she was on her way to the hospital, like she should have, I went over and stashed all of our things into a bush and then caught the next bus to the hospital.

She was still in the emergency room when I arrived so I wasn't allowed to enter until Beth made sure that they let me in. It sounded like she was being a bitch, so I think they let me in so I could calm her down a bit. I knew she didn't want to be there, I certainly didn't. I had spent a fair share of my days and nights in that place and it's no fun for anybody. She needed to be there unless she wanted to die though.

They drew some blood and ran a series of tests before determining she did indeed have pneumonia and an underlying condition that she wasn't aware of. She had chronic bronchitis. That smoker's cough wasn't just smoker's cough it seemed.

Since Beth was going to be in there for a while, I decided to hop back on the bus and head back to hide our things a little better. I found those two beers that I had purchased previously and decided to go ahead and drink them down before I headed back to the hospital. There was no telling how long she was going to be in there.

When I returned to the hospital Beth asked me where I had been. I told her I went and moved all of our stuff to make it less visible. She asked me, "Are you going to stay the night here in the hospital?"

"Yes, that's why I came back," I explained.

"They aren't going to let me go for a while, and I need somebody here with me to listen to what the doctors have to say. I don't understand all of it."

"I know that Beth. I'm right here to ask the doctors all the questions that need to be asked. Don't worry about it."

She was in the hospital for two more days before she was released. She still had to take it easy though. She was very ill and didn't realize how bad off she was. When she got out of the hospital she wanted a beer, of course. The doctor had told her to stop smoking, but I knew that one wouldn't stick. Things finally got back to normal. Well, whatever normal was for us at that time. They were more normal as far as before she was hospitalized anyway.

We walked over to the mini-mart and bought a couple of beers then walked over to the fence to discuss how difficult it was going to be out in the open field again. This certainly wouldn't last forever, and neither of us really wanted it to. We just didn't have anywhere else to go at that moment. I glanced over at Nasty Neighbor's house and didn't see his *Subaru*, so we were alright standing there for the time.

CHAPTER 14

CAMP TIME

This would be only the second night that we had to sleep in the open. With Beth being in the hospital and all, we got out of sleeping under what would be the stars on a clear night. I stayed with her in the hospital every night until she was released. They tried to kick me out one night but I told them, "I'm not leaving until she does. Call security if you want!" They got the picture and let me stay. But now we were back in the field with nothing but cardboard between us, the ground, and the elements.

Beth had never really been out in the open for any length of time. She, of course, has been camping in a tent for recreation, but that is a lot different than *cowboying it* where there is no escape from the elements. When you don't have a roof of any kind, and use cardboard for a blanket, it leaves a person with a definite sense of insecurity.

We had some money so we went over to the store and bought a bunch of beer and some snacks including jerky. I liked to chew on jerky when I was cold. I don't know why, it just seemed like the thing to do. We had a few visitors stop by and visit us before it was time to start to get ready for night, so we spent a lot of time bullshitting with people.

One person who stopped by was known only as Cowboy Bob. He was an old fart that was deafer than a stump but so funny that he made me hurt from laughing every time I talked with him. He had no teeth whatsoever and had the gift of gab that would put a smile on the Mona Lisa. We were getting a little low on funds since we shared all of our beer with him so he told us he was going to make a few bucks.

Beth and knew exactly what he was going to do. He was going to pan-handle people in the parking lot. It wasn't ten minutes later and here the old fart came with about twenty bucks. "Unbelievable!" I told Beth. "He just walked up to people and asked them for money." I guess it was his age that made him so successful doing that. I couldn't, and wouldn't do it; I didn't have the nerve to. I walked over to the store and bought three bottles of high octane red wine as per Cowboy Bob's instructions.

We all got pretty well shit-faced that night so Cowboy Bob stayed out in the field with us. It didn't feel that cold until morning. My alarm went off and I peeled my ass out from under the cardboard to stretch. I could see my breath and my face was numb. I told Beth to get up so we can get out of there before daylight. Cowboy Bob had already gotten up and headed for the bus station to go for a ride. Beth crawled out and slowly stood up. She still had about a quarter bottle of wine left, and I had about a third. We were both shivering so I told her, "Head to the fence line with this stuff while I get rid of this cardboard." She wandered off so I picked up the mess and put it away.

When I got back to the fence line Beth was attempting to roll a cigarette. Her hands were so cold she wasn't having any luck so I offered my assistance. She accepted, handed me the tobacco and rolling papers, took a swig of her left over booze, and put her hands in her pockets. My hands were warm from carrying the cardboard over to the recycle bin so I rolled a smoke for her. It wasn't a piece of art but it would smoke. She thanked me as I lit it for her. Even the small amount of heat from the matches felt good on my hands.

We stayed there and finished out our bottles so I stuck the empties in a paper sack to carry to the garbage can. It was almost time for McDonald's to open so I suggested we walk on over there and hit the restrooms. That seemed like a logical thing to do to. Beth thought so too. So off we went to use the restrooms. I wasn't in too big of a hurry to leave because, after all, it was warm in there. I also took my time and cleaned up a bit before heading out into the cold again.

I bought a cup of coffee and met Beth out at the rock. She had already made a couple bucks and was only out there about three minutes. It wasn't surprising though; a little gal, cold, holding a sign outside McDonald's. It did look, above all, pathetic to a lot of people. I sat down with her for a moment then I walked over to the bus station to read the paper. It was Saturday so the auto section was included. That was my favorite part. I read that and then I read the free weekly paper that came out every Thursday.

I kept my eye on Beth while I sat there, I saw her get a couple hits; it was probably a few bucks. I could tell it was paper and not change by the way she handled it, so I knew she would want to get up and leave. I put the free paper back in the rack and put the newspaper beside one of the posts at the bus station for someone else to enjoy. I was done with it and it would save somebody fifty cents.

As expected, as soon as I started walking over towards Beth, she jumped up and tucked the sign under her arm. I knew where she wanted to go. The mini-mart was the obvious choice to get a beer. I told her, "You go ahead and grab me one too. I'm stopping at the other store for some orange juice and some more beef jerky. You want some orange juice?" I knew better than to ask her about the jerky since she not too long ago lost that cap on her tooth. But I just couldn't resist asking, "How about a Snickers bar?" That actually put a smile on her face and it became a common joke between us from then on.

"Do you want me to have them put a couple in the freezer for you?"

She just laughed and told me, "You're an asshole!"

"I know it, but at least I have my teeth," I jokingly replied.

That seemed a little below the belt but she knew I was just jerking her chain.

I met up with her at the mini-mart after I circled back from the spot behind Burger King. As I approached I noticed that on the Shell illuminated sign, the (S) was burned out so all of the westbound traffic could view perfectly the word, *hell*. It was comical to say the least. I went inside and informed Sarah, the manager, about the strangely illuminated sign and calmly informed her that the sign is probably not very good for business. We all got a kick out of it, and from there on when someone said they are going to hell, we all knew what was meant. Sarah gave a chuckle when she said, "Of all the letters to burn out, it had to be the (S)."

Beth and I headed over to where I had just come from and then proceeded to go over to the rock. I brought up the mini-mart's sign again. Beth really got a kick out of that. We took the long way around behind Albertsons to head back to the rock when a lady in a silver Lexus pulled up. The power window went down and the lady handed us each ten dollars' worth of McDonald's gift coupons and a ten dollar bill. She asked if we had eaten yet. I told her no so she invited us to McDonald's to eat with her.

While we were eating she said, "I have seen you two out in that field. Is that where you sleep?"

"Yes, how did you know?" I asked.

"I just thought maybe you didn't have any place else," she explained.

We continued to eat when she offered to take us to a sporting goods store and help us out. Beth and I were astounded so off we went in the Lexus to go shopping. We ended up with a brand new tent, two new sleeping bags, and a Coleman propane stove with two bottles of propane.

We thanked her over and over. She asked if we would like to ride along the next day with her grandson to put in job applications. I said, "Sure that sounds good to me." She told us to meet her at eight in front over by the bus station. I told her, "I'll be there! Thanks again!"

Beth and I unloaded the items and thought about where we were going to set up camp. "The only place I can think of is up the road a bit behind those two ponds," I told her.

"Before we go to set it up, we need to get a tarp to put under it," she added.

"You go ahead and fly sign for a while and I'll run over to the hardware store and get one," I told her.

Beth sat on the rock while I counted my money out then waved at her signaling that I was going heading over to buy a tarp. She waved back so she knew that we were about to head up to our new campsite. I also wanted to purchase some more tent stakes to properly secure the tarp down that would be under the tent.

As I crossed the street towards the rock I saw Beth heading towards the mini-mart carrying the tent and the sleeping bags. I rushed over to her and grabbed the heavy load from her. She said she had to go pee, so I dropped the items outside the door and waited. I knew she wanted a couple of beers to take up with us. I wanted to stop at Albertsons and get some food but I changed my mind and figured I'd purchase that later in the day after we had our camp set up.

We headed up towards the place I thought would be a good spot to set up camp. It turned out I was right. The brush was growing thick providing fairly good seclusion and the trail wouldn't be too hard to push through. Blazing the trail wasn't too bad at first but once we got past the ponds, I had to take out my multi-tool that I obtained from a bizarre Ford Explorer rollover incident, and started cutting blackberry vines, small tree limbs, and other small brush at eye level. I didn't want either one of us to injure an eye when traversing the trail in the dark.

We reached the spot I had in mind, kicked a few downed tree limbs and rocks around thus opening an excellent flat spot for our tent. The tent measured seven by ten so we had about three feet on one side and the back, five feet in front, and ten feet off to the trail side. That would be perfect for a cooking and eating area.

We spread the tarp out and I staked it to the ground while Beth unpacked the tent. We spread the tent out carefully so the bumps that were unavoidable would be at a place that neither of us would be sleeping. That turned out to be the most difficult challenge of all since she had her side and I had mine. After the bottom was positioned, it was then time to raise the top and evolve the folded piece of nylon fiber into our new home. I had set up many tents before but this was my first experience with a dome tent. Luckily, Beth had experience with that style so it went fairly quickly.

We stood outside our fine tent, cracked a cold beer and toasted a warm, dry, inconspicuous place to rest at night. Before we put our sleeping bags inside I unzipped the door and stepped in. I could almost stand up without crouching. Without my hat, my head just touched the roof. "There's plenty of room for us and our gear," I excitedly told Beth. She handed me the sleeping bags and I spread them out.

We finished our beer and then headed back down to the rock, both of us excited for evening to arrive so we could enjoy some solitude and comfort during the night. I was already looking forward to cooking on the new stove. We had a skillet already but needed paper plates and utensils. That's wasn't much of a problem though. I'd get that when I bought groceries. We both thought we were shittin' in high cotton now with a brand new tent and sleeping bags.

CHAPTER 15

CRACKER

Not much time had passed until we were back down to the rock to tell the others about our new living quarters. Everyone wanted to know where we set up camp but we both kept it a secret. Not letting everyone know exactly where we were camped was a good policy so that word didn't travel and neither would our belongings. The only thing they knew was the general direction and it would stay that way.

We flew sign until about two hours before sundown. I told Beth, "I'm going to Albertsons to get some chow and paper plates. You go to Shell and get us some beverages for the night." I went one direction and she went another. We met up on the road heading to our new camp.

Once we arrived at camp, I fired up the stove and fried up bacon then some sliced potatoes with eggs cooked into them. Beth took all the other groceries inside because it looked like rain was just about to set in. We sat down on a couple of logs that I had dragged into camp and ate dinner.

"Pretty tasty huh?" I asked her. "Grab me one of those beers please." We finished dinner just as it started to rain and get dark at the same time. It wasn't raining hard, just enough to get things wet.

We crawled inside the tent and I unscrewed the head off my Mini Maglite, turned it upside down, and placed the barrel into the head forming a candle. Beth had never seen that done before and thought that was the neatest thing she's ever saw. I then moved things around on my side of the tent to make things convenient while Beth dug through her stuff and retrieved her tobacco and matches. She rolled a smoke while I tuned my Sony Walkman onto an AM station that forecasts every hour, on the hour. "No shit!" I said out loud as I listened to the obvious forecast and the rain tapping the roof of the tent at the same time.

"Blow that fricken smoke outside," I yelled at her as she coughed and gave me a sour look. "Maybe it doesn't bother you to die from that shit, but don't include me in it," I added.

After I listened to the weather forecast I tuned into a country music station, cracked a cold one, and leaned back to enjoy the music. Right after a song ended, it was the final piss break so outside we went. A brief walk for a final look around then back inside I went. I turned on the key-chain Maglite that I had hanging from the ceiling of the tent, and then out came the cards. "Kings Corner or Rummy?" I challenged Beth as she wiggled her sleeping bag around. I screwed the head of my Maglite back onto the barrel and stuck it back into the belt holster.

"Kings Corner I guess," she responded while I shuffled the cards with confidence knowing I would whoop her ass at the challenging game. After all, I taught it to her. Game one I took with ease, so naturally I must rub it in. Game two provided me with a little more of a challenge than I expected, so I lost that game due to my own over-confidence. Game three was mine, and game number four didn't go to the finish due to my winning and her whining.

The cards went back into the box then into the backpack for another time. I finished my beverage as Beth rolled a final smoke and put fire to it. I told her, "No smoking in the tent unless you somehow make the smoke go outside. I don't feel like dying of cancer just because you don't seem to mind the idea!"

After that was said, she did prevent most of the smoke from lingering inside. That would have to be good enough. I placed my headset off to the side and buried myself into my sleeping bag then peacefully drifted off to dreamland.

All of the sudden she yelled, "Kirk, there is something in here!"

She kept jabbing me in the side until I struggled out of my sleeping bag to see what the hell all of the excitement was about.

"No there isn't, go back to sleep, dammit," I said as I rolled over and proceeded to drift off again.

"KIRK! It's moving around over in the corner of the tent!"

Now on the verge of being pissed off, I reached for my Mini-Maglite that I keep holstered on my belt. I shined it in her eyes and explained that there was nothing in the tent and that the door was zippered closed so nothing could get in. I told her, "You're nuts, go back to sleep for God's sake! Its two-thirty in the morning, now get some sleep."

Now wide awake I reached for my Cheez-Its and a beer and slipped my radio headset over my ears. I was singing along contentedly to an old country tune when she had the tenacity to bitch at me for singing. After that episode about something in the tent, she had a lot of nerve complaining about *me* keeping *her* awake.

I ate a few more Cheez-Its, finished my beer and then went to sleep. Just as I drifted off again, I heard a noise and felt Beth moving around. I raised my head from my makeshift pillow and asked, "What the hell are you doing over there?"

"I'm clearing out all this dirt," she answered.

Bewildered, of course, and thinking she had hit her head or something, I again twisted the lens end of my Mini-Maglite and aimed it over at her sorry little ass to check out what pile of dirt she was bulldozing in the middle of the night.

After taking a quick look at what she was actually doing, a small ball welt up in my throat as I asked, "Where the hell did all the dirt come from?" She turned at me with that *you piss me off* look as she shook her finger at me and said, "I told you there was something in here! Look at that hole in the tent!"

Apologizing was not easy, but I did it anyway. "I'm sorry for not believing you. Let's get some sleep and tomorrow I'll get some tape from Al to fix it. I know he has some for me, he told me so,"

I told her as I rolled over knowing there wouldn't be much sleep from there on.

When morning came, Beth was already outside puffing a smoke and performing her morning gag ritual. I stepped outside towards a clump of bushes and proceeded to take my first morning yeller piss when Beth called, "Come over here and check this out."

I walked over looking at the ground discovering a trail of Cheez-Its. Turning around to look at the hole in the tent and all the dirt recently piled up by Beth's work in the middle of the night, I turned to her with a half shit-eating grin and said, "My God! I have been eating after a gopher!" She thought that was quite hilarious getting her jollies out of my misfortune. I found it to be quite revolting, the first thing in the morning, finding out that I just the night before enjoyed a tasty snack out of the same box as a large rodent.

I decided to take the remaining portion of the snacks up the hill about fifteen feet and dump them out behind an old log. There was a small trail where something had been, and it appeared to have dug under the log. Maybe it was the same something that enjoyed chewing a hole in the tent and helping itself to my Cheez-Its.

"Maybe it will get its belly full and leave our stuff alone," I yelled down to Beth. That was wishful thinking on my part of course; I knew it would be back.

As we packed our gear and headed down the trail, I told Beth, "You know, we now have a pet gopher, it will probably come back."

"We gotta give it a name," she commented.

"That's an easy one; how about Cracker?"

"Wait till we spread this one around. No one is going to believe us you know." she said as she chuckled and grinned from ear to ear, missing cap on her front tooth and all.

"Wait till I catch that little bastard and put a small leash around its neck and lead it around like a little dog," I told her.

She thought that was funny and was laughing as she pictured it in her mind. She also knew I would do it too, given the chance. The opportunity was there; I just needed to catch the little shit. What would people say if they saw me leading a gopher around?

We laughed then headed down to McDonald's to use their facilities and warm up with a cup of coffee. Then it was off to another day of flying sign and dealing with whatever else might arise on that somewhat rainy day. We ran across the usual people throughout the day filling them in on our latest discovery. The story of Cracker was sure to put a smile on the faces of pretty much everyone we told. Most people did not believe the somewhat bizarre story at first but after asking each of us individually about Cracker and receiving the same exact story made each and every one of them a believer, especially the employees at the mini-mart. The story of Cracker's existence put a little life into their ordinarily boring day. It's one of those stories that generate interest even trying to comprehend such an odd incident. It wasn't a common thing to be able to adopt a gopher.

One of the employees at the mini mart presented us with a nice gift that evening. He gave us two-way walky-talky radios with the appropriate quantity of Duracell batteries. He thought it would be a good thing to have in case we got separated and needed to get in touch with each other, such as when I am ready to head out and Beth takes her usual time and dilly-dallies around. That drove me nuts.

Since my long time C.B. handle was Torque-Wrench, I stuck with that. We needed a handle for Beth. What could have been a better fit than *Gopher-mom*? It stuck, so that would be her call sign.

The day went well so off to Burger King we went to eat supper and then it was over to Albertsons supermarket for a new box of Cheez-Its and some other snacks. Then up the road to the trailhead we walked. We talked about the little menace that now thinks our tent is his new castle the whole way up. "What are we going to do with it? How are we going to get rid of it? We can't

86

really keep it, it is a wild animal," I questioned Beth. For one thing, I wasn't entirely sure it was a gopher until that night.

We settled in for another cold, wet night of more Kings Corner and then some Rummy. Then it was time to check the weather forecast while Beth coughed on another cancer stick. After the forecast, I tuned my radio to the country station for a few minutes before putting it away and stuffing myself into my sleeping bag for the night.

I had just fallen asleep when we both heard some scratching noises on the outside of the tent. It was on her side so she hit the tent with the palm of her hand and yelled out a few obscenities. The noise stopped for a moment then the little fart was on my side scratching the tent up near my head. It obviously wanted inside but had only one way to easily get in. The bottom zipper on the tent came off track leaving enough room for the large rodent to wiggle through. Knowing this, but ignoring it at the same time, I thought we probably scared the little shit off. "It's not going to come in here knowing that we are aware of his presence," I comforted Beth. "Besides, I dumped all those crackers up behind that log. Surely he found them, and the new box was securely closed propped up near my head. I would definitely hear that and wake up."

About two hours into sleep Beth abruptly woke me screaming, "It's in here dammit. It's in here down by my feet!" She slapped towards the bottom of her sleeping bag in total panic. I sat up half awake and the little shit ran across my legs. I reached down to grab it and the gopher slipped right through my hands. "Man he is slippery!" I yelled excitedly. Then I knew for sure it was a gopher. It squeezed its plump body right through the broken zipper and down through the brush it went. The whole time Beth was yelling, "Did you get it, is it okay?"

"Just a damn second," I replied.

"Did you catch it?"

"No dammit, it got away!"

I grabbed my flashlight, un-did the tent, and looked to see where it went.

"It dove right off into the pond about twenty yards from our tent."

"Can you chase it?"

"Hell no! I didn't know gophers could swim but that little shit's moving right along in that water," I added as I reached up and turned on the light hanging from the ceiling.

"Well now that we both are wide awake we might as well sit and talk about what we should do about the little pest," I told Beth.

"It's not going to go away on its own, after all, there is always going to be some kind of food here and plenty of warm blankets for it to curl up in. In a matter of words, the gopher found itself a pretty nice home," she said.

We talked for a while until the excitement had calmed, then we went back to sleep. I was so worked up about the episode that I never did go into a deep sleep but I managed to rest though.

Morning came a little sooner than I would have liked it to but I had to piss anyway. I told Beth to get her ass up and get moving. I stepped out for my morning ritual including brushing my teeth, combing my hair by putting on my hat, and taking a first morning yeller piss. Not necessarily in that order. Beth came climbing out and started her ritual of coughing and gagging. I nagged, "Can't wait for that first smoke huh?" That pissed her off right out of the gate. I gave her time to do her dry heave thing before sloshing down the muddy, wet trail.

It looked like the rain was going to let up. I started the conversation by telling Beth we needed another tarp. It should be a green or brown one to throw over the tent to camouflage it better. She agreed then the talk moved onto Cracker.

"What are we going to do about Cracker?" She asked.

"I don't know. I don't want to poison it or kill it, after all. It is the little asshole's home territory. *We* are the newcomers. That'll give us something to think about today," I answered.

I knew that Cracker would become a good topic of conversation for some years to come.

CHAPTER 16

BOOK OF JOHN

As the cold season quickly replaced the summer heat, it brought more and more people that came along as strangers but left as friends. It seemed the warmer it became, the more people hung around the rock just to try their luck at gaining a few bucks. There wasn't anything anyone could do about it because none of us owned the place, therefore anyone could be there.

John somehow ended up with a dog. This wasn't just a dog; it was a big, big dog. John named him Sam. Now you might say that Sam had a little bit of an attitude problem. If he liked you, he liked you. If he didn't like you, he hated you. He wore a mandatory red collar that said, *Dangerous Animal*, around his neck. I never had a problem with the large beast, although Sam did have a problem with some people no matter how many bacon-cheese burgers they would give him.

John really cared for that dog. In fact, he bought several kinds of dog food for him but the massive animal wouldn't eat it. The brute was stuck on McDonald's bacon-cheese burgers. John brought that dog from his camp down to the rock daily to keep him company.

The large animal was really an attraction for a lot of people that drove by. Sometimes I would sit at the bus station and watch John lean back and go to sleep on the rock, partly due to heat and partly due to too much beer, sometimes a combination of both. People would drive by and see that dog and throw money out at

John while he slept. It was hard to believe but it happened on more than one occasion.

That all came to an end one night when Danny and John decided to sleep in a condemned house a few blocks away. It was a two story house so if they slept on the second floor who would know the better? Well, after a few nights someone did.

In the middle of the night, the cops came up the stairs with their K9. That highly trained German Sheppard took one look at the snarling beast named Sam and took off down the stairs and had no plans to return. Police dogs are fascinating animals and this one definitely wasn't stupid. Sam would have gutted that dog in ten seconds or less. One officer told John to keep that dog back or he would shoot to kill. John was able to calm Sam down and hold on to him long enough until the animal control team showed up and hauled Sam off forever.

Losing Sam took the wind out of John's sails for a while but in time he came around. He knew it couldn't and wouldn't last forever. Being on the streets is just no place to have a pet, especially one that needed a special home, like Sam.

John resorted to other hobbies while spending time on the rock, one of which was his wrist rocket. He was pretty good with that thing. He would put a small target across the entry from the rock, and could nail it almost every time. He had to make sure that no cars were coming and sometimes he cut it just a little too close for comfort. I know people slowly driving by in their cars saw him take aim and shoot across the access road.

One day John had been passed out for about twenty minutes while Beth and I were on the rock with him. I had noticed a burgundy color PT Cruiser stopped where the busses turn in at the station. One guy and one gal were there and the guy was poking a slim jim down the window. I thought nothing of it as they unlocked it and drove by us into the parking lot then went out the exit on the other side.

John finally woke up just as a police cruiser pulled up and stopped right in front of us. We thought he was there because somebody turned John in for being passed out or playing with that wrist rocket. We thought wrong though. The officer wanted to know if we had seen somebody break into a vehicle at the bus station a few minutes ago. Being a helpful citizen, I jumped up and explained to the officer that I did in fact see someone, and described the car and the two people to him. He thanked me and took off.

John cracked a beer and minutes later another cop showed up and stopped. I thought we were busted for sure but the officer asked the same question as the previous one did. I explained to him that another officer had just come by and that I told him what I knew. That cop then sped across the parking lot. I told Beth, "I did my part, let's go have a brew. It's hot and I need a break." We got up, stashed our sign, and walked over to the mini-mart.

By the time we returned, John was getting ready to head up to his camp so Beth and I would again have the rock to ourselves. But then Jumpin' Jack came hopping down the pea patch with his sign. "Great!" I told Beth. "That just shot this all to hell."

"Oh quit it. He's not so bad when he's not jumping out into traffic," she defended.

I just sat down feeling like we just weren't going to make that much that afternoon. I had some money stashed and I was sure Beth did too.

"Hi kids! Doing any good?" Skippy asked.

"Nope," I answered, "Mostly just killing time, hiding from the boredom. You know what I mean."

We flew a little while longer then made plans to head on up to camp. I decided to just get some lunch meat and cheese and some pop. I like to drink pop in the morning, and sometimes I liked to drink it instead of beer on a hot day. It seems like beer goes flat faster than pop as it gets warm.

I walked to Albertsons and Beth walked over to the mini mart. We met outside about twenty minutes later. I'd been standing there with my groceries for several minutes. Then we walked up the road to the trailhead trying to hurry as much as possible. I wanted to sit down and crack a beer. We got to camp and had a beer then made sandwiches. I had the Cheez-Its inside the tent so I grabbed them to go along with dinner. Luckily Cracker hadn't found that box yet.

We talked about John and how bad he was looking. Danny wasn't paying a lot of attention to him at the time and I think the loneliness was getting to him. Losing Sam, plus the death of his son, made him think of going to Texas even more. He was drinking a lot more than usual and hardly eating at all. John not looking healthy was a very large understatement.

John came down the next day while Beth and I were already on the rock. A couple other people joined us so John said he was going back out on the freeway. Off he went with his sign. We watched as he sat on the concrete divider and made a few bucks. He came back with his hair soaked with sweat. He was wearing a rough looking black leather jacket and wouldn't take the damn thing off. I have no idea why he wanted to wear that thing in such hot weather.

A few days went by with more of the same thing, nothing new except the temperature was even higher. It was now summer and the temperatures were soaring into the upper-nineties. All I had was short sleeved shirts. Before I knew it, I had one hell of a sunburn. I had blisters on my arms all the way up to the part where the shirt sleeves covered. It was painful at times even though I applied lotion frequently.

Even though John was as hot as the rest of us, probably hotter with that damn jacket, he always had something to tinker around with. It's hard to explain but he could come up with the most unusual item and make it fun for everyone. One item was a strange looking hat. It resembled a cross between a Green Beret hat and a thirties style hat that gentlemen wore while driving their ladies around in their 'motorcars.' It was a dark brown color, sort of military brown. Every day for about three weeks there he came with his back pack and his baseball cap. As soon as he sat down on the rock, the backpack came open, and off with the baseball cap, on with the other hat. He would yell, "Taliban!" and place it on his head. Every one there would yell, "Taliban" as well. We all got a kick out of it, and it always made John laugh. That was good to see him smile and enjoy the moment.

As the days passed by, it was then time for the fireworks booth. Every year a fireworks company set up a large tent selling fireworks for the fourth of July holiday celebration, and we all took turns checking everything out. The boss at the sight saw us on the rock daily and always waved at us. He knew we weren't going to harm or steal anything, if nothing else it was a little more protection for him knowing we were there and had a pretty good idea of what was going on around there on a daily basis. Hell, we were there before he got out of his trailer in the morning and after he crawled back in it for the night.

The owner walked over to us the day the tent and equipment was being torn down and hauled off. He said that the site boss told him we looked after the place at different times. Which was true, if anything looked a little suspicious we would take the appropriate measures. In return, for doing basically nothing but being there just in case something did happen, he gave each of us a fairly large bag of fireworks.

That was a lot of fireworks, so we had our own celebration a little late in the season. John held on to a few of his favorites to set off as he pleased. That quickly evolved into a potential disaster.

In front of the rock was a series of speed bumps about five feet apart. That was one of the reasons why the rock was such a prime spot to fly sign. The vehicles had to pass by very slowly so the people inside wouldn't be thrown all over inside the vehicle.

John got a wild hair up his ass one day to set off one of those spinners that as they twirl, they spew off other smaller spinners. He lit that thing and chucked it out into the road in the middle of the speed bumps and here came a car out of McDonald's drive thru. The timing couldn't have been worse. As soon as the car was directly over the spinner, it went into stage two and spat out all the little ones. They were dancing all over the place under that poor dude's car. It's a damn good thing he didn't have a fuel leak, he would have been blown sky high, taking us with him. The poor fellow didn't have a choice but to keep driving slowly over the speed bumps until he was out of danger. After he pulled out, John looked at me and laughed like hell.

We all had a lot of fun with John and likewise, he had fun with us. He talked of going to Corpus Christi, Texas for quite a while and started saving money for the trip. He had family here in the Pacific Northwest but wanted to go there for a season just to get out of the rain for a while. He always said he would come back.

John didn't ever get into what happened in his life that put him where he was. But by piecing together things that he told me, and what I found out from others, he was, at one time, quite successful and a model citizen. There was just something about John that always ticked in me that there was a lot more to him than he let on.

One afternoon while sitting in the shade and having a few beers with him, he let part of his past slip out. It was only a slight part, a tightly held personal secret, but it was significant. I had to gather the information together and chew on it for a while before I figured out what John's previous days had held.

It appeared John, in his past, was a well-established personnel training coordinator for a worldwide company that designs and manufactures products ranging from industrial electric motors to jet aircraft engines. His job was to train service personnel all over the world in troubleshooting and repair of large industrial electric motors and generators.

In short, John was no dummy. His not having a home had nothing to do with his intelligence level. He probably earned a fairly large salary during his career. The conversation changed to other things, so that was as far as I got that day. I didn't want to pry too far into his personal life. However, I was still curious as to what exactly happened to him.

I did find out later that he was a married man at one time with a son and a daughter. His daughter lived in the area where we were but he only saw her and her husband on occasion. John's son tragically died in an automobile accident during the time he was around us and homeless. It hit him pretty hard although he did hide his emotions quite well.

As the days passed by, a few more details came trickling in about John. He was happily married for a number of years in Tennessee and Indiana. He moved out to the Northwest as the divorce papers were being processed. Apparently when the divorce was becoming final, John decided to liquidate as many assets as possible so his wife wouldn't end up with the majority of them. One way that he accomplished this was by purchasing a new home for his recently married daughter and her husband. No strings were attached; it was paid for in full. I have seen the home. It wasn't a mansion but it was certainly not a dump either. The couple sold the home a few years later to move into yet a larger home across town to accommodate a baby. That was John's first and only grandchild.

I didn't dig any farther into John's past but to me he was one of the friendliest guys out there, although to him it felt like nobody cared for his existence at all. His self-worth went right down the drain as it happened to so many of us on the streets. It was not that he was stupid; he just got dealt a bad hand in life and lost out horribly. He could not see any way out. The deeper things got, the deeper he fell. He was just like a snowball in hell with nothing to do but simply melt away into more misery. I always felt compassion for him, mostly because I can relate with those kinds of feelings.

The day arrived when John announced to everyone that he would indeed be heading to Corpus Christi the next morning. Everyone was saddened of the news, even though we all knew that his plans were to come back the following summer. We all said our goodbyes and wished his journey well. John had a tear streaming from one eye when nearly everyone hugged him. I don't think he realized how much he actually meant to everyone that knew him. We were all on the edge of breaking down and crying.

That was the last time I saw John; in fact, not one of us ever saw John again. He never came back the next summer, or the summer after that. No news from him or about him ever came across in any form. Some people even gave him their phone number and permission to call collect, anytime. There had been no call, nothing. John's health was not good to say the least, so naturally we all think he knew he was dying and went to Corpus Christi to spend his final days. I, as well as many others, hope and pray that's not the case but the general feeling among us all is that none of us will see John and experience his wonderful personality ever again.

CHAPTER 17

FLYING THE FREEWAY

With John out of the picture, a substantial amount of life left the rock. The only regular people that showed up there besides me was Beth, Skippy, and on rare occasion, Danny. There were a few people here and there that showed up at different times but it was such a rare occurrence that I never remembered most of their names. The people walking by just to say hello was something of a treat. Some would come by daily and others just every now and then.

One of the more familiar persons that often walked by was Fran. He was born in Germany during the war, and had the accent to prove that point. He was a friendly fellow that always wore short pants. It could be twenty degrees outside, everyone layered up and still freezing our asses off and here would come that goofy Fran in short pants. Only twice did I ever see him with long pants, once for a funeral and another that I didn't find out what the occasion was.

It was still summer though and now the beer drinking had slacked off to more water, pop, and sports drinks. We all knew that beer will dehydrate a person pretty quickly. In fact, Beth didn't consume enough water one day and ended up taking the ambulance to the hospital. I could tell Beth to drink water or sports drinks but she wouldn't listen, she would drink nothing except beer and it almost killed her. She lived through it though, they just pumped her full of liquids, and potassium then sent her back.

Beth had gotten up to go use the restroom leaving Skippy and I on the rock. It was hot that day, so hot that we wanted to take our shirts off but didn't. We were sitting there patiently then here came a motorcycle cop. He stopped right in front of us, turning on his red and blue lights. As he opened one of his saddle bags and retrieved a ticket book, I turned to Skippy and whispered, "Oh boy, we're in for it now. Johnny Law looks like he's got a stick up his ass."

Skippy laughed as he shrugged his shoulders then nervously said to me, "We ain't got nothing to worry about, we ain't done nothing wrong."

"Maybe so," I said, "but he is not here to congratulate our efforts."

I looked at the approaching officer and greeted him politely by saying, "Howdy officer." The cop made us show our identification and then explained that the property owner did not want us sitting there anymore. Skippy and I just looked at each other and stood up. "We'll leave then," I said to the officer. He placed his ticket book back in the saddle bag and rode off without incident.

Skippy looked at me and said, "Well that sucks!"

"Yes it does," I agreed.

I watched the Betholizer as she stumbled over towards us asking, "What was that cop all about?"

"The rock is done. We've got to move on. I guess from here on out it's the freeway where John was flying before he left," I explained to her.

Beth said a couple obscenities and started walking with us over to the bus station to reflect on the situation. There really wasn't anything to reflect on; it was pretty much cut and dried. No more sitting on the rock was kind of an end to an interesting era.

"We have to fly the freeway now or nothing at all. Hot as it may be out there, it's the only other place I can think of close by. John did alright out there, you know," I explained.

The three of us sat at the station for a while and then Skippy stood up and walked out to go try his luck on the freeway. Beth and I decided to go get a brew and make a new sign then try *our* luck. We walked over to the mini-mart discussing what we should write on the sign while we walked.

We walked out of the store and over to the fence line. We both cracked our brews and looked at each other, wondering what else was going to happen that day. I wanted to chug the beers down quickly; it leaves less time to be exposed to someone that would squeal on us for consuming an alcoholic beverage on unlicensed premises. It's happened before, and I know that the jerk that lives in the house by the fence line is just the type to call Johnny Law. That's why he was nick named *Nasty Neighbor*, and fittingly so.

Low and behold the little weasel was home and spotted us. "Kirp," he yelled, "You better leave or I'm calling the cops!"

"That shows his intelligence level," I told Beth. "My name is Kirk not Kirp. Where the hell does he get Kirp? Second, this is not his property. It actually belongs to the state, and an extension to the freeway is in the engineering process at this very moment. He's just being a prick. Come on and drain that thing before shit-for-brains calls the cops on us." She did, so we got the hell out of there, carrying our empty cans with us.

By the time we crossed the street, Skippy was already done for a while. On the way by he told us, "It's hot out there kids but I've already made about five bucks." He walked to get him a brew and watch us from a distance in the shade. We got into position in between the east and westbound lanes and gave it a whirl.

"Whew! He's right. It's hotter than hell out here! Let's look as miserable and pathetic as possible," I told Beth.

It didn't take long, maybe twenty or thirty minutes, and we had raked in almost nine bucks. That wasn't too bad for a first time out there, although standing amongst the traffic there took a little more guts than the rock. More people came through there that were more likely to recognize me. The pride I had to swallow was a lot more than I would have liked to but I did it anyway.

"I'm well known for what I've done in this community you know; with my kids' ball games, cub scouts, and such. It's hard to stand out here all exposed like this," I told Beth.

"Oh well. You gotta do what you gotta do," she said.

"Yeah, I guess so, but it still isn't easy," I replied.

We left the freeway, did our usual shopping, and then headed back up to camp. When we got there I noticed that Cracker had been back to visit. Not uncommon for the little rascal. I spoke again about harnessing the little fart and walking him around just for laughs. We laughed about that for a few minutes before focusing our attention on more important matters.

The leaves were starting to change signaling that fall wasn't too far ahead. That meant our camp would be more vulnerable due to the loss of underbrush, only present during the summer, which kept our tent less visible. Another thing to consider was the two ponds below. What would they be like when the heavy rains hit? Those were all things we had to consider in advance.

The two ponds ran parallel with the road, all behind the locked gate. The only way up to our camp at the time was to walk along a small ridge between the two ponds. I didn't know it at the time but during the start of the rainy season the two ponds would fill up and overflow into each other making one large pond. That process would give me fair warning as I watched the water level in the ponds every day. As the level reached the merging point I would be forced to cut a new path into camp. That was a chore I was not looking forward to.

We played cards again that night before going to sleep. Cracker didn't make too much of a mess. I was making general conversation when I told Beth, "I need to save some money for some new batteries and socks."

The conversation suddenly turned into an argument. She informed me, "You can buy batteries for one a buck per package at the dollar store."

"I do *not* trust cheap batteries. I don't care what anybody tries to tell me, you are better off with paying a little extra and getting Duracell or Energizer, period. That's especially true when you are out in the woods every night, all night. You need batteries that you can trust; end of story," I explained to her.

Beth knew how I felt about cheap stuff that you need to depend on and she also knew that she wouldn't win the argument. She accepted the fact that I'm hard headed about certain things, and batteries just happened to be one of the major things. She decided to just keep her mouth shut.

The next morning it was the same thing, the same morning ritual. Beth doing her gag thing and me pestering the piss out of her. We stopped on the way down and I looked around at the ponds. I decided that the best way to travel once the water levels rose would be the far end of the ponds. That ultimately meant a substantially further walk but it appeared to be the best choice.

We went down to fly sign for a while and gained enough money for a couple of brews after buying some lunch and some batteries. We headed over to Burger King and ate a bite before going to the mini-mart for a couple brews. We purchased our beers and met Linda Lou on the way out. I explained to Linda that the rock is no longer available. I didn't tell her at the time but she was partly to blame for getting us kicked off the rock. She was about half snookered one day at just about mid-summer and took a piss right behind the newspaper drop-box. Not a good thing, people have a tendency to frown on such behavior.

Beth and I went over to the fence line to crack our beers and noticed Nasty Neighbor's Subaru was still in his driveway. We decided to walk behind the loading docks at Albertsons and drink them there, away from his highness.

The afternoon heat was coming on strong so I hammered my beer down before it had time to become warm and flat. As usual, Beth was taking as long as Beth wanted. Then here came the ice-cream delivery truck. Beth smarted off to the driver asking him, "Hey, where's our free samples?" The guy just smiled and went about his business.

Beth finally finished her beer and rolled a smoke, and then we were on our way. As we approached the intersection, I noticed Linda Lou out on the freeway flying. That immediately pissed off the recently transformed Betholizer. She said with a snarl, "Look at her; now that bitch is out there in our spot!"

"That it is *not* our spot Beth. She has every bit as much right to be there as we do." I told her. "Let's just go sit in the shade for a while."

"Well, she needs to leave there, she's the reason we got kicked off the rock,"

She only bought one beer before, so as soon as she makes some money she will no doubt head to the store for another," I explained.

When Linda had raised a few bucks, she left just like I said. Then it was our turn again. It was getting close to supper time so people were getting off of work. That is when the freeway became the busiest.

We made several dollars so we packed it up and headed for the dollar store. Beth wanted to get a flashlight for herself and I wanted to get batteries. We went inside and Beth found a barrel full of flashlights that took two D-cell batteries. The flashlight was a dollar, and the D cell batteries were a dollar for four. I, of course, was extremely skeptical of the quality involved in both of those products.

"A dollar for a flashlight? High quality item this must be," I told her.

She gave me a glare and made her purchase. When we walked out that door, I went straight into the hardware store and bought some Energizers for my Mini Maglite. Of course that pissed her off because I could get four shitty batteries for less than the price of two Energizers.

In my defense I told her, "In the middle of the night if something happens, I'm the one who has to deal with it and I don't want to fart around with replacing batteries. I want something I can trust. That's that! You know I can be pretty hard headed on things like that. I only buy items I can trust."

We stopped at the little store and purchased the usual items before going to Albertsons for some supper fixings. After that, Beth just had to stop by the little shop where she buys her tobacco and picked up a box. Then it was on up the road to the trail head. I wanted to go further and check out the idea that I had for a new trail but time was running out. We went back to camp and I had a bite to eat while Beth rolled a few smokes and stuck one in her mouth and packaged up the rest for later.

After she was finished with her cigarette, she stuck the batteries into the new flashlight she had purchased. She screwed around and screwed around with the damn thing before she concluded that it didn't work. She had her fill of it for a while, so she handed the thing to me.

I farted around with that flimsy fricken light for ten minutes before I figured out how to modify the ground strap running down the inside of the case so the piece of shit would work. I bitched, moaned, and complained the whole time. She heard me; I made damn sure she did. Then I really let her have it. I told her, "I'm really anxious to see just how long this cheap piece of shit works. Will the light even last as long as the crappy batteries? It won't take too long to find out!"

She gave me a disgusted look but down deep, she knew I was right.

"For crying out loud in the dark Beth; the damn thing didn't even work brand new!" I scolded her some more.

She had nothing more to say to me on the subject.

There still was a little daylight left so I ventured out from the camp to find a new spot for a trail-head from the camp end. I discovered a decent path with very little holes but the brush was really thick. I took a piece of ribbon that I'd found previously and marked the spot where the trail would start. Then it was getting so dark that I had to head back so I wouldn't have traverse with only the use my flashlight in unfamiliar terrain. When I got back, Beth was already in the tent drinking a beer, smoking a cigarette, and ready to play cards. I wasn't much into playing that night but I did just to keep her happy. I kind of wanted to listen to my radio but I could always do that later, I thought.

The next morning it appeared like it might rain. I cleaned up around camp and made sure that everything was prepared in case it did get wet. Beth came out so we stumbled around a bit and headed on back down the hill. By the time we arrived at the freeway to fly sign it was raining. Neither of us had rain gear but it was so warm that a person would just get wet on the inside from sweat anyway.

We were out there for quite a while without a hit. We both came to the conclusion that people just don't want to roll down their windows when it is raining. We stood there and stood there when finally a guy rolled down his window and handed us a couple bucks. We decided to leave for a while and take a break.

After we visited the Amber at the mini-mart, we walked over to the fence line. Nasty Neighbor wasn't home at the time; at least his car wasn't there, so we were all right. We had just cracked our beers open and started bullshitting. Another fellow we knew, Dusty, just happened to be walking by and stopped to visit, and then I heard that annoying voice; "Kirp! I'm calling the cops!"

I looked at Beth and our friend Dusty and said, "You know, that fricken jerk is really beginning to chap my ass! Come on, we'd better leave." We left that area and sat between the shopping mall and the freeway construction site in the field. I saw a black and white snooping around by the fence line so I knew that prick did turn us in.

The weather cleared up and the sun came out. It became so muggy that I thought I was back in Illinois. There was no breeze, so that made it feel even worse. It wasn't typical for the humidity to be so high in the Pacific Northwest, although it did happen occasionally.

I told Beth, "Let's go for a walk before we go back out to fly. I want to see what's going on down by Safeway. Besides, I'm kind of hungry for them nachos with jalapenos over at that little store."

"Okay, I haven't been down there for a while," she replied.

We walked into the little store and purchased a couple beers and I dolled up some nachos then we went down the alley more commonly called *the field*. It was a quiet place and at least it was away from Nasty Neighbor.

We had to stand because the grass was damp from the rain but the sun was shining. A friend came walking down the field on her way to the bus. She worked at the market research firm where I applied at when the lady in the Lexus took us. I asked about work and she told me it was slow and that she wasn't getting many hours in. We chatted for a while then she said she had to catch the next bus.

After she left, Beth and I made small talk while we drank beer and I ate the nachos. She couldn't eat them because of the jalapeno peppers. I finished them off and put all the garbage in a bag. As we headed over to the freeway I spotted Linda Lou out flying where we wanted to go, again. That immediately pissed Beth off. She already had a pretty good buzz on so she was well on her way to transforming into the Betholizer.

As we sat down at the bus station a few more people showed up. Beth went to use the restroom but instead came back with another beer. I leaned over to another person that I was talking to and warned, "Uh-Oh, she's going to get real mouthy real quick."

Beth finished her cigarette and was drinking the last part of that beer just as Linda packed up and walked off the freeway, headed towards the bus station. I didn't think anything of it; I was getting to the point of needing a piss break anyway.

Linda took a seat at the bus station and Beth figured she would give Linda Lou a piece of her mind about flying on the freeway. Linda shrugged it off for a while but Beth wouldn't stop. I knew it was going to get awfully ugly soon if she didn't shut her fricken mouth. Me and the lady I was talking to got up and headed towards another small store, turning around only to see Beth in the face of an ex-body builder who outweighed her by nearly seventy pounds, and whose temper had just about reached its peak. I told the person whom I was talking to, "This ain't going to be good." It wasn't.

Linda got her fill and picked Beth up off the ground, carried her over towards the parking lot, laid her down, and proceeded to slap some sense into her. Beth, whose mouth was a lot stronger than her fists, was basically defenseless against Linda Lou. I just kept on walking only looking back to make sure it wasn't going to get really bloody. I could have stopped it, I supposed, but Linda was just going to smack some sense into Beth. She wasn't going to kill or maim her; she just wanted Beth to know that she won't put up with her shit.

Some guy with a cell phone called the cops so by the time I came out of the little store with a cold one, they already were there and talking to both Linda and Beth. They put the cuffs on Linda and hauled her off.

When I approached the bus station, Beth then lit into me, yelling, "How come you didn't help out? You just walked off!"

I looked Beth right in the eye as I cracked my beer and said, "You started it."

That was all I said as I headed towards the fence to drink my beer. Beth went and got her another beer, like she needed it, and then headed over to join me at the fence line. I could tell she was pissed off at me but I figured I was right. I was friends with both of them. I finally spoke up and told Beth, "What you did was not only wrong, it was stupid! You're lucky you didn't end up in the emergency room. She could have put the warp right on your skinny little ass right there in front of God and everybody!"

That pissed her off even more but it needed to be said, and so did this: "The truth hurts," I told her.

I finished my beer, walked over and grabbed the sign, and went to the freeway. I was out there for about a half hour and made about five bucks. I could stop now and be way ahead of the game but here came the Betholizer stumbling over to join me. I mumbled, "I hope she keeps her fricken mouth shut." As I got a closer look at her, somehow, I knew she wouldn't.

"I hope they lock her up and throw away the key," was the first thing that fell out of Beth's mouth as she grabbed the sign away from me.

The only thing I could think of to say was, "They aren't going to keep her Beth, and you'd better just learn to control that hole in your face when you've had a couple of brews!"

All the sudden she was pissed off again. I'd had enough, so I left leaving her screaming, "Where the hell do you think you're going?" I didn't say a word, I just quietly walked away.

As I crossed Main Street I saw Linda get off the bus. I walked over to her and she walked towards me with a smile on her face. "Where's Beth?" She asked. I just pointed towards the freeway. Linda gave a small laugh and asked, "Would you buy me a beer?" I couldn't help it. I started laughing as I walked towards The mini mart. I bought one for her and one for me. I walked with Linda over behind Burger King, laughing the whole time.

When we got there we cracked our beers as she explained, "They didn't even take me to jail! They took me to the police station and questioned me then told me it was a mutual confrontation and stay away from her and then let me go! I talked the bus driver into giving me a ride."

She was chuckling while she said it. I was laughing so hard that I couldn't drink my beer. I told her, "You know, Beth thinks they are going to give you the electric chair."

We both got to laughing and Linda couldn't resist saying, "Who does she think she is, Wonder Woman? God, I could have beaten the shit right out of her!"

At that point, the laughter was uncontrollable. I just shook my head. I was laughing so hard I couldn't say anything.

When we finished our brews, I walked over to the bus station only to see that Beth was on her way. We were done for the day and headed over to the mini-mart and then to camp. Not a word was said the whole time about the day's events. I wanted so badly to crack a few jokes at her but I knew there would be no sleep that night if I did. It had been a long day and we were both tired anyway.

CHAPTER 18

LET IT RAIN

When the summer of 2007 was over and fall was knocking on winter's door, in the Pacific Northwest, that meant rain, and lots of it. Unless we had a rare Indian summer, it rained. When it started to get wet it seemed like it would never give up until summer finally hit. It's like a switch. It's on or it's off for the season with no happy medium. We may get a dry day or two, here or there, but mostly just good old fashioned rain.

I woke up early the next morning from the sound of the wet drops hammering the top of the tent. I had to pee but didn't want to step out in the dark to do it. I checked my wristwatch and discovered that it was only four thirty, way too early to get my ass soaked just to take a piss. I had an empty Gatorade bottle stashed over on my side for just such emergencies but as soon as I dug it out, I heard Beth start rustling around. That idea was shot to hell so I figured on stepping outside into the rain and getting my ass wet.

I carefully placed my Maglite so it was aimed at the direction where I would relieve myself. Very gently, I stepped out into the rain and darkness and immediately slipped and fell right on my ass. I landed right in the mud, right in front of the tent. "Son of a bitch!" I yelled as Beth poked her head to see what the commotion was all about.

"You sure are noisy," she smugly said.

"I'm alright, nice of you to ask," I snapped at her.

"Are you okay?" She finally asked.

"Yes, and thank you for your concern. Now I'm really awake. If you gotta go, now is the time," I told her.

She came crawling out so I grabbed her arm so she wouldn't do a repeat of what I had just done. As I took a firm hold of her, I said, "We gotta do something about this; it's slicker than shit right here."

Then we were both wide awake and chances of going back to sleep were slim and none. Beth said she was going back inside to roll a smoke. I wasn't going to crawl back inside that tent, so I asked her to hand me my rain jacket. She fumbled around for a moment then handed it to me out the tent door.

"Is there any pop in there? I'm thirsty from that jerky last night," I asked.

"No, but there are two beers left," she informed me.

"That'll really put us off to a good start. It is raining like crazy, and all we have to drink is beer. Oh well, you twisted my arm, go ahead and pass me one. If I'm going to be wet and cold today, I might as well feel warm on the inside," I said.

I grabbed a piece of cardboard that we had brought up previously, turned it over, and placed it on a log to sit on. As soon as I sat down, I felt my jeans suddenly start to stick heavily to my ass. That's always a wonderful sensation to have the first thing in the morning.

By the time I stood back up I saw Beth poke her beer out of the tent. I grabbed it with one hand and offered my other hand to her so she wouldn't end up on her ass. She made it out and had to go piss again. I shined my light over towards some brush so she could find her way.

After she got all buttoned up I asked her, "Are you ready to head on down? It won't be light for another hour but we've made it up here in the dark before, and I've gone down there and back in the dark without a light."

"Yeah, let's just go ahead and go," she said.

"Wait, my flashlight won't come on!" she complained.

I held my tongue as long as I possibly could as I checked out the cheap piece of shit. Then I just couldn't hold it any longer. I aimed my Maglite into her eyes and boldly said, "See this? Mine works huh? Imagine that. Maybe we should go and buy four or five of these dollar ones to carry around so the odds of one working would be better!"

That comment definitely did not score any points with her and she didn't speak to me the rest of the way down. I didn't care though, sometimes the truth hurts.

Not having the best of mornings so far; I couldn't *wait* to find out what else could get screwed up. Well, it got worse. I had a burrito the day before, soaked with hot sauce. I knew damn good and well how those things affect my bowels but I ate it anyway regardless of the consequences. The McDonald's lobby wasn't open yet so I eased on over to Albertsons to use the restroom there. A sign on the men's room door read, *Out of order . . . Sorry for the inconvenience. No problem*, I thought. *I'll just use the lady's room.* Problem! The door was locked. "Well horse piss," I mumbled to myself as I walked right on out the door. I walked back over where Beth was at the bus station clenching my cheeks just as firmly as I could. Finally I saw the doors at McDonald's come open.

I took care of business and cleaned up a bit while I was there. I veered over to the store for some stuff to munch on while we were waiting for daylight. After I ate some goodies I told Beth, "Well, if you aren't going to eat anything just put these snacks in your coat pocket for later, and we'll head on out there." She stuffed the snacks in her pockets and we walked over to the freeway. The rain had settled down to a slight drizzle and the traffic was picking up.

I grabbed the sign that we had stashed in the bushes and handed it to Beth. I told her, "I'm going can hunting. You'll do well out here in the rain by yourself." She nodded and I went to pick up cans. I found a few cans here and there and brought them back. I stashed them in the bushes then walked over to Beth.

"How much do I have?" she asked as she handed me some change and a couple of bills. I counted it behind her so no one could see me count.

"A five, a one, and a dollar seventy in change. See Beth, I made about thirty cents in cans. That's what happens every single time that I go looking for cans," I told her.

She put a grin on her face and asked what time it was. I knew what she wanted. She wanted another beer. I kind of wanted another one too after the rough takeoff I had that morning.

I told her, "Don't worry, its after seven. You should eat something though."

"Beth will eat when Beth wants to eat." she said.

She already said that little piece and she wasn't even buzzed yet. I could tell from the looks of her that this was going to be one of those days. You consider ninety pounds, an empty stomach, and two twenty-four-ounce malt liquors before eight in the morning, and it adds up for the perfect ingredients to produce the Betholizer.

We went over to the mini-mart and listened to April for a while. She was a sweet gal that was dangerously close to getting her nice looking twenty one year old body into a deep pile of crap with some guy that I had the pleasure of meeting once or twice. He appeared to be in his mid to late thirties. I didn't pry too far into her business but just to let her know to be careful, really careful. Why would a guy that is still legally married, but getting a divorce, be attempting to pick up on a sweet, young, good looking gal her age? That situation had a big red flag waving all over from it.

Beth hadn't evolved into the Betholizer quite yet, so she was interested in April's wellbeing also. She went to the restroom so I went and put two beers on the counter and paid for them. Beth came out so we told April goodbye and off we went. Just as we hit the fence line I saw Nasty Neighbor going down the street. "Good, he's leaving. Hide until I see him hit the main road," I instructed Beth. We did, so now all we had to consider is the school kids walking by, and the people from the adult foster home in the area. We cracked our brews and started talking.

I wanted to test the waters with Beth's attitude so I remarked, "Still packing that flashlight huh? Might as well pitch it. It ain't no good. Save the cheap batteries though, we can throw them at someone we don't like!"

That did the trick. She turned at me like a rattlesnake ready to strike and blared out, "Shut up about the fricken light. It only cost one dollar! Yours cost almost ten dollars!"

"Yeah, but mine has either Energizer or Duracell batteries in it, and a belt holster, and most of all, mine works!" I struck back.

I guzzled my beer and quickly turned to walk off. I knew that would put her over the edge. She yelled out, "Yeah! There you go with all my money!"

The Betholizer was back. It was really no surprise; it always happened when she didn't eat anything and then dumped a bunch of beer in her otherwise empty belly.

It started to rain a little more than a drizzle so I walked over to read the paper at the bus station. "Hey buddy!" I heard as I turned to look over my left shoulder. There was Al. "Need some tape? I got a roll for ya. I been carrying it around but I haven't seen ya. Haven't had any more them seizures have ya?" he asked as he smoked his pipe.

"No Al, I haven't, but thanks for the tape. It always comes in handy."

"You're welcome. I got more at home; I'll bring you some more."

I thanked him as he turned to get on the bus. He always asked about the seizures. He was a harmless man, very good hearted, and never forgot tape. I never could figure what the passion was between him and tape but he definitely had a thing for it.

Since it was raining, the only people who went out on the freeway to fly were me and Beth. We took turns so one of us could have a break while the other flew. We both managed to get fairly well soaked so we figured we would get something to eat before heading back to camp. Beth had this thing for cream of broccoli soup and wasn't about to leave until she had some. Thank God Albertsons had some that was fresh and hot from their deli section. I bypassed that and got some sardines and a fresh bottle of salsa. We already had some Cheez-Its up at camp, as long as Cracker didn't get into them.

As we approached the two ponds, I surveyed the situation carefully. The two ponds were filling up fast. I walked down to the far end of the ponds and there was nothing really flowing out of them. All the water was contained without drainage. It was mostly just sort of spreading around with no particular ditch or steam. Anywhere the lowest place happened to be was where the water would settle.

"This isn't good," I told Beth. "If it keeps raining like this all night, we're going to be coming out of her by blazing a new trail tomorrow morning."

"How long do you think it will take you to cut a new trail?" she asked.

"I don't know. It will probably a couple good hours of daylight."

"Why don't you run back down and get us some beer for tomorrow?"

"You mean go down and get some beer so you can drink while I blaze a new trail," I quickly corrected her.

"Well yeah. You'll want one when you get done with the new trail," she said.

Being a good sport, I headed back on down to the mini-mart. It poured the whole time I was gone. I figured while I was the one making the trip, I might as well stop and have a couple tacos. I did just that and enjoyed them very much. Then I headed back up to the road. I stopped before I got to the ponds and drank a beer by myself. Sometimes a person just wants to be alone for a little while. As I walked to the ponds I shined my flashlight between the two ponds where the trail was. The two small ponds had merged themselves together forming one big pond. I sloshed my way through the water that was only about an inch deep at the time and finally made it to the tent.

I thought I had better sleep well because it was going to be a long, hard morning punching a new trail through with nothing more than my multi-tool and a couple strong sticks. I wasn't looking forward to cutting the new trail at all.

I sat up talking with Beth for an hour or so. She wanted to play cards but I didn't want to. I just wanted to finish my brew and go to sleep. My plans were to sleep all night until close to daylight. I would need all the energy I could gain to clear the new trail.

Beth didn't want to go to sleep then; of course she didn't have to get up and blaze the new trail either. Her morning was pretty simple. Drink beer until either it was gone or I got the new trail punched through. It kind of pissed me off. I went down to get her the beer but knew she wouldn't lift a finger to help out in the morning. I just got covered up and went to sleep anyway.

Morning came and it sounded like the rain had stopped. I crawled out of the tent, took a piss and looked around. I walked down to the pond and sure enough, it was impassable without wading almost knee deep. I walked back to the new trail head and started in. I saw Beth crawl out, take a piss, and then come over to watch, beer in hand. That was all she did. I already figured as much so I just kept at it. I finally made it to the road then turned back to camp. When I got there Beth handed me a beer. It was only about ten o'clock; I had made pretty good time. I cracked the beer open and drank it down. At least she saved me one; I was pretty thirsty. Then it was time to show her what I had done as we walked down to the freeway to see what was going on.

We packed up and headed down the new trail to the road, then to the freeway to fly sign as usual. It started raining again and the temperature dropped dramatically. It almost felt like it could snow. We both flew for a while, and then we walked down to a friend's house to visit. She was kind of a different gal, you really couldn't tell where the truth stopped and the bullshit began. It just kind of flowed together so quickly that until it got so deep it was unbelievable. I would then piece it all together and draw the line between reality and bullshit. I have no doubt that when she started a story it was true, but somewhere along the line, the truth would stop and go away with any glimmer of reality whatsoever. She figured she must add to the truth to make her appear a little more knowledgeable or interesting, I guess. Well the interesting part was right. The knowledgeable part was somewhat questionable.

We were at her apartment for about an hour until I just could hardly stand it anymore. Those two were on the date hotline yapping like a couple of school girls before a high school dance. I told them, "I'm headed to the store to get a beer."

Beth jumped right in of course, "Get me one!"

"Naturally," I said.

As I walked over to the store, not too far away, I ran into a guy I hadn't seen in a while on the way. He was going there as well. Great, I'll buy two for me and one for Beth. I figured I'd just stand outside and bullshit with my friend and pound one down. She wouldn't even know about it. After all, I did all the work that morning while she stood and watched.

I stood there and talked with my friend for quite some time as we went over some old memories. He told me about his life after his divorce. I explained the mess that I was left with and he was sympathetic to that. He took off so I headed on over to see what the two gabbing women were up to.

Later towards evening we left her apartment and headed out to the freeway to fly for a while. It was cold and raining so I wasn't into staying there up into the darkness. We left early enough to stop by the mini-mart and make it up to camp and still have some daylight left.

By the time we crawled into the tent I was tired and just wanted to lay back and listen to my radio, have a couple more beers, and relax. It wasn't too much later until I got up to take a piss and noticed it was snowing. "Oh great," I said to Beth. "It's snowing. I'll set my timer to go off at two hour intervals and we'll take turns scraping the snow off the tent tonight," I added.

That didn't sound too appealing to her but it didn't sound like much fun to me either. But it sure would beat the hell out of having the tent collapse on us in the middle of the night. I have had that happen before, and it is not fun.

She knew as well that it was something that just had to be done, whether we wanted to or not. It's always fun getting up in the middle of the night and leaving your nice, warm sleeping bag to step out into the cold snow. There were no options though, and we both were dreading the all-night interruptions.

CHAPTER 19

THE VISITOR

B eth and I took turns getting up all through the night to scrape snow off the tent every time my alarm went off. It wasn't any fun, to say the least, but it had to be done. It didn't snow that much but we had to check it anyway just to be on the safe side. It was becoming daylight, and neither one of us was too anxious to get up so we both fell back to sleep. It wasn't deep sleep by any means but it was sleep all the same.

Suddenly, we both heard a voice say, "Hello! Anybody in there?"

The first thing that came to mind was cops. I answered, "Yes, just a second while I get out of my sleeping bag."

I peeked out before I unzipped the tent. To my surprise it wasn't a cop but a fellow in his mid-sixties dressed for the winter including a stocking cap, scarf, and hip-waders. I turned and whispered to Beth, "It's alright, it's just some guy. I'll see what he wants."

I stepped outside carefully so I wouldn't end up on my ass in front of the fellow and asked, "What can I do for ya?"

"Well, I wondered if there was somebody living in there. Are you warm enough?" he asked.

"Well, it got a little wet yesterday and with the snow we're a little cold but we're alright," I answered.

"How many are there that stay in there?"

"Just me and my friend, Beth."

He pulled his hand from his glove and stuck it in his back pocket inside the hip-waders retrieving his wallet. He pulled out two ten dollar bills while he said, "Here, go to the Goodwill and get yourselves some blankets!"

Totally amazed by this, I gladly reached out and took the money into my hand. The fellow placed his glove back on as I retrieved my wallet and carefully stuck the money inside.

"Thank you very much," I told him.

"You're welcome, are there others staying up here?" he asked.

"Not that I know of, maybe a little farther on up the road."

"Well, I hope this will help you out."

"It will, thank you again."

"You're welcome, again."

"Did you hear that Beth? Get out of there and let's get going!"

The gentleman then offered, "My wife and I are fixing Thanksgiving dinner on Thursday, I can meet you at the gate and give you two some if you would like."

"That would be wonderful. We would really appreciate a home cooked meal," I quickly replied.

"Alright, you have a nice day," he said as he turned to leave.

"You do the same and thank you again," I said loudly.

"You're welcome, again," he yelled and waved as he disappeared beyond the ponds.

Beth was standing behind me when I turned to her to ask, "Can you believe that?"

Beth was almost without words when she asked me, "Well, you do believe in angels don't you?"

Still flabbergasted by the early morning visitor we got our daily items ready to head down the hill. On the way down I reached for my wallet and handed her ten dollars and told her, "I think to save money we should go at separate times so we only have to buy one buss pass. We could make plans and do that tomorrow."

I knew I probably wouldn't buy blankets, two or three warm shirts or another coat would replace a blanket or two and be useful all day instead of a blanket during the night.

I needed three bucks for a bus pass, Beth would need to kick-in half of that if she is going but I somehow figured I was on my own for this one. I planned to make a trip of it and go to the employment office and the library as well as Goodwill as long as I had a day pass. I thought I that I'd might as well make good use of it.

We walked out to the freeway as usual grabbing the sign stashed in the bushes on the way there. We weren't out there very long until a lady came by in a Dodge mini-van full of kids and handed us three bucks while saying, "Here you are! Go get yourselves some hot coffee; you must be cold out here."

The light was already green as I jumped out and grabbed the money saying, "Thank you." I had to make it quick since there were cars behind her. That didn't take very long at all, the cold weather and the snow brought sympathy from some people who were more fortunate than we were.

I knew Beth wanted a beer, it was still early, but I figured if we both got one maybe she wouldn't bust that ten yet. Maybe she would keep it for what it was intended for. It was Saturday after all and we usually made some decent money out there on weekends.

It was cold, and I almost thought of making my clothing run that day. I could do everything except go to the employment office because they were closed on weekends.

"Dammit, I'm cold," I told Beth as we stashed the sign and headed towards the mini-mart. "I would sure like a dry coat to put on; this one is thin and wet," I added.

While we were in the mini-mart, Beth used the restroom, as usual, so I stood under the heat register. I knew Nasty Neighbor was probably home since it was the weekend, so I was already was planning to go somewhere else to drink our beer. As Beth walked by I handed her the money so she could get the beer and pay for it while I sucked up as much heat as possible.

Out the door we went to the location behind Burger King. It was actually a field with a wooden fence protecting us from visibility, almost entirely. We cracked our beers then Beth rolled her last smoke. I asked her, "You are going to go and buy tobacco aren't ya?"

"It's my money," she snipped.

I had my ten bucks folded up tightly in my wallet so that I would really have to think about it before I blew it on something stupid. I wasn't saying that I wouldn't spend a small amount of it but I at least wanted to make it difficult instead of easily available.

We finished our beers and stashed our cans at a place where we could retrieve them later and headed towards the freeway island. We were almost across the parking lot when a guy pulled up in a white Chevy four-by-four and yelled, "Hey! You guys want some cans?" I quickly changed direction and walked towards the truck. The guy was a regular, always saving cans for us. He already had the tailgate down by the time I got to him. One peek into the bed of that truck and I turned and told Beth, "Go and get three carts and push them here. I'll get these unloaded so he can get on his way."

We had all the cans unloaded before Beth got back. As the guy climbed into his truck I told him, "Thank you very much!" He looked at me and said, "Thank you! I hate turning these fricken things in but the guys are coming over to my shop tonight to make more empties."

I laughed as I said, "Have fun." He drove away as I started loading cans into the carts.

I pushed one cart and pulled another while Beth pushed one. We started plugging them into the machines at Albertsons when another guy came in with a paper bag full and laid them in the top of one of our carts and said, "Here, I don't want to mess with these. You can have them." I thanked him as he walked away. "The Lord works in mysterious ways!" I told Beth as I plugged a can in one machine and a Budweiser bottle into another.

We had almost finished the chore when Beth informed me that she had to piss. "Naturally," I told her as I was just finishing my two carts to her unfinished one. She walked to the restroom as I mumbled, "God she's slow!" It just drove me nuts sometimes how she could be slow.

I had already finished the cans, washed my hands, walked to Customer Service and turned in the slips before Beth was even done in the restroom. "Jeeze! What did you do, go for a swim?" I asked sarcastically.

"I had to go to the bathroom," she replied.

I just shook my head and kept walking. We walked over to the mini mart since we were in the neighborhood and grabbed a couple brews and some beef jerky then headed over to where we were before. When we got there, Beth remembered that she was out of tobacco. "Well shit!" I told her, "I'll go get it; you'll be the rest of the fricken day!" I took a swig of beer then beat cheeks to the little store that sells her brand of tobacco and gives out free matches. They would give out as many books as was asked for, unlike the little market down the street that made me pay ten cents per book. That was still under my skin.

After we finished there I decided to partake in some tacos. Beth thought that sounded pretty good so we waltzed into Taco Time and ordered them up. I just got the regular tacos for a buck each but for some reason, Beth always had to pay the extra and get sour cream. I knew that would take forever so I just sat down and started eating. Three minutes later, here came Beth with her taco, napkins, hot sauce and all that. I watched her carefully decorate her one taco as I unwrapped my third.

"My God!" I told her. "We'll be in here for an hour!"

"Shut up," she responded. "I like my tacos the way I like my tacos!"

"You only have one and it will still probably take you a half of a fricken day to eat it," I told her.

Then she wanted to take it back because it didn't have enough sour cream but I was getting fairly irritated and told her, "Just eat the damn thing! Let's go already! Jeeze!"

We *finally* made it out of there, only after she went to the restroom, of course. We grabbed the sign again and headed out on the freeway. We had enough money to call it a day but that would mean boredom up at camp and probably getting on each other's nerves. It was best to stay there and if nothing else watch the traffic go by. Just as I was thinking up something to talk about, a guy in a pickup, with a gal sitting so close next to him that they almost had to be sharing the same seat belt, stopped right in front of us. He rolled his window down as she handed him something black. The light turned green and he tossed it out the window. It was a jacket. A black jacket with an American flag patch sewn onto the right shoulder. It was an extra-large, just my size. I was excited about it; it meant I wouldn't have to buy one at Goodwill when I decided to go.

I was just about to get into another one of my stories just to keep occupied. It wasn't raining so here come Skippy. He looked wired, so Jumpin' Jack was definitely going to be out there with us to create a show. I've seen a lot of people do some pretty crazy things, but talking to cars? That pretty much frosted the cake. It wasn't the people inside the cars, I mean talking to the cars! That ran pretty high up there on my weird shit-o-meter. Since it was cold, people had their windows up. The people at least would think that he was speaking to me or Beth while looking at their car, not that he was indeed trying to carry on an honest conversation with their Chevy.

I had enough of that weird shit. We weren't going to make mega-bucks anyway with Jumpin' Jack there asking a car if it was feeling okay. I told Beth I was headed south. She followed me across the street then to the mini-mart. I told her, "I want to get enough supplies so we don't have to come back down today. I am going to do some more work on the trail and clean up around camp. We'll grab some cardboard to make a front porch and that will keep at least some of the mud out of the tent."

"Good idea. Let's get another flashlight in case mine goes out," she said.

I tried not to let it get to me but there was no stopping it. I could not change her mind no matter how hard I tried. The more I thought about it the more pissed off I became.

We walked over to that damn dollar store again, and she bought another plastic flashlight. I felt the anger knocking at my door but I tried to remain calm.

"Here we go again," I told her while gritting my teeth.

We then walked to the mini-mart and bought a bunch of beer. We then hit the trail up to the tent. I was still fuming about her buying another fricken flashlight that probably won't last through the week. I couldn't tell her anything though, I just had to shake it off and let it run its course.

When we arrived at camp, I started on the trail right away. Beth cleaned up around camp while drinking a beer. I completed my tasks and sat my ass down on a log. I told her, "I'm going to get a pair of gloves tomorrow."

"That's a good idea," she said.

I cracked a beer and enjoyed the scenery before asking her, "You saw hide or hair of Cracker? I haven't seen him in a while."

"No, now that I think about it, I haven't," she answered.

"I wonder what happened to the little bastard. I hope he is alright. He's a pain in the ass but he makes for a good story to tell," I said as I stood up and looked around. There wasn't a sign of the little fart anywhere. There were no tracks, dug-up spots, or anything showing that he had been around. That kind of worried me a little. The little stink kind of grew on me just a bit.

I retrieved my radio from my inside jacket pocket and turned to the weather station. The report was for rain with possible snow as low as three hundred feet. That meant we could get some flakes again that night. The last night's snow had melted off so everything now was just wet. I unscrewed the cap off my Maglite and installed some new batteries. I replaced them with some more good ones, not those cheap things that can't be trusted.

I told Beth I wanted to play cards if she was up to getting her ass whooped. She reached for the cards and dealt a hand of rummy. We both drank one more beer before it was time to get ready for sleep. I set my watch for midnight so I could look out and check for snow. I must have fell asleep first because the last thing I remember was Beth bitching about that root under the tent that poked her right on her tiny ass when she was laying down. I was glad I didn't have that on my side, although there was a small rock that would be a nuisance on my side from time to time.

My alarm sounded at midnight so I turned on my flashlight and peered outside the tent. It was snowing but had not accumulated anything. I set the timer on my watch for two-hour periods then went back to sleep. I was wakened by the two hour timer so I again turned on my light and looked out. The snow was starting to stick but not enough to worry about right then. Two hours later, the timer went off again. This time Beth woke up too and she had to piss.

I told her, "You might as well knock the snow off the tent while you're out there."

"No shit, Sherlock," she scolded me.

"You don't have to get so nasty about it, jeeze," I told her. I went to sleep and slept until daylight. I was a little more tired than I originally thought.

I crawled out of the tent and took a piss while enjoying the snow-covered hill behind us. Beth came crawling out soon after and took care of her morning ritual. I reminded her that I planned to buy a pair of gloves so we had best head on down and secure a spot on the freeway. I told her, "People might be quite generous because of the snow."

She didn't say a word. She just reached inside the tent and pulled out a couple of beers.

"I thought we drank them all last night! Do you want them now or save them?" I asked, knowing already that was a stupid question. I suggested that we walk down to the road so we can enjoy different scenery while we finish the beers off. That's what we did, and didn't regret that move. The snow on the trees was absolutely beautiful. It was so peaceful; I could have stood there for hours.

We made tracks, literally, down to the freeway. I grabbed the sign and out to the island we went. The roads were clear although there was snow everywhere else. It was still spitting some flakes on as we stood out there. It didn't take long until we made a few bucks and decided to sit down somewhere warm for a while.

We walked over to McDonald's and used the restroom then I ordered a cup of coffee. I read the paper while wondering what we were going to do the rest of the day. It wasn't snowing at that moment but it sure was cold.

CHAPTER 20

ALL WAS LOST

The passing day went by so slowly that it felt like dragging an anchor up a brushy hillside and I was flat-ass tired. I already had gone and looked at gloves but didn't find any that I liked for a decent price, so I didn't buy any. Boredom was getting the best of me so Beth and I went and bought some beer and snacks for the night and headed up to camp. When we got to the ponds, and I looked at the tracks in the snow, I immediately came to an abrupt halt and gazed at Beth out the corner of my eye.

"Uh-oh, somebody has been up here. Look at the tracks."

I walked off to the side of the trail as I studied the footprints carefully. I looked up the hill and didn't see anyone around although I put my finger to my lips to signal Beth to be extra quiet just in case the people were still in the area.

"There are three sets, but only going up, none coming down. Let's sneak on up towards camp a little further," I whispered to her.

I led the way farther up the newly cut snow covered trail towards the tent to find our camp in total ruin. The tent was dropped and cut to shreds, the stove had been kicked apart and scattered everywhere. All of our clothing was thrown about and all of Beth's paperwork was scattered onto the snow. Even our food was opened up and dumped out everywhere. It was just a mess, a total disaster. Nothing was salvageable. The tent was beyond any means of repair. The stove would never work again. I could not, for the life of me, understand why someone would do such a terrible thing. Nothing was taken as far as we could tell;

everything was all just utterly destroyed. It was an act out of pure, bitter, meanness.

"Whoever has done this probably has a nice warm bed to sleep in, with their belly full of hot food, and clean clothes to put on," I told Beth as I nudged part of the dismantled stove with my boot.

That was everything we had. It wasn't much as far as comfort but at least we had some cover to protect us from the rain and snow, but it was all gone. We had absolutely nothing. We would have to resort back to cardboard and pray the weather didn't become too awful.

As we stood there in total silence and disbelief, Beth started to cry. I got pissed, really pissed. Not much rattles my cage to the point that I feel like I could lose control and do bodily damage to someone but that crossed the line. Everyone has their limits, and whoever did that found mine. I carefully studied the footprints that lead up the hill. I didn't say a word to Beth, there was nothing to say. I followed the footprints until they came out on a road at the top of the hill, and then the prints disappeared. God help them if I would have caught up with the low-life individuals who had performed that terrible act.

We dug through the ruins and gathered up as much as possible. I informed Beth as I dug around some more that we were going to have a rough night ahead of us. They even cut the tarp we had spread over the tent. It wasn't even salvageable, so we had no cover to sleep under and it looked like it could snow again, let alone maybe the freezing rain. I have slept in that before and it's no picnic. When it comes to being bummed out, we wrote a new chapter in that book.

It was starting to get dark so we headed on back down the hill to try and sort things out. We walked over to the mini-mart and bought a few beers while telling them about our misfortune. Both of the employees were in total disbelief.

Amber offered, "You can stay in my car until I get off work in the morning."

"No Amber, that's really sweet, but that would be a risk against your job. That's a risk that we won't take. I've survived worse situations than this, believe it or not, we'll be alright," I explained to her as we walked out the door.

Beth spoke up to me, "I'm glad you told her that, we don't need to get her in trouble."

We went over to the fence line and each cracked a brew. I looked at Beth and said, "Well, it looks like we're spending the night right here under some cardboard huh?"

"Yep," was all she had to say.

We decided to walk over to McDonald's for a while and sit in the warmth. I asked Beth, "How much you got in your pocket? It sounds like a good excuse for some high octane wine." We had plenty of money, so I made plans to go to Albertsons to get a bottle of the fortified grape juice before I gathered cardboard. We sat there in McDonald's for about twenty minutes, sucking up the heat as much as possible.

The Christmas tree people had set their lot set up right outside McDonald's in the shopping center parking lot. As we left McDonald's, here came this figure running around the Christmas trees yelling directly at me, "Kirk!-Kirk!"

It was Tim that worked at the mini-mart. It was his day off but he stopped in at his work for something and apparently had gotten filled in on what had happened. He turned around and waved his wife over with their Ford Escape four-by-four and told us to get in. I had no idea what was going on as we pulled out of the parking lot and onto the freeway.

"Where are we going?" I asked as his wife as she took the small SUV up to about seventy.

"Wal-Mart," Tim turned and replied.

"Oh," I said.

Beth and I looked at each other and wondered what he had in progress. We both had an idea but we both let on as if we were dumbfounded.

We pulled into the parking lot and they both got out telling us to stay put, and that they would be right back. Beth asked them, "Can we drink a beer while you are gone?" I just cringed then nudging her as I loudly said, "Beth!" They both said it was okay just as long as it's gone before we get back on the road. I guzzled mine right down, not wanting to have any left when they got back.

When I heard the knock on the rear of the SUV, we both piled out to see what the fuss was about. Those two were so excited they could hardly stand it. They purchased; a new tent, new stove, tent heater, propane, sleeping bags, flashlights, and a wrist rocket with a box of steel shot.

Tim eagerly said, "Let's go set it up!"

Needless to say, Beth and I were speechless.

We all were in good moods as we piled out of the SUV at the locked gate. We all carried the new items up to where we were camped. Neither Tim nor his wife was prepared for the wet, slushy path they were about to experience. Both of them had regular walking shoes on but they said they didn't care, and that they had dry shoes at home.

Up the trail we all went, in the dark, sloshing in the mud and water the entire way. Tim was surprised at what as challenge it really was to get up there, especially by flashlight only.

"You guys come up here every night, sometimes in the dark?" Tim asked in disbelief.

"I've left here to go back down for something at dusk, and returned in total darkness," I told him.

"How did you find your way?"

"He has night vision. He can see if there is any light at all. But one time you got lost didn't you Kirk?" Beth interrupted.

"Yes, I did. Thanks for bringing that up Beth," I told her half-jokingly.

"You're welcome," Beth said.

"Usually when I come back down and expect dark soon, I leave a working flashlight with Beth. Usually mine!" I explained to Tim.

"Now you have some new flashlights," Tim proudly announced.

I didn't bother going into the thing about Beth and her damn one-dollar flashlights; the ones they bought us were of pretty good quality. They didn't want us to have items that we couldn't depend on. Flashlights are important while living in the woods, and Tim knew it. If only I could have made Beth into a believer.

We set the new tent up in a snap, threw the new sleeping bags inside, and thanked those two over and over. They were just happy that we had someplace dry to lay our heads again. That made the whole ordeal a lot more tolerable. I didn't even buy any wine that night; I didn't want it either.

CHAPTER 21

BEING CAREFUL

Beth and I crawled into the tent and spread out the new sleeping bags, this time making sure neither one of us had an annoying lump right under the spot where we each would sleep. We arranged the items inside of the tent the as they were before. She had her side to place items as she pleased, and I had my items placed strategically where I could get to them quickly. I made sure she had one of the new flashlights on her side, the other went between us, and of course I had my trusty Maglite in my belt holster. I also had the wrist rocket and ammo ready to load, draw back, and fire within a few seconds.

We found ourselves engulfed in a discussion about keeping a better eye on our camp from here on out and how to go about it. I didn't know how we could keep an eye on camp when neither one of us wasn't keen on the idea of staying up there all day.

"Well, we do have the walkie talkies, and they do reach down to the freeway just fine. That's one option we have although neither one of us wants to stay up here all day," I proposed.

"You could come up here once or twice a day and check on things," she responded.

"Yeah, it's kind of a long walk but I can round trip it in about forty minutes if I really had to," I said in a negative tone.

I put my headset on and checked the forecast then rolled over and said, "We'll have to play it by ear. It's late; let's get some sleep. Goodnight."

Beth was already out. Too much excitement for one day; I guess she was exhausted just as I was. It had been a long, long day.

The next morning we woke up and stepped out of our new tent. She went one way to piss, and I went the other. We then met back at the side of the tent praising ourselves and our friends for doing such a fine job in the dark, and thanking God they came when they did as we watched the falling rain which contained small, wet flakes of snow. We weren't at much of a higher elevation than the freeway, but at times it was high enough that we would see snow at camp but not down where we flew sign.

I was ready to head down, so I attempted to get Beth to move along a little faster. Silly me, to think that was going to happen. I was hungry and ready for a cup of hot coffee. Right then is when I came up with the phrase that lives to this day: "C'Mooooown Beth!" She finally completed her dilly-dallying around and started to walk towards me.

"You got your radio?" I asked her.

"Yep, right here."

"Turn it on and leave it so I can test it in a little while."

She reached down and rotated the switch to the on position while I jumped out ahead of her about thirty feet and then keyed my radio in, "Gopher-mom. Do you copy?"

"Ten-four torque wrench."

"I'm clear," I said as I slowed and let her catch up.

Our plans were for her to go up later to watch over camp while I stayed down and flew sign. I knew she wouldn't even think about that without a good supply of beer so we grabbed the sign and flew for a while. There was no food up there either; the jerks that destroyed everything dumped it all out, and I needed to check the radios and make sure the batteries were fully up in case she did run into trouble.

It was winter break time and the schools were out of session. It was prime time for some ornery teens to show their macho shit and come back to destroy our things. I didn't say for sure that it was kids that had done the damage in the first place but I couldn't see a grownup trashing our living area like that without taking anything at all. Also it is prime time to fly sign. Christmas season, Christmas bonuses, and people in a good mood overall were good reasons to make decent money out flying sign at that time. We both knew we had to keep a sharp eye out though, just in case some nasty people motivated themselves into a destructive mood.

We both flew on the freeway for about a half an hour when I told Beth, "I'll go get some beverages and snacks for you. I'll call you on the radio and we'll meet over at the fence line. I want to check the radios out and make damn sure they are working properly. I don't want you up there by yourself with a radio that isn't up to snuff."

"Alright, I'll wait for your call."

"It won't take long; just throw the sign over in the bushes."

I headed over to the mini-mart and got her some cookies, two Snickers bars, and some beer; items I knew she would consume. I stepped outside and keyed in my radio, "Hello gopher mom. You gotta copy?"

"I got ya torque wrench," she replied.

"Pack it up and head to the fence line, the radios are working fine."

Then someone broke in on our frequency and stated, "Yeah gopher mom, go to the fence line!"

Dumbfounded, I keyed in again, "Someone is riding us gopher mom. Identify yourself please."

There was no answer. I could have switched channels; Beth knew the alternate channel but decided against it. Nothing important was said, so I keyed in once again, "Gopher mom, I can see you now, I'm out."

"I'm out too," the subtle male voice broke in. It was kind of funny; at least someone was having a good time with us.

We met at the fence line and drank a cold one while we discussed when we should make contact. She didn't have a clock so I took my Walkman radio out of my coat pocket and handed it to her.

"I'll stay hot on my end in case something happens. You can just go hot every hour on the hour so you can check in. That'll save on batteries."

I showed her how to pre-set the radio so she could listen to any channel and easily switch over to check the time. The plan was then all set so she left to go to camp with enough beer, food, and my Walkman radio to keep her occupied for a while. I went back out and flew sign on the freeway as we had planned. At five minutes till ten o'clock, I reached down and rotated the on-off and volume control a bit because I knew she would be calling and waited for the call while cars drove by. I sat the radio down on the concrete divider beside me waiting.

I was paying close attention when a log truck went by upsetting the silence. It flew past then I heard, "Torque wrench you got a copy?" Before I could grab my radio and respond, the intruder broke in for me.

"Yeah gopher mom, I'm sure he's got a copy."

I keyed my radio in frustration, "I got ya gopher mom. This is torque wrench." I replied. "Intruder, identify yourself," I snapped.

I waited a few minutes then keyed in once more, "Gopher mom. Remember what we talked about?" I switched channels then waited. I waited for what seemed to be five minutes, but in reality it was only a matter of seconds, then I heard, "Torque wrench, you copy?"

"Yeah, gopher mom. Talk at ya later, stay on this channel. I'm clear."

I clipped my radio back on my belt and turned the volume all the way up. I held the sign up for the oncoming cars to see, wondering just who it was that no doubt was having a blast riding Beth and I while we tried to communicate on our radios.

Beth checked in as gopher mom at eleven, then again at twelve. I told her I was ready for a break so she decided to come on down for a while. I thought she was probably out of beer. I made a few bucks out there so I left the freeway and headed for

McDonald's. I had to piss like a Russian race horse on steroids, so I made pretty fast trip of it.

I radioed Beth to see if she wanted some McNuggets or something but received no reply. She apparently had turned her radio off to save batteries. It wasn't a problem; she could always get something later. I was hungry so I ordered two bacon cheese burgers to go. I had one gone and was working on the other by the time she approached me.

When Beth showed up I asked her, "Do you want to go to McDonald's and get you something to eat?"

"No, not right now; I want a beer," she answered.

"I figured about as much; after all, I only sent you up to camp with three. Alright, let's head over to the mini-mart," I said.

We entered the mini-mart and filled Amber in on our new camp gear. She was excited to hear that we had a tent again and didn't have to sleep out in the weather. In a sense we still were in the weather, just not out in the open without any kind of shelter whatsoever. I didn't elaborate on that though. We bought a couple brews and headed over to the place behind Burger King. When we got there I started a story about Billy and John that I'd forgotten for a while. I pointed towards a clump of trees across a small field and told the amusing story as we drank our beers.

"Back when Billy was alive," I said. "Danny and John were staying here in those trees. They invited Billy, Linda Lou, and me to go there with them to have a little bullshit session and have a good time. I don't know if you knew this or not but John liked to get drunk and fall down. We were all having a good time when John said, 'I gotta piss.' He stood up and wobbled around a bit then staggered off towards the blackberry bushes. He got about four steps and said, 'Here I go!' as he fell to the ground. We were all laughing so hard Linda spewed beer out her nose. That made us laugh even more. John was on his knees taking a piss when we finally got calmed down. It started again when John finished, zipped up, and said, 'Screw it, I'm crawling back!' And he did. Here he came crawling back on all fours. We laughed and laughed. About an hour later he had to go again. Billy said,

'I'll help ya John!' Not a good idea. John held on to Billy while he took a piss, then started back, fell, and took them both down landing on top of Billy. Billy stood up and said with a laugh, 'I'm going to be sore tomorrow!' The hysterical laughing began all over again," I finished telling Beth as I sipped my beer.

Beth was laughing at the story but not as hard as we all were on that evening. I told her, "I guess you had to be there."

We went to the Burger King and used the restroom before heading back out to fly sign again. I reminded Beth that I wanted to get back soon. I wasn't into staying really late. We stayed out until we made about ten bucks then headed on a beer run, and then to Albertsons for food and water before we walked back to camp. I told Beth on the way, "I hope nobody messed around up at camp."

We walked a brisk pace up to the tent, both wondering what we would find. That is a hell of a feeling, not knowing if you will have a place to sleep at night, wondering if someone may have ripped our new tent all to shreds therefore forcing us to sleep under cardboard. Thank God, it turned out to be alright. Nobody messed with anything. I sat my ass down on the log and cracked a beer in total relief, and then tore off a chunk of peppered beef jerky that I had just bought. Beth rolled a smoke and couldn't get the damn thing lit.

"Give me the fricken matches," I told her.

She handed them to me so I struck two at once giving her a hot flame to ignite her smoke with. She thanked me and began puffing on her cancer stick while gazing up the side of the hill.

She crossed her legs with her cigarette between her fingers as if she was into an intense conversation, and then asked, "What would you have done if you would have caught up with them up on the hill there?"

"I don't know. My brain was going a million miles an hour. I don't know what I would have done but it wouldn't have been pretty, I can tell you that much."

"Well, I hope we never have to go through that again."

"Hand me your walkie-talkie so I could swap batteries around."

"Why don't we just swap radios?"

"I'm not changing all the batteries, just half. Putting some fresh in mine, leaving some fresh in yours," I explained.

I could tell she saw no logic in my plan but she didn't understand that I had to keep mine powered up all day. It wouldn't do any good if she had a situation and needed to call for me, and I didn't have mine turned on. She handed it to me anyway. It was something for me to fiddle around with and kill some time.

We then talked about how I could fandangle some sort of an alarm system or trap on the trail. Our guards were up now, knowing that whoever trashed our stuff before knows the way up without snow tracks to follow. It wouldn't do any good to rig up a tin can alarm though; nobody would be around to hear it, and surely they wouldn't have the balls to come up there when one or both of us were there. Of course, one never knows.

CHAPTER 22

MOVING CAMP

The winter had been rough and we still had a couple months to go. Trying to be optimistic around Beth created a challenge at times. I knew down deep that the weather could be cold and wet right up until early June. The two ponds had overflowed and the drainage from the ponds wasn't a ditch anymore; it was more like a long spread out marsh. It seemed like every time it rained I had to pick and choose new stepping spots that were shallow enough not to let water go in the tops of our boots. Our feet were always soaked anyway but it felt better not allowing cold water to run down our ankles.

Both of our socks were shot. That goes with the territory which is no doubt why whenever some charity operation sets up a place to hand out items to the homeless, socks are the first thing to go. A person can go without other undergarments but socks are a must. If a person doesn't have any protection between the foot and the shoe, severe blisters will break out and probably infection along with the blisters. As far as we needed to walk every day, just to get to and from our tent, our feet were always sore anyway.

We cruised through the holiday season without incident. We celebrated Christmas by walking around and looking at the lights and decorations. I walked Beth down my parent's block showing her the magnificent display they put up every year. She was impressed, and so was I. My dad couldn't pass up something new on the market; he had to have it for his display.

Around Christmas we did very well flying sign on the freeway too. People were in a giving mood as usual. I received some money from family back east so I bought a few items for myself and stuck the rest away. I knew it would come in handy later, and it did.

This was just about the time I started feeling like I should worry about the child support thing again. I hadn't made any payments for quite a while. Jobs were hard to come by and that was an understatement. On top of the unemployment rate, it was really difficult to obtain employment for someone who is dirty, lives in a tent with no address and no telephone. I thought a cellular phone would be nice but how could I afford one, and where the hell could I plug it in to charge? I didn't even have money for clothes. I only bought clothes when absolutely necessary because it takes one day in the sticks and new clothes are filthy anyway. When they were ripped up beyond repair, then it was time to hit Goodwill to buy clothes.

I knew that soon the good old state would again put a warrant out for me for being behind on child support payments but that was nothing new to me either. You can't squeeze blood from a turnip. My kids were fine; I kept track as much as possible. They lived in a four bedroom house, each with their own room, a play room, a boat . . . Yeah; you might say they were just a little more comfortable than I was. Although, I was grateful that no one had messed with our new tent. A few days later, that changed.

Beth and I slept in late just a little bit one morning because we stayed up late the night before. I just woke up when Beth told me something was hitting the tent. I sat up and listened. It wasn't wind, and it wasn't Cracker. It sounded like somebody was throwing things at the tent. Something hit the tent at high speed. It poked a small hole in the top of the tent, above my head. I grabbed the wrist rocket and slid out. As soon as I stood up, four teenagers went running down the hill. I followed them so fast that I ran right through the pond and didn't even realize it. I stopped, pinched a steel shot in the leather, aimed, and fired missing one kid by about three feet.

They ran like hell. I chased them clear down onto the road. One kid stopped and turned. I right knew then what they were doing. They were firing gas powered pellet rifles at us. He took aim at me as I walked towards him. I yelled, "You fire that thing at me, you better make it a damn good shot! I'm not stopping!"

I didn't stop either. The kid tucked tail and ran towards the others. They went through a hole in a fence into a mobile home park. I watched as far as I could, then turned back to find Beth. I was sure she was horrified by that time. I returned to find Beth almost shaking. I told her, "This is no game; they were shooting high powered pellet rifles at us!"

"You're kidding me!" Her eyes were as big as quarters.

"No," I said. "I'm not kidding. It's time now to get the law involved. I think I frightened them enough that they aren't coming back right away though."

"How many were there?"

"Four I think, I chased them into that mobile home park down there."

"How did you get so wet?"

"Oh, I wasn't paying attention and ran right through the pond."

I looked around and found several blue, red, and yellow plastic pellets lying on the ground near our tent.

"Who knows how long they were taking pot shots at us," I told her.

"What should we do?"

"I don't know, but this is serious business. They could have injured one or both of us while we were still inside the tent," I explained.

I filled her in with more details as we headed down the road. I showed her from a distance where the little assholes went through the fence. We were both upset, and really didn't know what to do other than contact the police. But what would they do for a couple of homeless people? That was *really* what was going through our minds.

The people at the mini-mart could not believe it when they heard about the shootings. Amber called Tim at home and filled him in on the morning events. He was not happy at all. In fact, he told Amber that he would be right there.

Beth and I purchased a couple brews to calm down our nerves before Tim arrived. I kept looking over to see if he had shown up. By the time we were finished and started to walk over, Tim did arrive. We headed up to camp telling him on the way where and when it happened. We took him up to the camp and showed him the pellets and the small hole in the tent where one pellet could have struck either me or Beth in the head. Needless to say, Tim was very concerned for our safety.

We walked down to the road and I showed Tim where I chased them to, the hole in the fence, and the yard that they cut through. Just as Tim and I were looking towards the mobile home park, I saw one of the teens poke his head out the door of one of the mobile homes.

"That's one of them, right there," I loudly told Tim.

Tim ran towards the fence but the kid ducked back inside. Tim grabbed his cell phone and called the police. I stood there thinking that I should probably split because I knew I was in trouble over the child support thing again.

Just as Tim completed his call with the local police, Beth came down the trail and around the pond. She asked what was going on so Tim told her, "Kirk saw one of the kids so I called the cops. They'll be here in a few minutes."

Hearing that, I broke the conversation and said, "Oops! I'll be on my way now."

I went walking down the road at a fast pace. Later I found out that Beth filled Tim in on my situation with the back child support and that I probably had an arrest warrant out. I made myself very small in the heat of all of this; I stayed away as much as possible, not finding out the details until the cops had taken a report from Beth. She met up with me later and told me what happened at the officer's visit.

She said, "When the officer asked about you, I told him I didn't know where you were; you had a warrant out, so you left."

"Dammit Beth!" I yelled. "What the hell were you thinking? You didn't have to give him that detail!"

"Can I finish now?" she asked and then continued, "I took him right through the mud and up to the tent. I showed him the tent that was torn down, and all the pellets that were lying on the ground next to the tent. He wrote it all down then told me that we were on private property and we needed to move somewhere else."

"Well, I have connections with the company that owns this property; I've told you that before. As for moving, I think it would be a good idea anyway, don't you?"

"Yes, it's not safe here anymore, that's for sure," she agreed.

We walked over to the mini-mart, then over behind Burger King to further discuss the situation. We cussed and discussed until we finished our beers then I said, "We better go make some money now so later we can go scout out a new place. I think we may find a place up on the hill where I told you that Dennis and I stayed. We'll have to go check it out. It's a long way from here though."

"As long as we're left alone," she replied.

"Yes indeed, we don't need any more shit like that to make our lives even more difficult than they already are."

People were fairly generous out on the freeway island; we raked in almost ten bucks in less than an hour. I told Beth, "Let's go get something quick to eat then head up on top of the hill I was telling you about and see if we can set up there." She agreed so we left the freeway and headed over to get a small meal at the little store and then over to the mini mart for a couple beers to take with us for the long walk there and back.

We both found ourselves staring up the trail to what would soon be our former camp as we walked past it on our way to the place I described to her. We got about two thirds of the way there when she said, "This is a long way up here; let's crack a brew now."

"You'll need to have it gone before we start up the hill because I'm taking a short cut."

"What kind of short cut are you talking about?"

"How's your climbing skills?" I asked knowing it was going to freak her out when she saw the steep hill that was the shortcut. It was steep and nasty but it did knock about ten or fifteen minutes off taking the long route.

Beth finished her beer just as we approached the short cut. I took a left turn, crossing a ditch and through some brush, then started up the muddy hill. Beth took one look at that muddy hill and took a long, deep, disgusted breath that let what was left of her front teeth, from the frozen candy bar incident, show.

"No fricken way, you gotta be shitting me! I can't make that! You're fricken nuts," she complained.

"Just get your scrawny ass over here and latch on. Do as I do and use the tree limbs with one hand and hang onto me with the other. You'll make it. I didn't say it was going to be easy," I told her.

She bitched moaned and complained all the way up. I asked her, "See, That wasn't so bad now, was it?"

"No fricken way we can do this every day. My toes hurt," she snipped.

"This is only a short cut. The main way is not *nearly* as bad. You just have to watch out for ruts," I explained.

"Fricken hell! This is too much," she further complained. "People have to be mean, so we have to put up with *this* shit!"

We walked towards the end of the large meadow when she said, "This is too far, it'll take forever to go down there and back everyday"

"Got any better ideas? God Beth, give me a break! Besides, I've done it before with Dennis. We were camped right over there by the railroad tracks," I told her while pointing across the meadow.

"Tracks! You didn't say anything about train tracks!"

"It only comes through about four times a day, rarely during the night," I explained.

I took her up near the east fence and showed her a spot. "I was thinking somewhere right in here in these trees. What do you think?" I asked.

"Well, it looks okay. It's pretty flat and it's out of sight for the most part," she said.

"Yes, and there is a good place for a restroom over there by those bushes, and right over there is a stump where I can sit down and see anybody coming up the road or anywhere near here."

I was glad that she was *finally* on the same page as I was; it wasn't like we had a whole shit-pile of choices to choose from. It was either up there on the hill, or go way up the river to where Matt and I were camped until Beth showed up.

We both agreed on the spot so we made plans for the move that would take place the following day. I took her down the long way to show her that it wasn't all that bad. I pointed at the short cut as we passed it and said, "I took that shortcut down one time on my ass." She thought it was funny.

We meandered on down the hill with plenty of time to fly sign for a while before heading back to our camp for one final night. The chances of those kids coming back were pretty slim. I think I put the fear of God in that one kid who was going to shoot me and I kept coming at him anyway.

As we approached the trail head to where our tent should be I decided to walk up the path to make sure it was still there. I reached the area and looked around. No one had messed with anything; everything looked the same. I walked back down the path and told Beth again, "They aren't coming back today, if ever. Let's get a move on so we can make some more money."

The past few days nobody had been around and flying sign. We didn't have any competition, but that afternoon Jumpin' Jack was out on the freeway *power signing*.

I had only seen him do that a couple of times but when he did it meant he wanted a beer really bad and needed money fast.

Myself, I couldn't do it. I wouldn't stoop to that level. Power signing is the method used as vehicle is approaching; you hold up your sign and aim it right at the person driving, making eye contact at the same time. It is one step above outright panhandling. I don't know which one should be more embarrassing for him, power signing or talking to the cars. I wouldn't have anything to do with either one.

I told Beth, "You go out there if you want, I'll watch from the bus station. If you get a hit, give him enough of it so he will go get a beer, then you and I will fly sign as usual."

She crossed over to the island so I walked over to the bus station to observe. As soon as she got into position I saw her reach into her pocket and hand something to him. *She's paying him off,* I thought. He must have been short a little bit on change so she gave him what he needed, because he headed across the street with his sign. He crossed the parking lot as I got up to join Beth. "Have fun," he said as our paths crossed.

As soon as I approached Beth, she said right away, "He was short a quarter so I gave him one just to get rid of him."

"I figured as much; smart thinking. Now let's make some money so we can go back and enjoy our last evening at that camp," I told her.

She looked kind of sad, so I kept going on about how nice the new spot would be. I think she was just afraid of new territory. It's kind of the same as moving to a new house or starting a new job. I was pretty used to moving around but Beth was not. Even though she was raised as an Air Force brat, she wasn't used to moving like that.

We flew sign for about an hour and made sufficient money for the night and the next morning while we moved. That way we could get it done without heading down there first thing in the morning. We would have food and beer, the two main ingredients for a successful move. The only thing we wouldn't have is water for coffee, and I wasn't about to take any with us when we moved. I would carry a new jug up at a later time. We headed separate ways again; she went to the mini-mart and I went to Albertsons.

We met up in the parking lot and traversed up to the camp to stay the night one last time. We both felt kind of sad about it. If only people would mind their own business and just leave us alone. What they did and why they did it would trouble me for many years to come. It's hard enough to survive out in the sticks all winter long, let alone someone tearing down the only roof you have and destroying any possibility of a hot meal where you stay. It just didn't make any sense. What about poor Cracker? Even though I had not seen the little shit for a while, I knew he was probably still around. We no longer would have our pet gopher.

Beth and I sat and laughed about some of the things we endured that winter until I reminded her that it was still winter. That let the air out of her tires. We had a lot of work to do the next morning. I just hoped it would not be in vein and someone would come along and ruin the new camp also.

The next morning we sadly tore everything down. I carried things down to the road while Beth watched over it. It took about four large trips to carry everything down through the mud and the muck. The marsh was not easy to traverse on a normal trip so it was extremely difficult carrying all of our gear through it. I did it in pretty good time though. No sooner than we got everything organized, here came Tim. He entered from the other end of the road with his SUV. He had stopped at the mini mart and no one had seen us so he figured we were on the move. He decided he would come and help us. Thank God, we definitely needed the help.

We loaded everything into his SUV and off we went. We got to the new location and set up in record time. We were getting pretty used to setting up tents. I took all the wet items including the old sleeping bags and some clothes and hung them over tree limbs to dry. Tim offered to take them to his house to dry them but I refused. Sleeping bags are heavy and hard on dryers. It also makes the sleeping bags lumpy, as if that would matter to either Beth or me.

Once we got everything arranged, I thanked Tim for his help again. He offered to take us down to the freeway so we jumped in his rig and left our new camp all alone. We both had the jitters about that but it was something we just had to get used to.

Once arrived at the bus station Tim let us out as I surveyed the situation. Skippy was out on the freeway holding his sign. I couldn't tell from the distance if he was talking to the cars or not but he at least wasn't jumping around.

About twenty minutes later he got up and walked down the street in the opposite direction. He must have been going to the other store. Beth and I jumped on the opportunity and headed out to fill the vacant spot. We made a five spot right out of the gate. We flew for another hour, got some beer, and then headed for our new camp. It had been another very long day

CHAPTER 23

FINALLY SPRING

Now that our new camp was set up and everything seemed fresh and new, it couldn't be a better time for spring to arrive. I told Beth, "You know, just because it's spring doesn't mean the weather can't be downright nasty!"

"I know that; I'm not stupid," she said as she shook her head at me.

"I don't know. Sometimes I wonder," I said. She knew I was only jerking her chain.

I walked around for a while before returning back to see if Beth wanted to see where Dennis and I stayed. She kept on doing what she was doing without saying a word, so I took that as a no.

"Well, that's okay. It's not going anywhere. Besides, we need to take the almost dry sleeping bags down for the night anyway just in case it rains," I said to her.

We got everything organized inside and crawled in for the night not knowing if it would rain or not. The weather reporter said through the headset, "Cloudy and a chance of rain along with a cold front," but she wasn't always accurate.

Early the next morning I stepped out of the tent and was right away reminded of how cold it can get during the night when there is no cloud cover. It was fine inside the tent because while I was still in my sleeping bag I reached over and lit the tent heater. It put out a fair amount of heat, enough so that crawling out of the sleeping bag wasn't quite so bad. But once outside the tent, well that was another story. I took my first morning yeller piss over by some bushes and watched the steam rise from it. I much would have rather watched the morning news on television but all I had was the steam rising into the air for entertainment at the moment.

It wasn't too long before I heard Beth hacking her lungs out. She came crawling out dragging her back pack behind her. I said, "Morning. Kinda cold out here this morning."

She didn't say anything; she just staggered over towards the bushes to go piss then lit her a damn cancer stick so she could hack some more. I continued the one sided conversation saying, "I'm about hungry, how about you?" There was still nothing from her.

She reached down in her back pack and retrieved a beer. *Crack* I heard then she spoke in a low quivering voice, "You want one?"

"No, not right now."

"I'm not going to leave it here, and I'm not carrying it down either!"

"Jeeze! Give me the damn thing then if it will put you in a little better mood."

"I'm not grumpy!" She boldly exclaimed. That deduced my assessment about her attitude that morning, right down to level zero.

I took the beer and cracked it open while I walked to the stump that made an excellent view point of the road. I was talking to myself the whole time thinking that I might be the only one who would listen to me on the way down.

I looked at the frost on the ground and a puddle that had frozen overnight. I laughed to myself thinking how much fun it would be to watch Beth take the slick short-cut down the hill on her tiny little ass. I stood there picturing that in my mind. I'm glad she wasn't standing there. She would ask what I was laughing at, and I probably would tell her, and then be in deep shit the rest of the day.

I turned around to see Beth go deep into the bushes toting a handful of napkins. God I'm glad we had some sani-wipes there at camp. There are a few things that you just can't overlook when out in the sticks. One is toilet paper and the other is sani-wipes for your hands after the job is complete. Another is water. I would buy a new jug that day and carry it up so we would have it.

When she came back I asked her, "Did you wash your hands?"

"Yes!" She said, like a smart ass, as she knocked over her beer.

"Dammit!" she shouted while her beer spewed as she grabbed it.

I, of course, had to make things worse as I let her know; "You spill more beer . . . not a day goes by that you don't spill at least one." That didn't go over so well, I knew it wouldn't, that's why I said it. I just needed to give it a few minutes until the first part of the day's beer kicked in. She was usually fine up until a couple more, and then she will become the Betholizer again. I already had her day figured out as soon as she crawled out of the tent with that scowl on her face.

We got ourselves prepared and then headed on down the trail. This time we took the long way around so I could show Beth where Dennis and I stayed. There was still some stuff there. There was a torn down tent and some garbage. I figured he left without cleaning up. That just isn't right but there isn't anything you can do to change people's behavior sometimes. It's the shits for the rest of us but that's just something that happens.

We then went on down the hill to the road and walked to the bus station to check things out. We arrived early enough that there wasn't anybody around. I asked Beth if she wanted another beer, knowing it was a stupid question but I was trying to be nice. She nodded so we headed for the mini-mart. I checked my watch to see how long it took to walk down.

"Hey, Beth. It took us forty minutes to get down here. That was twice the time as it took from the old camp," I said as we kept walking.

"Huh," was all she said. She was in a pissy mood for sure, and I knew the Betholizer was just one more beer away. I knew I was in for a storm trying to keep her happy all day long, but I had weathered that storm before.

We walked over to the fence line to drink our beers down. I, of course, finished mine while she was about half done. I thought maybe I'd push her attitude just a little bit; it was usually fun watching her get all sideways over nothing.

"You gonna be like this all day or what?" I asked.

"Are you just trying to piss me off today or what?" She replied.

"Yes, and it's not that hard to do, you were pissed off as soon as you crawled out this morning."

"No I wasn't!"

"Bullshit!"

That lit her fuse; she grabbed her damn cigarette and smoked away. I wanted to laugh at her but I thought I'd better behave myself. She'd had enough for a while. I thought maybe I'd start in again after she calmed down a bit. When she finally finished, I handed her the sack with my can inside so she could install hers. As she placed it in the sack, as I watched Nasty Neighbor in his driveway on his cordless phone.

"Fricken jerk," I mumbled.

"Nasty Neighbor?" she asked.

"Of course, and he's on the phone. Let's go," I said.

There for a while he wasn't so bad. There was another car parked in his driveway, sometimes during the week, and sometimes it would be parked there overnight. Everybody thought that maybe he was getting a little, so he didn't have to be such a fricken jerk. But once that car quit appearing in his driveway, he was back to being a turd. She must have figured him out.

As we walked towards the island on the freeway, I stuck the empty cans under the bush where we had stashed the sign. I managed to get the cans in there but didn't retrieve the sign. There was no sign to retrieve.

Not again, I thought.

"Somebody made off with our sign again?" Beth asked.

"I think I have a pretty good idea who is doing it."

"I do too. Go get his sign," she ordered.

As I stood up and turned to walk away I whispered, "God help you Skippy today if Beth finds out you took our sign; she'll go ballistic on you."

I walked over to where Skippy's sign was usually stashed, and it was gone too. I walked back to Beth and informed her, "Either he stuck his in a different spot, or somebody got his too."

Beth turned and slapped the crossing signal button like she meant business and asked, "You got your marker don't you?"

"Yes of course," I replied as the signal displayed the funny looking little illuminated stick man that informed us it was okay to cross.

We traversed over to the nearest cardboard box and it was empty. They had just picked it up for recycling. "Well shit, let's go around back," I said knowing time was ticking away and someone else would be out there flying the freeway by the time we got back.

I jumped up on the large recycling bin and looked in. "Just as I thought. They're making the route. Of all the damn times they decide to pick up the cardboard, it had to be today. Let's hit the pizza place," I told Beth.

Off we went over to the pizza place. It was a little bit of a walk but we needed a piece of cardboard to make a sign. We walked there to find a dumpster full of prime cardboard for a sign. I grabbed a big piece and tore it down to a suitable size. "There, this is perfect. Let's head out there, I'll make the sign on the island," I told Beth. We boogied on over to find that no one there was out there yet.

I plopped my ass down on the curb and tore the cap off my marker. I wrote the tried and true phrase, "Can you please spare some change? Thank you and God Bless!" It's an oldie, but it worked. I was almost done with the art making when a Volkswagen Jetta stopped and the driver rolled down the window. Beth was on some other planet at the time so I yelled, "Beth-go!" She finally jumped up and grabbed the hit. It was two bucks that would have gone bye-bye if I didn't tell her to get up. That was two bucks without a sign. That was one for the history books.

It reminded me of a time not long before that I made a few bucks on the rock all by myself. The traffic was slow so I decided to share the story with Beth just like so many other stories I have bored her with in the past.

I told her, "On my way back from the mini-mart going to the fence, a guy pulled up beside me in a blue Ford sedan, probably a Granada, and asked if I was homeless. I answered him yes, and he handed me a half case of beer, a bag of hot deli chicken, and a ten dollar bill. I took it up to John's camp to share. What do you think about that Beth?"

"I don't remember anything like that," she said as she looked at me like I made it all up.

"When have I ever told you something that wasn't true? If John were here, he would tell you it happened. I took the chicken and beer up to his camp only to find him gone. I left half of the beer inside his tent for him when he got back from wherever he was. I took the chicken and some beer with me. No shit Beth, right out of the blue. I have no clue who that guy was," I explained in detail.

"That never happens to me," she complained.

"It just did, stupid! We just got a hit and didn't even have a sign out! We were just sitting here!"

The new sign seemed to have luck within it. We raked in about twelve bucks in less than two hours. It was time for a break anyway. We left the freeway and on way over to the mini-mart we ran into my mom and dad. We talked with them for a while then here came Dusty with his dog. He walked over to the car so I introduced him to my parents. Dusty was a really neat guy. He was a little rough around the edges and loved to talk like he was a martial arts warfare machine, but he was just a kid at heart.

After my parents left, all four of us, counting the dog, walked over to grab a couple beers and go somewhere to chat. Dusty filled us in on how he had to leave the mobile home park where he stayed. It was his mobile home but it was in a fifty-five and older park. Dusty and the manager just didn't see eye to eye anyway. I don't know why; I had been to his house on occasion and it was fairly well kept for a bachelor, especially when compared to the home across the road from his.

He didn't have much time to pack up and leave before the deadline was up so a large amount of his personal property went to a lot sale with the proceeds going to the park. It wasn't a fair deal at all, but Dusty was so devastated at the mess, he didn't even try to fight it. That sort of things happens in life when the bottom suddenly falls out.

Dusty was a welder-fabricator by trade. I remembered back to when we first met. I was over in the field beside Safeway drinking a beer when Dusty was walking his dog and drinking a beer. We got to bullshitting while we both sipped our brews and playing with his incredibly intelligent dog named *Nakita*. He was testing me, and I was testing him to see if either of us was just blowing smoke or really did know how to weld. As it turns out, both of us knew that each other was indeed a welder, so that set a firm foundation for a friendship, and it lasted.

We then continued on to the mini-mart and then walked back over behind Burger King to bullshit and drink our beers. We talked of different things that had happened in the area, but nothing too serious. I didn't want to pry into Dusty's personal life; I figured he would tell me when he was ready.

As I finished my beer Dusty polished off his. Of course ole slow poke Beth was still nursing hers. Dusty said, "I'm buyin' if you're flyin'." Well I had money but what the hell. "I'm flyin!" I told him as I stuck out my hand. He handed me a five and told me to get three. I didn't waste any time. Beth had still not finished hers and I was already back. I was thinking the whole time that soon we would be blessed by a visit from the Betholizer. We did, and as usual, it wasn't pretty.

After we were all done I asked Dusty, "What are you going to do? Where will you go with your dog, and what are you going to do with all of your belongings?"

"I'll probably be camped up around you guys. Work is getting slow and I'm probably going to get laid off soon. Piss poor timing," he answered.

As Dusty started to walk off he turned and said, "See ya later torque wrench, bye gopher mom," then snickered. I looked at Beth and she looked at me. I tilted my head for a moment then yelled, "Intruder! Dusty, it was you!"

"See ya at camp," he yelled.

"I can't believe it. It was Dusty that was riding us on our walkie talkies," I told Beth.

"It's a small world," she said.

We had kind of a rough time up on the hill for a couple days. The weather was wet, and then it turned cold. It turned really cold without any warning. Everything that had water in or on it froze. There were places on the trail up there that were so slick that even I had a hard time with it. I had on really good work boots too. Beth just had walking shoes. It wasn't easy or fun, but we had no choice but to stick it out until spring.

We both knew we were on borrowed time up there, and judging by the amount of heavy pipe stockpiled on the road below, construction was just waiting for the weather to become sunny and dry. With that in mind, we had to come up with another plan and a new place to move to. But for the time being, we had to be content where we were. Besides, Dusty had plans to join us, we just didn't know when.

CHAPTER 24

TIMES WITH DUSTY

It wasn't long until Dusty and his dog were staying up on the hill with us, although neither Beth nor I didn't mind much. He was always a decent camp-mate. He always brought his own food and beer and maintained a clean living environment. We actually had a lot of fun up there. We all three respected each other's privacy and left it at that. That dog, *Nakita*, was a blast up there; she had never had a large place to run before and was enjoying this immensely.

One evening Dusty came walking up the back way. He always wore a brown khaki jacket so he was not easily visible. I was practicing with my wrist rocket and firing at a tree. I didn't see him coming up the short cut. I drew back on the rubber and launched a shot at the target when I heard him yell, "Quit shootin' dammit! You 'bout hit me!"

"Sorry, I didn't see you!" I yelled back.

"What are you tryin' to do, knock me on my ass?"

"I said I was sorry; I didn't see you coming," I told him as him and his dog walked towards me.

He walked on over and turned the dog loose before him and I took turns pulverizing the cardboard target. Beth sat on a log and watched as she drank a beer and smoked a cigarette. When it got dark Dusty built a small fire. We usually didn't build fires at our camps but I figured one small fire wouldn't hurt anything. We all stood around and bullshitted until it was dark, and then we crawled into the tent.

It was a little tight in the tent with most of our gear but we managed. To my surprise, everyone was asleep by the time I was done listening to my headset to catch the weather forecast. That was alright though; I was tired anyway so I rolled over and fell asleep.

Dusty was the first one up and out and I followed shortly after. Beth wasn't ever in a hurry to do anything so naturally she took her own time. The sun felt good on the cool, crisp morning. It looked to be a wonderful day, just as the forecast said it would. When Beth crawled out we got together and headed down the hill.

As we walked down the paved haul road towards the freeway, all Dusty and I heard was Beth's voice from behind us, "Wait up guys. My toes! My toes!" I was so sick of hearing about Beth's toes I was just about to scream. Dusty caught on pretty quick about her toes and he too was getting a belly full of hearing about it.

When we arrived at the bus station Dusty decided he would go one way while me and Beth went another. Dusty didn't fly sign. He was getting unemployment so he had income. It just wasn't enough to get him into another place to live. Beth and I grabbed the sign from the new spot where we stashed it and headed out to the island. It turned out to be a normal type day until we started to head back and Beth ran into her so-called fiancé. I could not believe the look on her face. I told her, "Oh no, not again. Beth don't do it!" She did anyway. She spent the night somewhere with him so Dusty and I had the camp to ourselves.

That night Dusty and I partied down with food, beer, and the dog. We laughed and joked until almost midnight. Dusty even asked me, "How can you stand to be around her all the time?"

"I don't stand it, I only tolerate it to a point," I told him.

"How?"

"Well, when she starts to get mouthy, I tell her to shut up. If she hits me I grab her and shake the shit out of her."

"Does it usually work though?"

"If she keeps it up I walk off and leave her little ass to herself. She usually gets the picture after I'm gone for a while and then finds me later to apologize."

I took a swig of beer then went on to say, "You wouldn't know it but she is actually a good person. She just thinks that the whole ninety pounds of her can handle as much beer as the guys can. God, Dusty, I weigh over twice what she does, and she tries to keep up with me. That's how we came up with the nickname, Betholizer," I explained.

I went on and on with some of the stories I have in my memory and we laughed until our bellies hurt. Then he called his dog and tied her up while I wiggled into my sleeping bag.

"There's a lot more room in here now," he said as he got into his bag.

"Yeah, we should just throw all her shit outside."

"Do you think she'll be back?"

"Oh yeah! She'll never learn about that guy. He only comes around when he strikes out elsewhere and then he knows he can get a piece from Beth," I explained.

"Does he really do that?"

"Yep, it's been that way ever since I've known her. Pleasant dreams now!"

"Shut up! You didn't have to tell me that," he said as he slipped off to sleep.

The next day was more of the usual with the exception of the ending. I hadn't seen Dusty all day but Beth did come back. I didn't want any details of her romance and she didn't offer any. I just could not believe how gullible she could possibly be. I stayed down the hill most of the day then I spent some money on food and beer for the night. When I got to camp Dusty was playing with his dog out in the field. I walked up to him to talk for a while. He told me, "You better not go near the tent!"

I cracked a beer and walked around thinking Beth must be changing clothes or something. Finally I walked back to Dusty and said, "Wait a minute, that's my tent. What gives?"

"When I came up here, I saw two sets of feet sticking out of the tent so I left. I don't know who is in there now," He explained.

I blew my temper and threw a rock over into some nearby bushes and told him, "I'll go get this squared away right now, dammit. Heads are going to roll."

I walked over to the tent ordered, "Out of the tent. Now!"

Beth poked her head out. "What's wrong with you?" she asked.

"Get out here, and bring your friend with you," I ordered.

"He's not here!"

"Bring him anyway!" I re-ordered. Beth could tell by my voice that I was pissed.

"Don't be screwing in my tent!" I bluntly told her.

She stayed inside so me and Dusty started drinking beer and joking. I wasn't there to witness what happened, but I knew how that character was. We kept talking to each other and laughing at the same time.

Beth yelled, "Our tent, and you guys shut up about me!"

"You need to get your ass out of there and go someplace else. Take your boyfriend with you," I yelled back.

She denied everything but Dusty told me there were two sets of feet and I had no reason to not believe him. Beth came out with her sleeping bag and said she was leaving to sleep somewhere else.

There wasn't anyone else in there then. I didn't know exactly what happened but I couldn't make her sleep outside. I told her, "Put your shit back in there. We'll all sleep inside. Everybody is about three sheets to the wind anyway. This is definitely not a good time to make *any* kind of judgment."

The next morning we all crawled out one right after another starting with Dusty. He was in the mood to get the hell out of there. I think he thought the shit was going to hit the fan so he beat cheeks down the hill.

Beth tried to explain her actions but I cut her off. "I don't give a shit what you do with your body as long as it doesn't affect me. Don't bring his ass up here and into my tent."

"Our tent," she cut in.

I cut her off again, and then and told her, "Don't do it Beth, have a little respect! End of conversation. I don't want to hear any more about it."

Even though I was still pissed off, I kept my mouth shut. We gathered up our gear and walked down to the road when I remembered I had stuck a couple beers beside the tent. "Crap! I got to go back up. I left a couple of beers up there in the open. I'll catch up with you," I told her.

I took the short cut to the tent and was back within ten minutes. I didn't realize it at the time, but that would be the last time I would see that camp again.

CHAPTER 25

THANKS NASTY NEIGHBOR

The weather report proved to be right on track that day. It was shaping up to be a good day, for a while anyway. The sun was shining, we were doing fairly well flying sign on the freeway, and I had an egg McMuffin and coffee for breakfast. Overall, things were going good.

Dusty showed up about lunch time so I walked over to the bus stop with him. We decided to grab a couple beers and head over to the fence line. It was just me, him, and the dog; Beth stayed out on the freeway. That was fine by us, neither one of us wanted to listen to her whine about her beloved boyfriend leaving her again. Everyone tried to tell her that he was a lover and a leaver.

We just got to drinking the beers and talking when the old familiar voice rang out across the street and through the field, "Kirp! I'm calling the cops!" He stuck his cordless phone up to his ear.

I told Dusty, "I can think of a better place to put that phone."

Dusty freaked out, stuck his beer in the fence, and made tracks with his dog. Me, I stayed there and stared at the prick and pushed it as far as I could. I pretty much knew I had a warrant out for the child support thing anyway. I waited it out and antagonized the asshole as long as I felt was justified before I grabbed both of the beers and headed over to the freeway. I sat down beside Beth and sat the beers between her backpack

161

and her legs. I turned around when I heard a low deep voice say, "Could I see your identification please?"

I looked up to find that there was a cop standing right behind us. I pulled out my wallet to show the officer my ID as I told Beth, "Goodbye."

The officer asked me to step over to his car. There sat Beth with two open beers. I giggled about that as I spread my legs with my hands behind my back. Needless to say, I got a black and white taxi ride to the jail. I had a warrant again for not paying child support of course. It was the same thing as twice before.

It didn't really bother me much that I got arrested again; I knew it was going to happen. I went through the book-in process at the jail then they housed me in a dorm. I felt like a fish out of water listening to the other inmates and their individual reasons for their present stay. Some of the stories were incredible to say the least. I was eavesdropping on a chit-chat session where one guy knows just how to steal a Honda Accord. He must know how, this is the third time he was caught in the act.

When chow time came and me, being the new kid on the block, I had to hunt around for a table to sit at. Low and behold I heard a familiar voice from behind me. I spun around with my tray and there sat Dennis the thief. I sat with him and we talked while choking down our tasty lumps of mac-n-cheese with green beans on the side.

Dennis asked, "You back in for child support again?"

"Of course," I replied, "and you?"

He took a big bite of green beans while he told me, "I got busted for shoplifting again. Since it's my fifth time within two years they are going to try it as a felony. Habitual they say."

I laughed as I asked, "How many times have they caught you in total over the years Dennis?"

"Oh, I don't know, nine or ten I guess," he answered as he chewed his green beans.

I tried my best not to laugh even harder but I could not control it. I said with a chuckle, "I'm sorry Dennis, it's just that . . ." I couldn't finish what I was going to say.

We talked for a while before I was suddenly moved into a single cell where I didn't have to associate with the big boys. Two days later I was moved to the work release center in my own clothes and a lot more freedom, plus the opportunity to get a job.

This time I latched onto a job at a market research firm doing telephone survey interviews. It didn't pay worth a damn so I saved as much money as possible. I knew it wasn't enough to get a place to live and that I would have to resort back to camping but at least I would leave with some cash in my pocket. I was determined this time I would be better prepared. I saved money to buy clothes, a military duffle bag, a sleeping bag, and more items I would need when my day came to walk back to freedom.

Within four months my release date finally arrived. The guys in whom I had developed sort of a friendship with all asked, "Where are you going to stay?"

I told them straight up, "Out in the woods again, I have nothing else to rely on." On my way out the door I shook everyone's hands and left to cash my check. I was in a really good mood. *Freedom at last*, I thought.

I went to the bank where my employer did their banking to cash out my paycheck.

"You'll need an account with us before we can cash this. We can start a new account with a minimum of fifty-dollars," the snotty looking teller explained.

"Bullshit!" I told her. "It's your check; it's got your bank name right on it."

She wouldn't cash it without an account. I lost my cool and told her, "Okay, bitch! I'll just go somewhere else!"

I wasn't going to let that gal ruin my day so I jumped on the bus and stopped at one of those check cashing places to take care of it. It cost a little but I walked out with cash in my wallet. I jumped back on the bus and headed out towards the freeway. I saw nobody around so I figured I'd go stash my duffle bag and go shopping then see if I could find Beth.

CHAPTER 26

FINDING BETH

I walked over to the department store and purchased a new sleeping bag, a new package of double A Duracell batteries, and a tarp. On the way back to where I would temporarily sleep I stopped at the mini-mart for a couple cold beers. There was a new person working there that I didn't know so I didn't ask any information the whereabouts of anyone. I meandered back to my spot and sat back to have a beer and listen to my radio for a while.

As I sat there I began planning what to do for a camp. I knew I couldn't raise a tent where I was at; it was too close to where Danny and John used to camp and too close to the road. I got up and walked to their old location. What a mess they left that place in. Garbage was scattered all over the place. I shook my head in total disgust and then turned and walked away.

I knew it was getting late and needed to go down and eat some supper before laying out the tarp and my sleeping bag for the night. I walked down to Burger King and ate supper and then walked over to the bus station to see if anyone was around. No one was there. I wondered what happened and where everyone had gone. I walked over to the mini-mart and bought a couple more beers for the evening. It was silent and peaceful when I crawled into my bag and went to sleep wondering what had happened that nobody was around any longer.

I woke up fairly early the next morning and took my first morning yeller piss before packing everything up. I stashed everything behind some bushes before walking down the hill to have breakfast. I thought about going up the hill to Skippy's camp but knew if he was there, he wouldn't be awake yet. He was a late sleeper and didn't have a clue that I knew where his camp was. He thought he was hidden but he didn't realize that I knew that hill like the back of my hand. I knew that he would know where to find Beth, and I needed to find her. She had all of my things when I got arrested and I needed them back. I figured that I would check with him after I ate some breakfast.

I went down and ate before walking back toward the freeway to see if anyone was around. I still didn't see anybody there, so I just decided to get on the bus and go to the library for a while and catch up with my email on the computer.

I stepped off the bus then walked to the library where I checked my email then surfed the internet for a while before heading back. I made plans of walking to different places to see if I could find out where Beth had set up camp or had run off to.

I hiked up to Skippy's tent and announced myself about ten yards away. He came crawling out so we bullshitted for a moment then I asked about Beth. He said, "She's camped down the hill a ways in the trees behind those apartments."

He then pointed the general direction as he bounced on one foot while trying to get a shoe on the other. I knew exactly where he was talking about, it is the same place that John fell down once while a bunch of us were sitting and bullshitting, and then took Billy down with him a little while later. I knew that place well.

"I guess I'll go pay her a visit, she is supposed to have all of my stuff," I told him.

"She is with her boyfriend down there, he's been hanging around lately," Skippy told me as I turned away

I thought to myself, *Oh great! She is mixed up with him again.* I wondered what kind of a mess this was going to be, and maybe I'd be better off to go and search for a new spot to camp elsewhere. I needed a tent but I didn't want to spend money on one yet. After all, half the tent that she had was mine. Certainly not her beloved boyfriend's. No matter, he would leave anyway.

He always did. *A little smooch-smooch and a roll in the hay and he is on his* way. I thought.

It wasn't really a joke though, that was just the cold, hard truth and Beth was so gullible she really believed someday they would marry. *Whatever toots her horn*, I thought, *I just want what's mine.*

I decided to walk over to the mini-mart and grabbed a few beers to make my introduction a go little smoother. I'd never known Beth to turn down a beer. On my trip to her campsite I thought of what I would say especially if her 'one-and-only-love' would be there. I mumbled to myself, "Well screw it! I'll get what is mine and let her have the damn tent. I'll go buy a small one just for me and find a spot to pitch it."

When I arrived at the camp, there sat Beth with her shirtless excuse for a fiancé. I hesitated a moment as they spotted me and then I moved on in. Beth jumped up and gave me a hug while her wonder-love put his shirt on. I made things go as fast as possible when I reached in the sack and grabbed beers for everybody.

We sat around for a while and shot the shit when he jumped up and said, "Well I'd better get going!" My original thought was wrong. He hadn't been staying there; he would only come around for a quickie and then leave. He jumped on his bicycle and pedaled off.

Beth and I sat there for a while discussing the last few months events both hers and mine. She wasn't aware that I had money and I wasn't about to tell her that I had a substantial amount of cash on hand. She asked, "Well, are you going to stay here then?"

"Yeah. I guess so. I've got a new sleeping bag stashed up on the hill with my clothes and stuff. I'll get it later." We finished the beer then Beth suggested we go fly sign for a while.

Walking toward the freeway was a slow process. Nothing had changed in that department for sure. As we got closer to the rock across from McDonald's, I spotted a low-rider Japanese pickup truck high centered on one of the five speed bumps strategically placed there. The pickup was headed east and had already cleared two of the annoying bumps but got hung up on the third.

Never being a fan of low-rider trucks, especially Japanese low-rider trucks, I told Beth, "This is what you get when you drop a vehicle down that low."

I thought we would walk past the mess and watch the two Hispanics try to remove their very noticeable vehicle from an awfully embarrassing situation. The two men got out and carefully studied the bizarre incident. The driver scratched his head with one hand and pointed with the other. They were both engulfed in an intense conversation for about two minutes before the driver climbed back in and fired the engine.

The passenger stepped onto the back bumper and began jumping up and down while the driver gunned the throttle. The problem was that it was the brackets holding the leaf springs to the frame are what were hung up on the speed bump. Jumping on the bumper was going to do absolutely nothing to help their predicament. It was only going to make him tired.

When I was a heavy equipment mechanic for a rental company, I learned a few steps.

One: when the equipment is in a bad situation, to get it out of it, you; a) have to make sure nobody gets hurt, b) make sure the equipment doesn't get damaged more than it might already be, and c) do Minimal damage to the surrounding terrain.

Two: Whoever got the thing in that kind of a situation in the first place is a fricken idiot, so don't let that person be in charge to fix the problem. In this case, both one and two applied.

The driver stood on the gas and the automatic transmission shifted through all the gears then into overdrive, spinning wheel at a dangerously fast speed. It was only touching the asphalt just enough to create one hell of a smoke show. Then he would throw the shifter in reverse creating a horrifying *clank* that sent shivers up my spine. I thought he was either going to blow the tire, blow the engine, or break something in between.

I couldn't stand it any longer. I looked at Beth in total amazement and shook my head. As much fun I was having watching these to idiots try their best to get their truck out of this humiliating experience, I figured I'd better take over before something really bad happened. I waked over trying not to laugh while Beth followed to see if she could be of some assistance.

When I reached them, I quickly discovered that neither one of them could speak a lick of English so I had to resort to hand signals. I tried to explain to them that we had to lift the ass end off the ground and move it over about a foot to clear the speed bump. As I continued to explain this to the driver, the passenger was behind the seat digging out a cheap scissor jack that was no way going to fit under the body of the grounded vehicle. He found out for himself that it wasn't going to work so he threw the jack in the back of the little truck with a loud *bang* of anger.

Just as we got ready to grab the rear bumper, Fran pulled up with his Ford Crown Victoria and asked if we needed a hand. I told him, "Yes indeed, Fran. Good timing." Not knowing the two men didn't speak English he said, "Why don't I just push it off? No guarantees that I won't damage your truck though."

His Crown Vic was equipped with push-bars on the front bumper so he could only suffer Minimal damage. I flagged him forward until the two bumpers touched then signaled for the go ahead. The Crown Vic didn't even grunt as it nudged the little truck from the mess it was in.

The passenger quickly jumped in and off they went without a wave of thank you; kiss my ass, or anything. They ran away like a whipped dog with its head down and its tail between its legs. I told Fran, "Thank you Fran." He said, "You're welcome." and drove away laughing.

Beth and I sat down for a minute and laughed at the amusing situation while we rested. The event only added to what the unusual day would bring. We were only there at the station a few minutes before we decided to get moving.

We walked over to the freeway with Beth's sign when I saw three people sitting under the tree across from the island. I saw Danny, Skippy, and some guy that I didn't recognize. I asked, "Hey Beth. Who's the guy over there with Skippy and Danny?"

"I forget his name. He's new around here but he claims he's been here longer than me," she answered.

"Oh great, not another one of those guys."

"Yeah, he hasn't been around here very long."

We stayed out and flew for a while, made a few bucks and decided to go grab a few beers and join up with the crowd. As we walked back, I saw that the new guy was out flying. "More competition huh?" I asked Beth as I eyeballed him on the way by. He was flying Skippy's sign. We sat down in the shade and started talking with the others.

CHAPTER 27

ENTER NIMROD

The new guy saw everyone laughing and drinking beer in the shade and must have thought he was missing out on something. He crossed the freeway intersection without even using the crosswalk, let alone the use of the signal. *He's pretty gutsy or just plain stupid*, I thought. After I met him I knew the latter of the two was the more accurate.

He came over and sat down in the shade and then it started. He said, "Whose turn is it now?"

I looked at Beth and asked, "Who's turn? What does he mean whose turn is it?"

Before Beth could respond, the new guy turned to me and said, "We each have a half hour a piece out there before we have to switch off. Those are the rules."

"Whose rules?" I voiced. "There have never been any rules around here."

"There is now," he said. "I've been here longer than anybody and those are the rules!"

"Bullshit! This is the first time I've ever seen you, and I've been around here in and out for over three years," I argued.

I knew right then that him and I were just *not* going to get along. This guy was dumber than a sack of hammers. His nick name quickly became, *Nimrod*. It was fitting. I didn't even know his real name and didn't care to find out. A grown man that doesn't know the proper way to wear a simple baseball cap doesn't score points with me anyway. I guess he thought it looked tough or something, having his hat turned around backwards, but it just made him look even more ignorant than he already was.

We all got into a conversation when I said something to the effect of 'nice log truck' as one passed by. Nimrod said, "Yeah, but it's only a six cylinder Diesel, all the V8's have dual stacks and the sixes have one exhaust stack."

"Bullshit!" I corrected him, "They're all pretty much all six cylinders now with a splitter after the turbocharger."

"Oh! You know everything too, I see," he sparked at me.

"Well, there are a few exceptions, like Mack's Maxidine Diesel," I added.

He responded just like the total idiot that he was, "You don't know what you're talking about!"

I just looked him in the eye and let him know, "I haven't been a Diesel Mechanic for nearly fifteen years and not learn anything!"

I knew that conversation was not going to go anywhere with any sort of reasonable intelligence on his part, so I told Beth, "I'm going for another cold one. Want to join me?"

She got up so we headed over to the mini-mart then on to the spot behind Burger King. I couldn't help but vent a little bit on the new-comer now called Nimrod. I told Beth right away, "That guy is trouble. You just wait, he's trouble."

We conversed about Nimrod for a while thinking that things wouldn't be the same with a dumb-shit like that hanging around. I told Beth, "I have never seen him before. Not even before I started hanging around here. Basically it was just Danny and John. Occasionally Billy and Linda were here, but not that guy, he's full of shit. Besides, who died and left him to be king? I'll tell him where he can stick his rules!"

"You pretty much already did," Beth said. She knew I wasn't about to bow down to that clown at all.

We finished our beers and then walked on over to the freeway again to find that nobody was flying. They were all under the tree sitting in the shade. As soon as we walked out to the island, here that boneheaded dip-shit came. He yelled across the freeway at us, "You got until I finish my beer, then it's my turn!"

I wanted to yell back but Beth put the back of her hand to my chest as a signal to let him be.

I told her, "If that guy is that big of an asshole right now, I wonder what he's like after a few beers."

Beth and I made quite a few dollars in just a few minutes so we decided to pack it up. Nimrod had not come over yet but as soon as he saw me press the walk signal he jumped right up and downed the rest of his beer. He met us at the intersection and told us, "You can give me my share now and give everyone else theirs."

I looked at him in the eyes and put him strait, "No way! That's our money. You are only included for a piss break or to make change. Those are the rules. That's the way it's always been, and that's the way it is now! Let's go Beth."

I could feel that he wanted to start something right there. We just kept on walking. Nimrod was really starting to get on my nerves. Beth knew it too. She couldn't help but know that things had changed since I had gone away for a while.

We walked on back to camp to sit in the shade for a while before deciding what we were going to do about supper. Finally, I got up and walked to the store for some bread and lunchmeat. When I returned we ate then thought about going back out to fly sign for a while. It was too soon to call it a day; we still had about four hours of daylight left. I didn't feel like sitting around all that time and it wasn't all that hot then. In fact, it looked like it could rain. I was hoping Beth wouldn't give me a hassle to sleep inside the tent. It would be a lot drier than under that tarp in case it did rain.

We walked on out to the freeway to fly for a while talking of Nimrod, and hoping he wasn't out there anywhere near the freeway when we got there. That would just put a real damper on the whole evening if he was hammered and wanted to start a fight with me.

The traffic wasn't heavy at all, not even worth staying out there to fly, so we walked over to the mini-mart then headed back to camp for the night. We bumped into a guy that lives in the apartments nearby so we stopped and chatted with him for a while. He was a nice guy that had his leg in a brace due to an injury at work. He was bored out of his mind so we didn't mind talking with him.

I offered him a beer but he refused saying, "I have some in my fridge, you guys keep it."

That was nice of him but he was more than welcome and we let him know it.

When we reached camp Beth sat her ass down on a log. I just stood so I could walk around and see what went on around us. It wasn't long until here came Dusty. I hadn't seen him for a while so it was good to talk to him. When I asked him about his dog, tears welled up in his eyes as he said, "I had to give her away. When I lost my house I had no way to keep her. She likes to run so it would be cruel to keep her."

"I'm sorry, Dusty. That had to be rough," I told him.

He already had his own beer so I didn't even bother offering one to him. He loved that dog, and I could tell it was just tearing him up. He knew though that out in the woods and homeless is no life for an active dog like Nakita.

We talked for about an hour and Dusty started playing around with me. He pushed me on the shoulder and asked if I wanted to go for it. He was just horsing around of course, but when he grabbed me and tried to throw me down, then it was on.

We were both laughing and grunting as we tried to out-do each other. He got a good hold on me so I spun around and dropped him right into the blackberry bushes with me landing on top pinning him down. We were both laughing so hard we could hardly move as he said, "Get off of me, Kirk!" I jumped up and offered him a hand and he pulled me back down. We just laid there in the blackberry briars laughing and trying to catch our breath. Beth was laughing so hard I thought for sure she was going to puke.

It was a good time had by all so we sat down and enjoyed a cold beer while Dusty and I picked the stickers out of our clothing and skin. We were a mess. Blackberry briers were tangled in our hair and our clothing, scratches all over our arms, but it was fun. Something told me that he needed that kind of attention at the moment. He looked as if he was a little bit low on self-esteem. That happens when you are forced into living that way.

A bit later it was time for sleep. Dusty said he would sleep on the ground so I tossed him a sleeping bag and he found a flat spot to lie down. It didn't take long for me to fall asleep that night, especially after the brawl him and I had. That takes a lot of energy when you're laughing at the same time.

Morning came so I crawled out. There was a sleeping bag all neatly rolled up outside the tent. Dusty was already gone without a sound. He just woke up and walked off, but that was alright. There was no reason for him to wait until we were up.

"Well, Beth, Dusty has already hit the trail. Get your lazy ass up so we can get a jump on the freeway before Nimrod shows up with his damn rules,"

She crawled out and stumbled over to a nearby bush and did the dry heave thing. I told her, "I could swear you are pregnant. My God, Beth, this is not normal. You need to eat better or something. This is not normal."

She coughed and replied, "Don't mother me. Leave me alone!" She finally straightened up and walked towards me.

We finally got around and walked down to the freeway. Nobody was out flying sign at the time so we walked on out to claim our spot for a while. We made a couple bucks, not a lot, but enough to call it a good start.

The temperature was warming up quickly so we decided to rest for a while. I told Beth, "Let's go to the other little store and walk down the field by Safeway for a change."

Beth thought it was beer-thirty but I had biscuits and gravy with jalapeno peppers on my mind. When we got to the little store, Beth put a couple of beers on the counter while I doctored up the biscuits and gravy. Then she says, "I think I want some too."

"Do you want a full order or a half?"

"How much money do you have? Do you have enough for a beer later on?"

"Do you want a full order or a half, Beth? Answer the question."

"Half, I guess," she decided.

I knew she wouldn't eat a full order anyway but I thought I'd better ask. I paid for her order as she took forever doctoring hers up, then we headed on down the field to find a flat spot to eat the biscuits and drink the beers.

When we were done, we cleaned up all of our garbage and headed down to the freeway only to see Skippy and Nimrod under the tree. "That's just a really good spot for them right now," I told Beth as we walked out to the freeway island with our sign. I could feel Nimrod's beady little eyes penetrate us as we stood there with the sign. We stood there for about ten minutes before we got a hit. I told Beth, "There is the icebreaker, now let's show Nimmy how it's done."

We got a few more hits right away so we were doing fairly well. I saw Nimrod jump up so I knew he wanted to get in on some action. He had his hat turned around backwards, as usual. I guess he must have had the attitude thing going or something. As he got up and walked over to the off ramp from the freeway, I could see he had an attitude going with a cocky little half-ass hop on one foot. I bumped Beth in the arm and looked at her. She was already looking at me as I shook my head while she gave a half-ass sigh.

"What a moron," I told Beth.

He walked across the freeway exit and stepped onto the grass then proceeded to take a piss, right there in front of the people exiting the freeway onto Main Street. I bumped Beth and told, "Look at that idiot. He's taking a piss right out in the open! Oh boy, Beth!"

We stood there watching the dumb-ass drain his noodle when I saw that he was just about to get exactly what he deserved.

"Check it out, Beth!" I said loudly.

She looked just in time to see a black and white coming down the exit and coming to an abrupt halt just as the blue and red lights came flashing on. We both were laughing at the most enjoyable scene as the police officer talked on his radio with the mike attached to his lapel.

"Busted!" I yelled enjoying every second of it.

Skippy was watching the whole thing as well. I was overwhelmed with joy watching as the officer emptied Nimrod's pockets as a backup unit pulled up behind the other cruiser. "Nimmy is going bye-bye! Nimmy is going bye-bye!" I sang to Beth in a short little chorus.

We got a good chuckle out of that and then I told Beth I was going to the library to check my e-mail and stop by the employment office to see if there was anything I could apply for. Of course she didn't want to go, three dollars for a bus fare was too much for her. That was almost enough for a box of tobacco. I went anyway.

When I returned, I saw Beth out flying again with Skippy. Who knows what they talked about, if anything. They probably talked of Nimrod getting arrested for pissing in public. I didn't see him around, so I figured they probably would keep the idiot overnight at least.

Later on I walked out with Beth for a few minutes then we decide to head on up to camp. Dusty then came wondering around so we talked with him a few minutes. He asked, "Is there anywhere up where you guys are that I could set up my tent?"

"Sure," I said. "Let's go get it and I'll show you a place up past us just a bit. It's a goat trail, but it's not too bad." He agreed so we walked to the shed where he had his stuff stored and retrieved his tent.

We were walking back when he decided to make a stop at the mini-mart for some beer. He offered, "You help me set this thing up and I'll buy the beer."

"I already planned to help you get set up. I've got money in my pocket but if you're buying, I won't turn you down," I told him with a smile.

That was nice of him to offer the beer knowing I would help him anyway, but I think it made him feel better. He never came across as a person to just take and not give in any sort of way.

I helped him carry his camping gear up the goat trail to the flat spot where he could successfully set up a decent camp. We staked the floor down then ran the poles through the loops. When it was time to raise the thing Dusty was getting pretty wobbly. I thought right then that it probably go a lot better if I just did it by myself. I think him and the beer together would be a real mess if he fell onto the tent while we were trying to raise it. He just stood back and watched while I laughed and raised the tent. I, of course, found humor in it, knowing I'd been down that road before.

I walked on back to my camp and sat down for a while. Beth fumbled around with the task of rolling a smoke. It wasn't too much longer until here come Dusty down the hill to visit. He had his sack of beer with him so I knew it would be a lengthy visit. I turned to Beth and said, "The more the merrier; to an extent of course." We talked way up into the darkness when he decided he had better get up the hill to his camp. I knew that was going to be quite a show so I was prepared to help him out. I wondered how he made it down the hill without ending up on his ass. Now he had to go back up that steep goat trail.

He made it about a third of the way up the hill when he blurted out "Oh shit!" as he fell about ten feet down the side hill into the blackberries. I turned on my Maglite and headed up to rescue him. I almost got him up to the trail when he decided to fall again and take me with him. This time it wasn't planned, he just didn't have any coordination. I sat up and saw the glow of my Maglite off into the bushes so I went after it. Dusty finally crawled back onto the trail as I retrieved my light and stepped back onto the trail also.

I got him up to his tent and stayed there until I was sure he was inside and lying down. I didn't want to leave him alone while he was still vertical because he would probably fall onto rather than into his tent. I knew how it was; Beth had a tendency to do that on occasion. Of all my days of having a tent to sleep in, I had only fallen onto it one single time. It seemed Beth wanted to make a career out of it.

Dusty was safe then so I walked back down to camp, took a piss, and then crawled into my sleeping quarters for the night. Beth wanted to know what happened so I told her, "Dusty went for a walk in the blackberries. He's okay now; he's sleeping like a baby."

The next morning I crawled out to start the day. It looked like another nice one with not a cloud in the sky. I asked Beth, "You coming out? We better get a move on it; it'll be getting hot in a few hours and we need to make some money."

Beth crawled out setting two beers on the ground. I said, "Oh yeah, Dusty bought me some brews last night for putting up his tent. And he brought his own down last night. Speak of the devil, here he comes."

Dusty came slowly walking down the trail. When he got to our spot he stopped and asked, "Can I buy one of those off of you?"

"You can have one Dusty. I'll wait for a while. I need to head down and use the little boy's room anyway," I told him.

Beth handed him a beer and he cracked it while I turned and walked down to use the restroom at Burger King. It looked as though it was getting kind of busy in town, it would be a good day to get out on the freeway early to fly sign.

After I got out of the restroom I still didn't see either one of them so I walked back up to see what the holdup was. Beth wasn't done with her beer yet, imagine that, so I figured I'd clean up the cans and pick up some garbage while I was waiting. I had everything cleaned up just about the same time she was ready to roll. Dusty was already on his way. "C'mooooown Beth!" I said as patiently as I possibly could. She was used to me saying it that way by then anyway. Finally, we were on our way to fly sign.

I stuffed the trash in a garbage can and took the empties into Albertsons while Beth continued onward toward the freeway to start flying the sign. I cashed in the slips to get the refund money then headed over to the mini-mart. I just bought one for me a little later. I saw Beth out on the freeway so I figured I would just read the paper at the bus station and suck down the beer before I headed out to fly sign with her.

After I achieved that goal, I walked over to McDonald's and used their restroom before heading out to the freeway myself. An old fellow by the name of Paul was sitting at a table eating his pancakes and sausage, so I stopped to say hi to him, and ask how he was doing, before I proceeded out to the freeway with Beth.

As soon as I reached her, there came Nimrod. He walked to the edge of the freeway and yelled, "Fricken cop callers! I will get you for that!"

"They let the prick out of jail," I told Beth

"What did he yell?" Beth asked.

"He thinks we turned him in. We were standing right here the whole damn time. What a Nimrod."

"What? We didn't turn him in. He took a piss right in front of a cop!"

"What an idiot. Nobody called the cops on him. He pulled that little stunt off all by his stupid self," I said.

Beth just laughed and watched for windows. We made a few bucks here and there before leaving for lunch. That incident just proved his lack of intelligence, but in his own beady little eyes, he probably did believe that we had called him in.

It took time and an intervention from others in order to finally convince Nimrod that Beth and I had absolutely nothing to do with his getting arrested. I asked him several times, "How could have either Beth or me called the cops from the freeway? You know neither one of us have a cell phone."

A day or so later Nimrod approached Beth when she was by herself. They got into it over the idiot getting arrested out of his own stupidity and insisted again that she or I had called the cops. It ended when he hit Beth. It takes a special breed to pick on a skinny, somewhat defenseless woman when there is nobody around to defend her. I wasn't around when he did it, but found out shortly after. The nice guy with the brace on his leg, Devin, was nearby when Beth told me about the episode. He didn't take to the idea of Beth getting hit by a guy very well at all. He pulled his Mazda 3 up beside us and loudly said, "You go back to your camp. Kirk, get in and let's go find this asshole!"

Enough said. Beth headed back to camp as I crawled in the Mazda.

We took a ride to the bus station to look for Nimrod and there he sat. Devin was in a terrible mood anyway because his insurance company was jacking him around, so he was ready for a fight, even with his leg brace and all. I pointed over at Nimrod and told Devin, "That's him right there!"

Before I could figure out the somewhat confusing Mazda door release lever; Devin was already on his way over to have a little chat with Nimrod. He got right in his face and told him flat out, "If I ever hear of you messing Beth or Kirk again, I'll tear you apart!"

I stood about five feet back and could tell that he was dead serious. I didn't have to say a word, just watch. Devin wasn't screwing around either; I had a feeling that if Nimrod would have opened his mouth, Devin would have jammed his fist into it.

We climbed into his car and headed back. Devin walked up to our camp with me and applauded how clean it was as soon as he saw where we were staying. Then he looked at Beth and said, "I don't think that prick will be bothering you again, if he does, come and get me or leave a note for me. I know what he looks like now, and I'm sure he'll remember me."

"Thanks Devin, I owe you one," I told him.

"No problem," he replied. "You don't owe me anything, it felt good!"

"If you need a strong back or anything, just look me up."

"All right, Kirk, I'll see you guys later."

"Okay, Devin," I said. "Tell the little lady we said hi."

"Will do," He said as he hobbled towards his home with his brace and a grin.

I told Beth, "Only a brainless idiot would try that again."

"Time will tell," she said. "Only time will tell."

CHAPTER 28

LENDING A HAND

The summer days remaining could be counted using both hands. It was still unseasonably hot with daily temperatures soaring into the nineties. It looked like we could get an Indian summer if things didn't change but that usually only happened once every seven or eight years or so.

It was however time to start thinking about the oncoming season and the weather it could possibly bring. In the Pacific Northwest we never counted on what the weather should do, instead we counted on what it could do. I had seen days in January where people were wearing their shorts and tee-shirts the very same year that snow dusted the valley floor in early June.

At that moment though, we had to at least begin thinking about the weather patterns that could develop and be mentally prepared for what might come at us. That meant just thinking about what we would need and checking out the sales where we may get a bargain on the items we needed for a rough season if it came to that.

Beth and I were taking a break at the bus station one hot day doing just that. We were discussing what we should save up for. A less than adequate plan was better than no plan at all. We talked of clothing, shoes, that sort of thing. It's difficult to discuss winter items when it's summer like weather.

As we chatted away about those items, a guy walked up and sat down across from us. He looked as though he felt either lost or a little out of place. I made small talk with him and noticed the southern accent right away. It wasn't as strong as I'd heard before, but it was definitely noticeable.

His name was Bill and he was from North Carolina. He was out here on the west coast looking for work. He had been stationed in Florida in the United States Air Force. That won some respect from me right out of the gate. Any person who has an honorable discharge from any branch of the U.S. military automatically gets bonus marks in my book. Whether the soldier ever saw combat or not, those people deserve a pat on the back just for their efforts and dedication.

He wasn't having much luck finding a job. I told him, "Join the crowd, man. This is probably the worst state in the nation to find work at the moment." He rolled a cigarette that obviously came from tobacco he obtained from tearing up snipes from ash trays. I couldn't help but ask as I studied his duffle bag, "Where do you live?" He him-hawed around a bit, cleared his throat and said in an almost whisper, "I've been staying at the mission but I'm going to leave. It's too fricken depressing over there."

I gave him a half-ass grin and said, "Yeah, been there, done that. It's no fun."

Beth walked out to fly sign as we sat and talked for a moment longer. I asked him, "You want a beer, I'm buying?" He replied, "I don't drink much but what the hell. I've nothing better to do."

I figured Beth wouldn't mind, she was over flying sign by that time anyway. We headed over to the mini-mart where I got my favorite and he grabbed the same. I asked him, "Are you sure that's what you want? Some people don't like it; it has a different flavor to it, but I like it."

"I'll just get what you are getting," he quietly replied.

I paid for them both and we walked up towards our camp. We walked within spitting distance from the tent when we cracked the beers open and I asked, "If I offered a place for you to stay, will you promise not to pull anything off? That's our tent right there hidden just beyond those bushes. See it?"

"Yeah, I see it there. Is it big enough?"

"Oh yeah," I said with a smile. "It's a six man tent. There's more than enough room for just me and Beth. With our gear and yours, it might be a little tight but not too bad. It would get you away from the mission anyway."

"Yeah, I gotta get out of that place," he said.

"I know how you feel. I told you, I know what that place is like. Look, we don't bite. Every now and then Beth gets a little mouthy and I have to tell her to shut the hell up, but other than that, it's pretty calm and easy going around here," I explained.

We headed back to the bus station and saw Beth on her way back from flying. When she got there I first asked her how she did. "I did alright. Now I'm ready for a beer," she said.

I thought that was prime time to fill her in that we now have a temporary roommate. I didn't figure that she would mind. If we could help somebody with anything, we usually did. I didn't see any problem with inviting him to stay with us; we really didn't have anything of value to steal, even if he would have turned out to be a thief.

All three of us headed to the mini-mart and Beth headed for the restroom. I asked Bill, "You want another? I've got some money but I'm going to see if I can con Beth for one anyway. I'll see if she will spring for you one too, I know she has the money, she does very well out there by herself."

"No thanks," he said. "That last one went right straight to my head."

I chuckled and told him, "Oh yeah. I didn't tell you that those have a little kick to them. If you're not use to them, they'll bite you right in the ass."

I heard Cabby in the background say, "You ought to know Kirk. That's all you buy!"

"No it's not, sometimes you're out of it and I'm forced to buy the other stuff," I denied.

"Not very often!" she chuckled.

"Leave me alone Cabby! I'm trying to impress a new friend!" I fired back at her.

Beth came out of the restroom so I automatically grabbed two. She asked Bill if he wanted one. I didn't tell her that we just drank one about a half an hour ago. What she didn't know wouldn't hurt her. Bill said, "No thanks." She dug into her pockets very carefully as not to expose her hidden fortune and then paid for the two beers. Cabby, at the register, bagged them, so off we went. "Bye Cabby!" I said loudly as I held the door open for Beth and Bill.

We cracked the beers on the trail that leads to camp then I broke the news to Beth. I gently told her, "Bill is going to shack-up with us for a while, the mission is about to drive him fruit loops."

I studied her actions carefully when she said with no emotion, "Okay, as long as he knows the rules."

I rolled my eyes at her and said, "He does Beth, good grief!"

I then glanced at Bill and said, "Looks like you're in, Bill. Welcome to your new home."

"Thanks guys," he said nervously as he rolled a smoke.

Beth and I walked back out to the freeway and Bill took off somewhere. He didn't say where but it didn't matter; it wasn't any of our business anyway.

Beth and I flew sign for a while until Nimrod decided for himself that it was his turn. Instead of arguing with the idiot, I decided to leave. Beth followed, so we made our way across the freeway when Beth suddenly got a bright idea and said, "Let's try it over there on the other side." I studied the cars coming down the fairly new road and thought standing there might not be such a bad idea. That's what we did, and by golly it worked.

As we stood there where no one had flew sign before and was doing well, I kept an eye on Nimrod and discovered we were taking in almost double the hits that he was. He kept looking over at us and could obviously see that we were scoring fairly well. I wanted to stick my tongue out and put my hands to my ears wiggling them while saying, *Neener-Neener-Neener* but I thought that might be pushing it a little too far so Beth and I just pretended like it and said it so he couldn't hear, and laughed as another window came down with a dollar bill sticking out.

We went and bought some Chicken McNuggets and sat down for a while to decide what we needed to invest money in with the day's profits. I told Beth, "The battery on my watch is going south and we depend on it from time to time. They're about five bucks."

She agreed so I went to the department store across the street while she went back out to fly sign. As I crossed back after having the battery replaced, we bumped into each other near the mini-mart. I knew what she was there for so I decided to join her.

I broke the silence and stated, "All this time no one has tried to fly over at that spot, and look what happened."

Beth took a swig and said, "Yeah, but you know that Nimrod is going to be over there, because he saw how good we were doing there."

"I know," I said in a disgusted tone, "he's probably been flying sign there longer than anyone else too! Just ask him; he'll tell ya all about it, I'm sure. The fricken jerk!"

"I don't know where he gets off on that, he wasn't anywhere around back when Billy was alive," she said.

"Did Bill tell you he is on some kind of bi-polar medication?" I asked to change the subject.

"No, he didn't say anything to me about anything like that."

"He told me he is bi-polar and having a hard time getting his medication. We better keep kind of an eye on him. He seems okay, but you know how that condition can affect people."

She nodded her head and took another swig and replied, "Yep, I know."

"About done?" I asked.

"Yes, but I got to go potty before we go back out."

We walked out onto the freeway and stood there in total silence. Neither one of us liked to just stand there watching the cars go by one by one. I for one was getting quite bored.

I knew Beth was getting sick and tired of hearing about every truck that went by, but we had to have something to talk about. I could see her point; how would I feel if all I heard about is knitting, or making earrings, or something I possess no knowledge of and didn't care to learn. I thought about it and then decided to head over and get some propane for the tent heater since we had already made some money. That way we would have something substantial in our possession instead of blowing it all on beer. Besides, it's a lot better to wake up to a warm tent on a cold morning than it is to freeze our asses off, beer or no beer.

As the evening progressed into night time, all three of us gathered back at camp to finish the day with some bullshitting and beer drinking. Beth and I had tacos for supper. I didn't ask Bill what he put in his belly.

Beth was the first to crawl into the tent, with Bill soon to follow. He slept on the east side, Beth in the middle, and I on the west side. Everywhere we set up a tent it always seems that I am always on the west side. The side that gets the wind beating against it and therefore keeping me awake. Beth planned that out; she wasn't born yesterday.

We all settled in for a night's rest. About two in the morning Bill decided he needed to step out and go piss, waking everybody else in the process. Then Beth decided she had to go too. I mumbled, "Well shit, I guess I might as well go too since I'm already awake."

"I'm sorry, when you gotta go, you gotta go," Bill responded.

"No problem," I replied.

Beth cracked a beer and asked me, "You want to split this?"

"God, Beth!" I replied. "It's two in the morning. Oh well, what the hell. Maybe that will help me go back to sleep for a while; it's too damn early to stay up now." I chugged half of it and tuned in my favorite country music station on my Walkman radio.

It only seemed like a minute or two later but it actually was close to six o'clock when I woke up. "Up and at it," I said as I crawled out of my sleeping bag. To my surprise, Bill was already up and out of the tent.

I heard Beth snarl, "What time is it? Is it really time to get up?"

"Its six-fifteen, time to get your ass up. I got to hit the little boy's room."

Beth crawled out right after I did and started her day with that gag and puke thing. "You better go see a doctor, that ain't right!" I pestered her again. She didn't say a word; she was already sick of hearing me complain about it. Bill had already left before we started walking down the trail to Burger King.

After we both had finished, we moved on from Burger King to the freeway. We flew the new spot instead of having to put up with Nimrod's shit. We did pretty well right out of the gate. I asked Beth, "You want to head down to the store and get some biscuits and gravy?"

"I don't want any, but I would like a beer," she answered.

"Well, let's get a move on it then, maybe we can get back here before shit-for-brains shows up and ruins everyone's day."

We packed our sign over with us and stashed it where nobody would see it then proceeded on to the store. We walked down the path to the field and found a place to sit down. Beth didn't even want a bite so I ate all the breakfast while she drank her beer. Then I cracked mine and proceeded to drain it. After eating those jalapeno peppers with the hot biscuits and gravy, that beer went down fast and smooth.

We gathered our trash and the other beer and headed out to the freeway. Beth decided to go back behind a fence near the freeway and drink the other beer, so I went out on the main island to fly sign. I was doing alright out there when I saw Nimrod heading my way.

I thought: *Oh great, here that asshole comes.*

He walked to the edge of the freeway and yelled, "Beth is having a problem over here and needs your help!"

I immediately jogged across the freeway and threw the sign into the bushes and hurried over towards the fence.

I didn't even make it to the fence when Nimrod threw his hat down with his glasses inside and punched me in the face sending me on my ass. He then climbed on top of me and proceeded to beat the shit out of me before I could figure what was going on. I protected myself as best as I could, but he was on top of me just whaling away.

He finally let up some, so I got to my feet and started walking away. He followed me so I picked up the pace. He was calling me names the whole time but I just kept right on walking. Cars were driving by the whole time; someone had to see what was happening. This attack was right out in the open. When I got to the crosswalk I went over to McDonald's to clean up. As I looked in the mirror, I discovered a small cut on my left eye lid and my left eye beginning to swell and turn black. I cleaned up as best as I could and tried to figure out what the attack was all about. I thought: *Maybe his little pea-size brain still thought Beth and I called the cops on his stupid ass.* I didn't know, and I didn't care. All I knew is that my original thoughts about him being a problem were spot on, a direct hit.

Beth came over as I left McDonald's so we walked over to get a beer. I needed to think about this. There was no reason for the attack from nowhere. Beth and I walked over to drink our beers and talk. I cracked open my beer then I asked, "Did I do anything to deserve that dry gulch?"

"What's a dry gulch?" she asked.

"A dry gulch is when someone attacks with no warning," I explained.

"Oh, like a sneak attack."

"When someone lures another person in, then throws a pussy punch at him."

"I don't know what happened," she said.

"What did he say to you?" I asked. "He came over and told me that you were having a medical problem and needed me. Then he sucker punched me and dropped me on my back and kept punching me in the face. He even punched me in the nuts but I was able to protect myself."

"You're kidding me! He punched you there?"

"Yeah, several times!"

"What an asshole," she said as she turned red and was madder than hell.

"Sucker punching asshole is more like it," I corrected her.

When Bill came around and saw my eye he asked what happened. When I told him he got pretty upset.

"For no reason?" He asked.

"Yeah. Just dry gulched me right there in front of traffic and everything," I said.

He pointed at the paper bag on the ground and asked, "You got another one of those in there?"

"Help yourself."

I could tell by the look in his eyes that he was not a happy camper. I told him, "Go easy on that stuff! You know how it will sneak up on you."

That was the conversation the whole time we stood there. I told them both, "I'll get to the bottom of this. Leading me to believe that she had a problem just to lure me over with my guard down is just being a pussy. No ifs ands or buts about it, just being a pussy." They both nodded their heads in total agreement.

When we were done with our beers we headed back out towards the freeway. I wasn't about to let Nimrod's little cheap-ass stunt ruin my day. I don't know where Bill went again but Beth's plans were to go and fly sign. As for me, I turned and looked at her and told her "I'll be right back. I'm going over to the department store."

CHAPTER 29

GETTING PREPARED

I walked into the department store and headed for the sporting goods section. I knew just what I wanted, and just where it was in that store. I grabbed the item, paid for it and walked out the door ten bucks poorer but with pepper spray clipped on my belt. I grinned as I thought: *Alright, Nimrod, I'm ready for you now you stupid asshole.*

I met up with Beth out on the freeway flying the new side. I walked to her with my new surprise, pulled it out, and then told her, "I dare that sucker to attack me like that again."

"I bet that'll teach him a lesson," she said

"How did you do; are you ready for a break?"

She picked up a sack of food someone gave to her and then stuck the folded sign under her arm. That signaled to me that she did alright and was indeed ready for a little time off.

As soon as we walked into the mini-mart, Cabby asked me, "What happened to your eye?"

Beth filled her in on the details while I grabbed three beers and placed them on the counter. Cabby just shook her head as she rang up the beers, Beth handed her the money and I held up the pepper spray to show it off.

I told her, "He tries it again he'll be on the ground gasping for air!"

She laughed and said, "I think he deserves it."

I grabbed the sack and we headed out the door, leaving Cabby with a smile upon her always pleasant face.

I drained my beer down while Beth was sipping hers like fine wine. I reached down and grabbed the other and cracked it open. "I suppose you going to kill that one too," she remarked in a pissy tone.

"No!" I snapped back. "I'll drain half of it while you tinker around with that one. Then you'll roll a smoke, and then you will have to go piss, so on and so forth."

"I'm out of tobacco. I have to go find some snipes," she fired back.

"Do you know how sick that is? You don't know who or what has been sucking on the end of those things. Think about it Beth, you are digging them out of a damn ash tray for crying out loud. That's fricken gross," I replied in disgust.

I picked up the cans and shoved them deep inside a bush so we could retrieve them later as we headed back down to the freeway. I saw Nimrod and Skippy out on the island so we stood on the south side of Main Street. It didn't bother us that Nimrod was there; we would mind our own business and leave when we wanted to. We stood out there until it was getting dark then headed back to camp for the night.

Sleep came fast for the three of us that night. I didn't know why we were so tired. I guess all the turmoil with Nimmy beating on me had some effect on it. I woke up to some noise at around eleven so I got out of my sleeping bag to see what was going on. I turned on my Maglite just in time to see Beth's little ass climbing out of the tent. I had to pee anyway so I followed. I probably wouldn't have been able to go back to sleep with her rummaging around anyway

We met back in front of the tent and Bill came climbing out. "What's going on?" he asked. "Nothing, Beth woke up so in turn, I woke up. We figured on sitting out here and enjoying the warm night. We haven't got a lot of them left you know."

"What's it like here in the winter?" he asked in his southern accent.

Beth and I laughed while I said, "Well, it's wet, just wet."

He shook his head like he wasn't looking forward to that at all. He had been stationed at the US Air Force Base in Florida, after all.

We all crawled back inside the tent when Bill asked, "What are you going to do about that guy?"

"Nimrod? Nothing right now. I'm going down tomorrow to talk to the pastor at the church and see what he says," I answered.

"Well if it was me, I'd beat his ass. You're stronger than he is, why not?"

"Nah, that's not my way. I'll get him back, but in a way he won't expect. Kind of like he did to me but on a scale that he hasn't got enough brains to figure out," I explained to him.

The next morning we all crawled out at the same time. Beth did her morning gag and puke thing again so I had to wait for her. Bill went ahead and hit the trail. I guess he didn't feel much like hanging around for the show. After she was done she turned around and reached inside the tent and grabbed a beer.

"I'm going to Burger King to use the restroom and clean up a bit," I told her.

"Do you want a pull off of this?" she asked. I figured what the hell. Besides, the more I drink, the less she will have. That was a plus at that time of day. I drained the top half of it then told her, "I'll meet you after I get out of the restroom."

We met up and proceeded over to grab our sign that was stashed between two water valve boxes near McDonald's. I reached down and found nothing. "Horse piss," I groaned. Beth knew right away that someone had taken our sign again. She said, "Probably Nimrod."

"More than likely; why not make a complete jerk of himself. He's already off to a damn good start," I grumbled.

After I searched for some cardboard and fabricated another sign, we went out and flew. About an hour into it I saw Nimrod head out on the island, sporting his little hat and his beady eyes, to fly sign as well. I just could hardly bear looking at the fricken jerk. His dark eyes always hidden behind those dorky round glasses, only magnify his evil globes making then appear twice the size that they really are. At least he was over on the island and not near us. *That fricken Jackass*, I thought in almost hatred. I was really beginning to dislike him, very much.

Beth and I flew for another half hour when Beth said, "Mother Nature is calling."

Off she went to McDonald's to take care of business, leaving me there to make some money. I saw Nimrod leave the island but to my surprise, he snuck up behind me and started calling me names and stood really close to me, right in front of cars and right in the open. What a dip-shit. Some lady pulled up to the intersection in a Toyota Camry and told Nimrod, "You get out of his face right now! I'm calling the cops!"

She already had her cell phone glued to her ear before she finished her threat. Nimrod realized this, and since he and the police were not exactly on the best of terms, he left in one hell of a hurry. "Thank you!" I said loudly as the lady drove away with the phone still stuck to her ear.

I walked over towards McDonald's to meet up with Beth. I told her, "Nimrod! What a fricken shit-head!"

"What did he do now?" she asked.

I filled her in on his little stunt and said, "We better go the other way just in case that jackass is over where we go to have a beer. Are you hungry yet?" She shook her head. I told her, "I could use a cold one after that little episode. That fricken idiot was challenging me right there in front of God and everybody. He's a fricken idiot, Beth!"

"I know," Beth said as we crossed the street and headed for the store and taking our sign with us that time.

The day seemed to be going by fast as we stood there and conversed about the problem with Nimrod. I told Beth, "You know, it's only going to get worse. That ding-bat thinks he owns this area. I gotta go piss so I'll be back in a minute." I walked over to Burger King to use the toilet.

When I walked out the door, after using the restroom, I noticed dark clouds to the west. As I approached Beth I began conversation as I walked and pointed, "Check out the clouds. It appears as though we might get a bit on the wet side tonight."

"Yeah, we need to get prepared at camp," Beth replied.

I agreed so we walked up towards camp. I looked at the small ditch crossing the path to the tent and told her, "You know, this drainage ditch might get a little tricky when the real wet stuff comes." I walked down the ditch a ways observing the water lines from the previous years. When I walked back to Beth I said to her, "I'm going down this way to see if there is another way in and out. I really don't want to swim out of here if it rains all night and this thing floods."

"Good idea. I'll go with ya," she eagerly agreed.

We walked along the ditch all the way down to where a dead end road met up with it. I looked around and told her, "Apparently, the ditch takes all the run-off from the hillside there." I pointed towards the foothill about twenty yards away. I walked around the barrier at the dead end and noticed a mound on each side of where the water would flow. I pointed at the mounds as I yelled at Beth, "We we'll cross here when the water gets too high on the main trail. Come here and let's see where we can cut a trail on the south side of the ditch."

She came over to me and we followed the ditch a ways then I took us through some trees then zigzagged through some blackberry bushes until the tent was in sight.

"There," I told her, "this won't be so bad. It will take a little longer, and difficult in the dark, but we can make it."

It was sprinkling when we reached the tent so we made sure things were prepared for rain. There was a small leak that I knew would need some attention so I climbed inside to grab some tape that Al gave me. I scrounged around for nearly five minutes and for the life of me I couldn't find that roll of tape. "Dammit," I said. "Beth, have you seen that roll of duct tape Al gave me about two weeks ago?"

"No," she answered.

"I wonder where I put it. Half the time I'm sleeping on the damn thing," I grumbled. "I've looked high and low for it but can't find it." I could tell I was getting pissed just by the way I was moving things around inside the tent. I was usually fairly careful but not that time. I needed to just stop looking for a while and calm down before I messed something up.

Just as soon as I was ready to crawl out I felt a lump jabbing me in the ass. I reached down and thought that I had found it.

"Shit, just an old chew can," I mumbled as I tossed it out of the tent and onto a clump of grass growing right outside our tent door.

"What?" Beth asked.

"Nothing."

I never did find the tape so I told Beth as I crawled out, "Oh well, maybe we'll bump into Al later on today. If we don't, I'll just go and buy a small roll. Good stuff though, none of that cheap shit that doesn't stick, and tears every way but the way you want it to."

"Yeah, yeah, yeah," she said as she picked up some stray garbage from the area.

"Well it's true. You get what you pay for. Personally I don't care to get out of my sleeping bag in the middle of the night and re-tape something because I was too damn cheap to buy the good stuff," I explained.

We made our way towards the freeway but when we came to the bus station. Low and behold, there was Al. "Hey buddy," he yelled as he waved with his whole arm and his hand well above his head. I walked to him as the magic words spilled out, "You need any tape?"

I turned and looked at Beth with a shit-eating grin, then turned back to Al with an honest smile and answered, "As a matter of fact Al, I do need some tape. Do you have any?"

He reached in his blue jacket pocket and pulled out a roll of packaging tape. The brown stuff about two inches wide that is used for shipping boxes. I looked him in the eye and sincerely told him, "Thank you Al. That is perfect for what we need. It's gonna rain and we have a hole in the tent. This will work just right!"

"I'm glad it'll work for ya. I'll get some more and bring it to you. You are going to be here tomorrow?"

"I'll be looking for you, Al."

"Okay, buddy." he said as he approached the bus. It probably made his day that I could use his tape. Al and his tape, a legend in his own time and didn't even know it.

I grabbed the sign that we had stashed in yet another location and we both walked out to the freeway to fly. We didn't have to worry about tape now but we were getting low on funds and we needed to buy some more sani-wipes. It didn't take long until a Hispanic fellow pulled up and gave us a five spot. I told Beth, "That didn't take very long."

I then heard someone yell from the parking lot, "Hey! You guys want some cans?" It was the same guy in the Chevy four-by-four that doesn't like farting around with them. I immediately pressed the walk signal and told Beth, "Get a move on it. Knowing this guy, we are done for the day after we cash these in."

Three shopping carts later we had enough cans to keep us busy for at least an hour. I told him, "Thank you, again!"

"No, thank you. I hate turning these damn things in. See ya!"

"You know, he's a regular now. He'll hunt us down with his cans," I told Beth. She just painted on a smile as she started pushing a cart towards Albertsons. I pushed one and pulled the other into the store and to the machines to start plugging them in. We took the slips up to Customer Service and walked out the door with twenty four bucks and some change. That wasn't bad for an hour's labor. I walked down the soap isle and got some sani-wipes and then we headed over to the mini-mart. We bought our beer and then we headed up to camp.

We sat down for a while to rest our legs while drinking a beer when I asked Beth, "What do you want for supper? We've got enough money to get something special for a change. I kind of want pizza. How about you?"

"Yeah, I haven't had pizza in a while. That sounds pretty good," she said.

197

"Well, I guess I'll go get a pizza then. I hope Bill likes pepperoni because that's what I'm getting. I'll be back in about an hour or so. It's a long walk, so you might as well repair the tent while you're waiting. Here's the tape," I told her as I tossed her the tape and left camp to go and get pizza.

The walk to the pizza place was enjoyable, mostly because I had a little time to myself. If I would have ran into Nimrod, I would have nailed the jerk in the face with the pepper spray and watched him cough. I walked into the pizza place and ordered a family size pepperoni with jalapenos on the side. When it was done baking, I took off and headed for the mini-mart to get Bill large bottle of Mountain Dew. While I was there, I grabbed me another beer because I knew Beth was indulging herself at camp.

When I reached camp I tossed Bill the soda and opened the pizza. We ate until our bellies couldn't hold anymore. There was only two slices left when we were all three done, but I thought if Dusty showed up, he could eat the rest. We talked and laughed for a couple of hours when Beth stood up to go take a piss. I could tell she was hammered when she lost balance and damn near ended up in the blackberries. I whispered to Bill, "Uh-oh, anymore beer and she will turn into the Betholizer." He gave me an empty look so I filled him in on the transformation that takes place with her when she gets her snoot full. He thought I was joking; I informed him that I was not.

When it was time for bed I yelled out, "Last call for piss break, smells like more rain, so be prepared." Everyone crawled in and got prepared for the night. Then it happened. The Betholizer started ripping on me for no apparent reason. I didn't even know what she was yelling about but she sure was making a lot of noise and calling me every nasty word she could think of. Then she started hitting me as hard as she could. Bill stayed out of it, although he did sit up watching and listening.

Beth kept hitting me so I gave her the ultimatum. "Stop it, you bitch, or it's going to get real ugly!" She wouldn't stop so I reached down and grabbed the pepper spray and gave her a good sniff, but also giving Bill a little dose by poor aim. They were both coughing and gagging with nowhere to go; they couldn't see their way out of the tent. Bill took off his glasses to try to wipe his eyes, only making it worse. Beth just called me a nasty name and tried to lie down. I leaned back and tried to go to sleep thinking to myself, *That'll shut her trap for a while.*

CHAPTER 30

BILL MOVES ON

I apologized to Bill for accidentally spraying him with pepper spray. He didn't say much about it until little later. I was almost asleep when all of the sudden I received a punch right in the eye that wasn't quite yet healed from Nimrod's cheap shot. I yelled out in total surprise, "What the hell?" I quickly sat up and shined my Maglite around and found out it was Bill that struck me. I blinded him with my Maglite which I had twisted the head to the spot-light position.

"What the hell did you do that for?" I asked.

"For spraying me in the face!" he exclaimed.

"That was an accident! I only meant for Beth to get it so she would stop hitting me and shut her damn mouth!"

"I'm sorry; I'll leave in the morning."

I took my light out of his eyes and told him, "No, we'll talk about it in the morning, there's no since in getting hasty over this, Beth obviously had too many beers and I know how she can get. She probably won't remember any of this. Get some sleep. I'll see ya bright and early."

The next morning it was kind of chilly and wet. It did rain a little bit, but the clouds had disappeared by then so the heat escaped from ground level. It looked to be a fairly nice day. My eye hurt like hell again, though. After I finished taking my first morning yeller piss, I went to find Bill to talk to him about what had happened. Bill was standing over by a large fir tree looking at something so I waltzed on over to see what was so interesting. He was loading a small pipe with pot.

When I approached him he turned and said, "I'm out of my medication so I substitute this."

"I don't care if you smoke that shit, just don't do it in my tent or be around me when you get weird. What you do is your business but don't bring any trouble," I told him.

"I'm going to have my sister wire some money to me and then I'm going back to Florida."

"Well, that's your choice, but don't let the episode last night influence it, I forgive you. I probably shouldn't have sprayed Beth but it is a lot better than me cutting loose and popping her a good one."

He laughed as he stated, "My God, you would have killed her!"

"Yeah, I know. I've had to shake the shit out of her a couple times before to shut her up, but I would never hit her. I'd send her flying into the next county, for Pete's sake."

Beth came out to see what was going on. I told her we just got up and were talking. She walked back to the tent, I chatted with Bill for a few seconds then I left as well. Beth and I picked up the garbage from the night before and headed down the trail. The ground was still not soaked, so no water built up in the drainage ditch. We grabbed our sign and headed out to the freeway.

We flew for about an hour before I spotted Al at the bus station. Beth told me she had to relieve herself anyway, so we headed across the street. I went over to talk to Al while Beth headed to McDonald's

"Hey, Buddy. I got ya some more tape!" I patted Al on the shoulder and told him, "You're a life saver, Al. The other tape worked great. This will come in real handy. Thank you." He looked me in the eye and grumbled in a low voice like he had a mouth full of cotton, "Welcome."

We decided to head over to the mini-mart when all of the sudden here was Beth's beloved boyfriend. I shook my head and thought, *Shit, not this again; he looks like he's plastered.* I was nice to him, but when Bill showed up I took my beer and walked up to camp with him; mostly just to get away from a situation that could become volatile. Beth's boyfriend being pickled and her well on her way was a bad situation any way you looked at it.

Bill and I were up at camp just tinkering around when we heard the two of them down there yelling. All the way from camp we could hear his loud voice. I told Bill, "He's going to get busted! People won't tolerate that kind of language around here. Those apartments are right there, and there are kids there too. He'd better cool it." Bill agreed so we just went on about our business.

Within the next half hour I peeked around the corner to see a black and white parked there and two officers talking with Beth and her loudmouthed boyfriend. I told Bill, "Let's get out of here before they attract attention to our camp area." We walked down towards the cops when one turned around and said, "Howdy! Do you know these people?"

"Yeah, kind of. We are headed to Burger King. Is there a problem?" I answered.

The other officer said, "May I see some identification please?"

I whipped out my wallet and withdrew my ID card while Bill pulled out his military ID. He called our names into the police database and then told us that we were free to go. Bill and I beat cheeks over to Burger King as fast as we could walk. Once inside, I bought Bill a hamburger and I got a chicken sandwich then we sat down where we could see out the window. All we could see is the rear of the police car so we really didn't know what was going on. Fifteen minutes later we saw two cruisers leave so we got up, put our garbage away, and walked out the door.

When we got to the sidewalk where Beth and her wonder man was sitting, we saw nobody. "Oops, it looks like they went bye-bye. But look, there are no cans here. The cops must have taken them for evidence," I said.

Bill was looking off into the distance when he finally spoke and said, "Well, looks like it's just me and you now."

"Well, at least I have all of the money in *my* pocket." We laughed then walked over toward the bus station.

We got almost to the bus station when I located Beth bent over retrieving our sign. I told Bill, "Well, she didn't go for a ride with the police. I wonder where her lover-boy is. I'll bet ya he went for a ride."

"Let's go see what happened," Bill said with a shit eating grin.

We eased our way over to Beth. She didn't look like she was in a good mood at all. She turned and looked at Bill and me, with fire in her eyes.

She said, "Well, he got arrested. I told him to quit yelling but he just kept it up."

I turned the heat up a little more and said, "Yeah, you're one to talk. Why did they put him in cuffs? Did he have a warrant or something?"

"No," She said. "He was yelling at me and he also yelled at Walter. He was walking his dog."

"Walter? He yelled at Walter? Why?" I asked.

Walter was an older gentleman that lived in the nearby apartments that had the striking resemblance of the late Walter Mathieu, the actor.

"He was drunk and waving his beer and yelling foul language at him. Walter just kept walking," she explained.

"That fricken idiot! I told you he's bad news Beth. Dammit, this looks really bad on all of us!"

"You better have some money left, because I want a beer."

"I told you I had money but I think it to be wise not to go down there given all the shit you guys caused over there. We'll go down to the other store and let things cool down for a while."

We walked down the street to the little store to buy our beer while Bill went the other way. After we made our purchases we walked down to the field to talk. I was interested in what exactly went down but I knew I would have to wait until she got about a half a beer down before I would find anything out. She rolled a smoke then let it loose.

"He started fighting with me over nothing, then Walter came out, and then shit-head told him to eff-off and mind his own business," she explained.

I gave her the rolled eye look and told her, "Great. I told you, Beth, he's trouble. How many people have tried to tell you that? You just-won't-listen!"

"Well, you don't have to worry now because the cops are going to ask the judge to put a restraining order of a thousand feet against him coming near me or that area."

I just kept my mouth shut. I wanted to comment so badly I could feel it ready to fall from my lips. But I just kept a lid on it, although I did say, "I wonder what Walter thinks about all of that? This doesn't look too good on our part you know." She nodded her head then took another swig of her beer and a drag off of her cigarette.

We walked back to the freeway and flew sign for a while. The day was getting away from us in a hurry so we decided to take what funds we had and sneak up to camp. It was already starting to get cold so we needed to get some things organized inside the tent.

When we got up to camp, I climbed in the tent and re arranged things so I could light the tent heater if it got uncomfortable in the middle of the night. With three of us in there, it was going to get a little crowded trying not to burn a hole in the tent with the heater. I also moved some clothes around to make more room for items we normally would have left outside.

It wasn't too long before Bill come wondering up to camp. We all sat down and talked about the day's events when I mentioned that I would like to go and talk to the Pastor the next morning. They both thought that would be good for all of us to go to church, so we made plans to do just that.

We all rustled around and prepared for sleep when I jokingly asked Bill, "You aren't going to climb over here and punch me in my sleep again are you?"

"Are you going to spray me again? I said that I was sorry."

"I know, I was just jerking your chain."

The next morning I crawled out before anyone else. It was a chilly morning and I should have taken time to light the heater. We just weren't used to the weather yet, so it felt a lot colder than it really was. Bill and Beth crawled out and watered the bushes as I checked my watch and told them, "It's almost time to start walking down to the church. It's about a half hour walk from here." We started walking down the trail then I said, "Wait a minute. If we cut through there, we can take about five minutes off our time. It's gotta be warm inside the church."

We arrived at the church and checked the door. It was locked. Nobody was around yet. "We must be an hour early, oops," I said, somewhat apologetically. We hung around the front of the church freezing our asses off for about ten minutes when some lady parked her car and went up to the doors. She walked right in. We didn't check that door. The Pastor was in his office the whole time. The lady taught Sunday school for kids and arrived early to prepare.

We walked in and the Pastor invited us to sit and get warm. He said, "Kirk, have you guys had breakfast?"

"No, we were in a hurry to get someplace warm."

He smiled and said, "Make a pot of coffee. I'll be back in a few minutes."

I walked to the restroom to wash my hands while the pastor walked around to the back of the church to get in his truck. The coffee finished brewing just as the Pastor came through the door with a dozen fresh doughnuts from Albertsons.

"Here ya go," the pastor said.

"What a guy," I told him.

We went into the pastor's office and talked with him for a while. I talked about the shiner on my face and that Bill didn't do all of it. Bill talked of his problems and Beth talked of hers. The pastor listened carefully to all that was said. His input was quite helpful to all of us. We were glad we went to church instead of doing nothing except thinking only negative thoughts about the things we had been going through.

We sat through both the adult Sunday school and the regular service. All three of us enjoyed the whole experience. We were offered a ride back to where we hang out but I knew Beth wanted to visit the little quick-mart on the corner a block away, so I made an excuse to refuse the ride.

We made our way down to the store and bought a couple of beers for Beth and me, and a soda for Bill. I joked at Beth and said, "I bet you had a cold beer on your mind the whole service. Shame on you!" She knew I was just joking. As a matter of fact I was ready for a cold one too. It got a little warm inside the church. We were just starting to get acclimatized to the cold weather.

As we left the store and started walking, Beth asked, "Where are we going to go to drink these?"

"Watch and learn," I told her from experience. We walked down a side road with wooden fences on one side and metal and wooden fences on the other. Basically all a person had to worry about was the traffic, which wasn't much on a late Sunday morning. I told Beth, "Just listen for my signal. When I say pull, I mean pull. No dilly-dallying around. Got it?"

We cracked them open while they were still in the paper sacks. I turned sideways and checked both left and right then said, "Pull!" I tipped my brew up and started chugging while I watched Beth fumble fart around with her paper sack. I took a breath, looked around and said, "Pull, I say. Pull!" I caught her in mid-swig and the combination of my words, Bill's laughing, and the mouth full of beer had the foamy liquid spewing out of her nose. We all were laughing so hard the people in the oncoming cars probably thought we were *all* nuts.

We finally calmed down and finished our beers and made our way back towards the freeway. We had to stop, of course, at McDonald's to use the restroom before heading out to fly sign. Nimrod was out on the island so we took the other side. The traffic seemed to be fairly heavy so we would probably do fairly well. Bill didn't stay for the fun at the freeway; he left to do something else that was more important, I guessed.

We stayed out for a couple of hours then took a break down at the field near the Safeway store. Beth went ahead and stayed there while I walked over to the little store and bought some nachos with jalapenos and three beers. I took everything down the path in the middle of the field and couldn't see Beth. I finally saw some tree branches move about twenty yards away and Beth came popping out of the trees. "What did you do?" I asked as if I didn't know. "We were just near a restroom not ten minutes ago."

"I didn't have to go then," she replied.

I cracked open the nachos and scraped a pepper onto one and crunched it down. I offered some to Beth, knowing all the time she wouldn't eat any. It was just a friendly gesture.

After I finished my beer, I cracked the other and drained half of it as usual, waiting patiently for Beth to finish hers so we could get going. When she was finally done with her first one, she said, "I can't drink the rest of that one, help me out please." I picked it up and drained it down to about two inches and said, "There. Can you handle that?" She grabbed it and finally finished it. Then we left there and headed towards the freeway.

We made our way back to the freeway just in time for Beth needing to go piss again. I just shook my head as I held up the sign for the oncoming traffic to see. She walked across the road to use the restroom. I raked in four dollars and some change in that amount of time. That wasn't bad for no longer than I was out there alone. We stayed a little while longer then we headed up to camp for a while to relax. After that we came back down for something to eat. That wasn't too bad of an afternoon really.

We made enough money for the night, and then some, so we decided to pack it up for the day. On our way over to the mini-mart we bumped into Bill. He walked over with us then followed us up to camp. We had just sat down when Bill told us of his new plan. He said, "I got a hold of my sister in Florida, she is going to wire me some money for a ticket home. I'll be leaving first thing in the morning."

"Well that just shot my mood all to hell," I said. "I was just getting to know you!" I told him.

"You don't know me at all. When I get to Florida I have to turn myself in to the police. I have an outstanding warrant for my arrest."

"Oh, well I guess it's better you go take care of it and get it over with then, huh?"

"Yeah, I've got to get on with my life," he explained in a saddened voice.

I took a swig of beer and walked over to watch the sun go down. I didn't want the day to end up entirely on a bad note and the sunset was a spectacular sight that evening.

The next morning I woke up at around five thirty to take a piss and Bill was already gone. He made no noise, said no goodbyes, nothing at all. He just up and quietly walked away. Beth came out of the tent, I told her, "He's already gone. He must have caught the first bus to where ever the money was getting wired to. We'll probably never see him again."

Beth had a tear in her eye as she walked slowly over towards me. I took a deep breath, gave her a small hug and quietly said to her, "Like a flower floating down a river, people come and people go."

CHAPTER 31

THE MCRAY RIVER

With the rain moving in with the winds of autumn, it was time to get really serious on preparation for the wet weather ahead. That meant careful study of the surrounding trees for limbs that could come down from snow, not to mention whole trees that could uproot from water saturated ground and fall on our tent. It also meant the challenge of the drainage ditch that crossed our path on the way to camp that would no doubt overflow with any heavy rain.

We started out the day as usual with the exception of needing to save money for items we needed. I elected myself to be the treasurer since Beth couldn't find her own hand in her own pocket. When we received the first hit of the day, that money went in one pocket for daily items but from then on, I split the income in half. I put half of it in one pocket for then and half for expenses that would help us through the wet, cold months.

The rain hit later that afternoon and we were soaked before we could retreat to any kind of shelter. We ended up at the bus station for a few minutes before heading over to McDonald's where we sat for a few minutes until the rain died down. I told Beth, "I'm going to walk over to the department store and get you a poncho. They can't be that expensive. I'll be back in a little while. I'll meet you out on the freeway when I'm done." She nodded her head so I went and purchased a poncho for her. Nothing was special about it; it was just a piece of thin plastic with a hood. The type I purchased didn't even have sleeves, just a basic poncho.

I went out on the freeway to fly sign with her for a while when she gave me a funny look. "What?" I asked. She reached in her pocket and pulled out a ten dollar bill.

"Great, let's keep at it so we can save that for propane and batteries."

"And a new flashlight for me," she said excitedly.

I shook my head and said, "Oh God, not this again. Are you going to save money and buy a good one this time?"

"We'll check it out before we buy it," she explained.

"Yeah, that worked out great the last two times," I argued.

While I was bitching about the flashlight idea, a minivan pulled up with the window down and a hand out. I jumped out and told the lady, "Thank you, I'll give it to her," which I did give the money to her. As soon as I turned around to step back on the curb, I spotted another window down with a hand sticking out. I grabbed it as the man drove by. I yelled, "Thank you!" I don't think he heard me though; the light was green and he was on the move.

When the traffic finally died down a bit, I reached in my pocket and counted out eight bucks. I asked Beth to count the money she had in her pockets but she handed it to me. She was having a terrible time with her eyesight then. I counted out fourteen dollars from her pocket, so we walked off the freeway over to the bus station to figure out what we would do from there. That would give Beth an opportunity to get out of the poncho before we went shopping.

We stashed the sign and her poncho over near the mini-mart and went inside to get a couple brews. We talked with the guy at the register for a while before going over to the trailhead to talk about what we were going to buy at the department store. We decided on one bottle of propane, some batteries, and a flashlight, as we had discussed before. We put our empty cans inside a plastic bag and stashed them in the bushes to gather later.

We went shopping and purchased what we set out to buy, with the exception of a good flashlight. Beth insisted on another cheap flashlight of that damn barrel at the dollar store. I shook my head as the lady at the register put batteries in it to make sure it worked. I did keep my mouth shut while we were in the store but that didn't stop me from running my jaws as soon as the door swung shut behind us. I told Beth, "That should be your first clue when you buy a flashlight, when the person that is selling it has to put batteries in it to make sure it works when it is brand new. Get a grip, Beth. Go next door and buy a good one!" She wouldn't listen even if you took a bull horn and yelled directly into her ears.

From there, we walked up the trail to the tent. What we found when we walked to our tent was there wasn't any tent. It was gone, and all of our things with it. I looked at Beth and sadly said, "Oh no, it's happened again." Beth was without words. The only thing we could find was our camp stove, food, and our sleeping bags that we had stored inside the tent. We had nothing to sleep in but wet, muddy sleeping bags that were lying in the muddy water. I sat down on a stump in total disbelief at the downright heartlessness.

"Why is this happening to us? We aren't even anywhere near where it happened before," I said in disgust.

Beth choked a bit and said in a crumbling voice, "What will we do now?"

I thought for a moment and said, "We have to make some more money, and a new sign that stresses that we need a tent. We can take what we make and go buy a tarp. I'm going to walk around. There must be come kind of clue as to where everything went. I'll be back shortly."

I took off down the trail to where the drainage ditch crosses. The ditch was then appropriately named, *The McRay River*. The first part is from Beth's last name, and the last part from mine. It was getting quite full and required a strong leap to cross it.

I walked off the trail where I saw footprints and drag marks in the grass. I followed them and found our tent; it was totally ruined. It was cut to pieces and the fiberglass poles were even broken in two. All of our things were wet, and muddy, even our bible was ruined. I walked back to Beth to fill her in on the horrible news, knowing that she was already on the verge of tears.

As I filled her in on the mess that the tent was in, the first thing she thought of was Bill must have done it. I told her, "He wouldn't do something like this. Even off his meds, it wasn't in his nature to create such havoc on people that were already in as rough a situation as we are, even with a tent. It doesn't really matter now who did it; they have to meet their maker sooner or later. Let them explain their actions to God. Let's go and make a new sign to fly."

We walked over to a cardboard recycling bin and I found a suitable piece of cardboard to make a sign. I took out my permanent marker and wrote, "WE NEED A TENT BUT ANYTHING HELPS! GOD BLESS!" We then walked out to the freeway with a lost feeling deep inside.

It was a new sign so we weren't really expecting any huge response at the time but we stayed anyway; we had nothing to go back to so what the hell. We did make a few dollars within a few minutes so we decided to go and grab a bite to eat. We decided then to go over across the street and buy a tarp. I went to take care of that task by myself while she went and flew sign some more. She didn't score a tent, but she did make some more money.

At the end of the day we set out to get some cardboard to lie on, and figure out some way to stay as dry as possible with one tarp to share between the two of us. It was going to be a challenge, especially when one of us had to go pee in the middle of the night. Trying to get out from under the tarp with pools of water on it was going to be tricky to say the least. We went and bought some beer and beef jerky for the long night ahead. Sleeping under a tarp and on top of cardboard wasn't anything new to us at that point; it was just uncomfortable as hell.

As we walked towards the trailhead, we ran into Devin. We told him of our situation and he had an idea. His friend owned a blue Dodge four-by-four that was parked near the end of the one way street. He was having a difficult time getting it running in order to sell it.

Devin knocked on his door and introduced us. Devin asked if I helped get the truck running if we could stay inside it during the night to stay dry. He said, "Yeah, that's alright with me as long as you are gone before seven." I tapped my watch and told him, "I've got an alarm; that will be no problem at all. By the way, I'm a former Diesel mechanic. Maybe I can be of some help with getting this thing running for you." He nodded his head once then went back inside his apartment to get the key to unlock it.

He came out the door and walked to the truck. "Just leave it unlocked so you can get back in," he said as he twisted the key.

"Okay, will do so, thank you."

"There isn't anything in there to steal, so people will leave it alone," he said as he walked back inside his apartment and shut the door.

Beth and I couldn't have been happier at the time. At least we had a dry place to stay for a night or two. We walked back to the McRay River to drink a beer since it was too early to get in the truck. I told Beth, "When we do get another tent, we're going to have to cross down at the other end. It looks like if we get much more rain, the McRay is going to jump out and flood this whole area."

We talked as we watched the rain fall from the sky as the droplets glistened on the asphalt from the light emitting from the street lights. It wasn't going to be the most comfortable place to sleep, but at least it was out of the pouring rain. I replaced the battery in my Sony Walkman and listened to my favorite country station before crouching down in the seat of the truck. We were in a warm, dry, and secure place so I was on my way to sleep. "Good night Beth," was the last thing I remember saying.

I was half awake when my watch started beeping to remind me of where I was and that it was time to get my ass up. We had to be out of there by seven so I reached over and shook Beth until she woke up.

"Beth, get up. It's almost seven, we gotta go," I told her.

"Okay, okay. I'm getting up, give me a break!"

"I gotta go to the little boy's room. You better go too."

"Give me a second," she said in a pissy tone.

She finally got her little ass up and crawled out of the pickup. We made sure everything was back where it belonged and walked over to Burger King. I used the restroom and sat down while I waited for Beth. I reached in my pocket and took out some money for a hot breakfast. We could share a breakfast sandwich, so I walked up and ordered one. When she walked out, she walked to the table.

"I'd rather have a beer," she said after looking at the breakfast I just purchased.

"Just eat half of this. We'll get a beer later," I told her.

It wasn't raining so we walked over and flew the sign in hopes of scoring a tent. It was actually a fairly nice day; the traffic was usually heavy on those days. The sun was shining and it wasn't all that cold. It wasn't exactly warm by any means, but it wasn't entirely uncomfortable either. We were out there for about an hour when Beth was firm about going to get a beer. "Okay," I said, so we carried the sign over to the mini-mart, went in and bought two beers and grabbed the sign on the way out. We went up the trail to the McRay River to drink them. The water in the drainage ditch had jumped out. It would be the long route up there if we did come across a tent. We finished our beers, took a piss, and headed back out to fly sign some more.

We were only there about ten minutes when I heard someone yell across the freeway from behind us. I guy was standing on the other side of the fence beside a parking lot holding what looked to be a large blue duffle bag.

"A tent!" I yelled at Beth.

"A tent, hurry up and get it," she instructed.

I was so excited I didn't wait for the crosswalk. I ran over to the man while he lifted the heavy carrying case over the fence. He was out of breath.

"I was hoping you guys were out here today. I dug this out of my garage. I saw your sign yesterday and told my wife I was coming down to town today to give this to you," he explained as he gasped for air.

"Thank you very much, this just made our day," I told him.

"I just looked inside and the poles aren't there. I'll go back home and get them. Are you going to be here in about an hour?"

"I can meet you right over in front of McDonald's," I said and pointed across the busy street.

"Okay, I'll meet you there in an hour."

"I'll be there, you can count on that," I said excitedly.

Walking back across was quite a chore but when I got there and filled Beth in on the situation. We were both so happy we couldn't wait to go to camp and set it up.

We took the tent up to the camp and laid it out and staked the floor, and then I went back down and waited for the poles. He came back with the poles just like he said he would. I told him, "You don't know how much this means to us. Our other tent got torn down and destroyed along with most of our other items."

He reached in his back pocket, opened his wallet and handed me a twenty as he said, "You're welcome son. Have a nice day."

My jaws dropped. I could hardly believe the kindness of this fellow. I nodded my head at him as he backed his car out of the parking place and drove off. I thought all the way back to camp, while carrying the poles, how some people are out just to destroy and make life more miserable on people while others can't seem to be helpful enough. It's a sobering thought how God positions these miraculous plans all in order.

I yelled at Beth when I reached McRay River so she could come get the tent poles instead of me carrying them all the way around to avoid crossing the flooded ditch. She grabbed them and instructed me to go and get a couple beers so we would have them after we raised the tent. I told her, "I wish you would have told me that before, it would have saved me a trip down there. I'll be back in a few minutes."

Off I went, again. On my return trip I walked up to the McRay and looked up and down it only to spot an old pallet down the way a bit. I sat the beers on the trail and walked down to the pallet. I drug the pallet to where the trail meets the ditch and made one hell of a splash.

"Kirk, Is that you? Are you alright?" Beth yelled.

"Yeah, just building a bridge. It worked too," I yelled back at her.

I grabbed the beers, crossed the Bridge over the McRay River, and walked right up to Beth and our new tent that she had already raised by herself while I was gone.

"Awesome," I said. "Let's have a brew!"

CHAPTER 32

HAPPY HALLOWEEN

We were both glad to have a tent to sleep in; it was wet and would only become wetter and colder as winter approached. Halloween was just around the corner meaning the rainy season was here to stay. No Indian summer that year, just good old northwest sunshine, rain, and lots of it.

It rained like a cow pissing on a flat rock all day and all night. It rained so hard that the bridge that I had just constructed over the McRay River floated down stream about forty yards. *So much for that*, I thought: *It's going be the long way in and out from here on.*

We were damn near out of money and our food stamps were close to being depleted. Beth's was near zero balance, and mine was close behind. I didn't know how much was on my card so I decided to call the number to find out what the balance was. We were saving all of our cash for just these kinds of times so at least we would have some kind of reserve. It wasn't much, but it was something.

The rain slacked off so Beth and I both walked over to the phone booth outside Albertsons to call and check my balance. I had a whole dollar twenty eight left on my card. That was barely enough to get something to eat so we began counting the reserves.

As we started to walk off, an older gentleman wearing jeans and a raincoat stopped us. We have had people on occasion approach us before so we thought nothing of it. As he came right up to us, I thought he probably needed directions or something.

The fellow asked, "Do you need some help?"

Beth and I looked at each other when Beth spoke up and said, "Well yes."

The guy reached in his shirt pocket retrieving his checkbook and asked, "Does either of you have a pen?"

Bewildered, I answered, "Yes, I do."

As I grabbed my pen and handed it to him, he scribbled on a check and tore it off then handed it to me.

"Do you have identification?" he asked.

"Yes, I do," I answered.

"I'll go in the bank with you just to make sure they cash it for you,"

The gentleman followed Beth and I into the bank and stood by the door as I presented the check and my identification to the teller. As the teller finished her business on the computer and opened the cash drawer, I turned around only to find the guy had walked out the door as soon as he saw the check was cashed. He was long gone by the time we walked out the door with five twenty-dollar bills.

I looked at Beth and said, "Can you believe it. A hundred bucks out of the blue. Let's go eat."

"God does work in mysterious ways," she replied.

I asked Beth what she fancied for a good hot meal. She said, "Cream of mushroom soup."

"Where do you find that?"

"Sometimes Albertsons has it."

"What if they don't? Then what do you want?"

"Tacos, I guess."

We walked over to Taco Time where they have my favorite type of burrito. One little taco was ordered for Beth, sour cream of course, and a gut bomb for me. It all came to a little over five bucks, but what the hell; we hadn't eaten like that in a long time. We sat down and ate and discussed how we were going to spend the money. Our tent heater was stolen about the time our tent was destroyed, and we had no cook stove that was functional anymore. But it's difficult to cook a good meal in the rain anyway; not impossible, but definitely difficult.

Beth brought up the fact that she needed a flashlight again because hers was stolen when the tent got thrashed. I was hoping that she would forget about that. I knew what she was about to say, so I tried to divert my attention on the fellow giving us a check for a hundred bucks. It didn't work; I still heard her say, "We have to go to the dollar store and get a flashlight and some batteries."

I pulled my Maglite out of its holster and showed it to her. "Why the hell don't you just get one of these? They always work! Ten bucks, with good batteries. Now they come with Duracell."

"I don't have a belt," she responded.

I threw my arms up and exhaled. "Whatever," I said in disgust.

I was still mumbling as we walked out the door, "Buy that cheap shit and it won't work when you need it most. That's crazy!"

We walked across the street to purchase some items at the department store, my favorite place to shop. Pretty much everything they sell is of good quality. I picked up some extra batteries for my Maglite and my Walkman radio along with some paper towels and sani-wipes. I priced a tent heater and decided to wait on that for a while. Beth wandered along beside me the whole time. I told her, "If you need something, like a flashlight, now is the time. I purposely took her down the aisle where they sell Maglite products. She passed. I knew her so-called logic before she even spoke.

"I can buy ten flashlights at the dollar store for the price of one Maglite," she spouted.

I knew that the middle of the store wasn't the place for me to get all riled up, but I fired back at her anyway, "You just go and buy your cheap flashlight, and make sure it works before you actually go out the door with it. If you're lucky and it works, we'll go over to McRay and I'll turn on my Maglite and throw it in the water; then you turn on your piece of shit and throw it in. Then you'll see the difference."

With that out of the way, but still not convincing her, we headed to the checkout to pay for the items before walking over to the dollar store. I could hardly stand to watch the steps again that one must take to buy something as simple as a flashlight.

Step one: Dig through the barrel. Even though they are all the same, you still have to dig through the barrel to get just the right one. Maybe she had some kind of trick that made her lucky enough to pull one out that might work the first time. I don't know. Step two: Take the piece of shit flashlight up to the checkout and have the clerk put batteries in it to see if it works. If it does happen to work, pay for it and leave. If it doesn't, proceed to step three. Step three: Go get another one and listen to Kirk bitch, moan, and complain. Step four: Repeat step two. It was a viscous, unnecessary cycle that I, for the life of me, just couldn't quite understand.

After a few tries, the two gals finally came up with a new flashlight that actually worked so we paid for it and out the door we went. I was hoping Beth would take me up on the water test, but down deep she knew I was right. I decided to just let it go. *There's no since in whipping a dead horse*, I thought. We walked back to the tent and put our stuff inside. We headed out to fly sign again, mostly out of boredom.

While we were out there I started thinking of what I was going to do for a Halloween costume. I asked Beth, "You remember those old television rabbit ears over by Don's truck?"

"Yeah," she said. "What about them?"

"I'm going to get a big cardboard box and those rabbit ears and be a television for Halloween. Wouldn't that give people a charge?"

"It'll be unique, that's for sure."

"Think about it. How many people do you see dressed as a television set? I think it'll be cool!"

She didn't say much about it, she only shrugged her shoulders like it was no big deal. What was a big deal though was that she was going to use an old wedding dress that she got from a clothing box somewhere and dress up as *The Bride That Was Left Behind.* I didn't say anything but I was thinking to myself: *Imagine that, someone leaving her at the altar.* I just concentrated on what all I was going to do to my costume.

We left the freeway when I looked west and noticed the black clouds moving our direction. We walked over to the mini-mart, then up to camp. It started raining but the trees provided some protection. I got busy around camp just cleaning up a bit and studying the trees some more. Little stuff that needs to get done but somehow gets overlooked.

I asked Beth, "I ain't seen Skippy for a while. Have you?"

"No," she answered.

"I'm going up the hill to see if he has been in his tent."

There was no trail up to where Skippy's camp was at; I just had to weave in and out of the clumps of blackberry bushes as I climbed the steep hillside. It was a difficult trek to say the least, but curiosity got to me. I didn't know what I might get into up there but I went anyway.

When I made it up to his tent I announced myself and waited for a reply. There appeared to be nobody around so I carefully undid the entrance to his tent. The zipper was broken so he had some kind of elaborate button system on it that took me a minute to figure out so I wouldn't damage anything. I finally got the thing undone for a peek inside.

He wasn't there. It didn't appear as anyone had been there for at least three or four days. Out of respect, I didn't crawl inside although I did go in far enough to grab a tent heater that looked remotely familiar. That was as far as I went before backing out. I tipped the heater upside down and found a crack in the base. The same crack I accidentally put in our tent heater when I stumbled and fell on it one night as I took it outside to install a new bottle of propane. I buttoned his tent back up and carried our tent heater down the hill with me.

When Beth saw the tent heater she naturally thought Skippy must have destroyed our tent and took the heater. I had to admit that it appeared as though that was the case. Although I didn't think Skippy would tear down our tent. Take the heater? He might have pulled that off. In one of his weird moods I could see that but not tear down our tent and cut it up. For one thing, he would have to have help dragging the thing down to where I found it. It was way too heavy with all of our stuff still in it for his scrawny ass to pull it. For another thing, I just didn't think he would do something like that.

Now that we had our heater back, I decided to walk down and buy a bottle or two of propane. "If it's still on sale, I'll get three." I told Beth as I started down the trail. My mind was still on finding our tent heater as I proceeded down the trail towards the flooded McRay River. "Damn I hate back tracking." I said to myself as I turned around and headed back to intercept the other trail; the one that crosses the McRay with a culvert.

I almost made it over to the department store when it started to rain. I walked around the store for a while just for something to do before purchasing two bottles of propane and a poncho for me. I paid for the goods and by the time I walked out the door, it was pouring down rain. It was raining so hard that it looked like the drops were bouncing back up when they hit the ground. I took the new poncho out of the bag and put it on. I knew the bottoms of my pants were going to be soaked, but at least I would be dry from the knees up.

I stopped by the mini-mart on the way up and bullshitted a while before buying a beer for the walk up to camp. I walked across the road and to where the dead end road intersects. That's where the McRay River ran off the hill and flowed through a culvert. I cracked the beer and took a big chug, then I progressed forward walking through the rain that was already creating puddles on the way to camp. Just out of curiosity I walked over to the McRay to see how it was doing. It was flooding about ten feet from where it was supposed to flow. I finished my beer and walked back to the tent.

Beth took refuge from the rain inside the tent. She wasn't exactly dry in there either. Both sleeping bags were still wet, and her clothes were somewhat wet because she didn't climb in when it started to rain. She stayed outside and smoked a cigarette. The rain didn't let up and I wasn't ready to spend the rest of the evening in the tent. I decided to stay outside for a while. I had my new poncho covering most of me, so I couldn't get all that wet. I told Beth, "Grab me another beer please."

"Another?" she responded.

"Yes please."

"What do you mean another? Did you have one already?"

"Does it really make a difference?" I asked.

She handed me the whole bag out the tent flap and told me she was coming out too. She crawled out, her poncho in her hand. She slid the poncho part way down on her narrow chassis and got tangled.

"My God," I said, "do I have to dress you too?"

"Shut up," she said.

I then quickly changed the mood back into how I was going to make my costume look like a real television. That would keep things mellow while the rain fell on us.

I told her that I was to cut holes on the sides of the box for my arms, then one in the top to poke my head through. The rabbit ears had a base that the individual antennas were secured to it, so I would have to modify it for clearance. The rabbit ear's coaxial cord I would stick through a hole in the back of the box giving it a functional appearance. Extended about two thirds the ways out, both antennas would protrude about twelve inches above the top of my hat.

"What do you think I should write in the screen section," I asked her while she smoked her cigarette.

"How about, 'Can You Please Spare Some Change? Happy Halloween!' That would work," she said.

It was starting to get dark so we decided to go inside and play cards until it was time to go to sleep. We were both wet, so getting in our sleeping bags was not exactly comfortable. Once I was situated in my bag and my body heat finally warmed up the inside the bag, I had to go piss. I told Beth, "I got to go piss, you might as well go too before we're both asleep." I stepped out first while she followed shortly after.

When morning came, I was glad to see that it wasn't raining. It was just beginning to become daylight, so I couldn't tell yet what the weather was going to do. Traditionally it rains like a cow pissing on a flat rock on Halloween but I was hoping maybe that year it would be different. I was counting on a somewhat dry day because my costume would fall to pieces if it got too wet during the day. If I was to go through the trouble to make the television costume, I wanted for at least a few people to get a good laugh out of it.

We got all of our shit gathered up and headed down the long trail to avoid the now severely flooded McRay River. As we proceeded down the trail towards the culvert, the puddles on the trail became deeper, wider, and longer until I had to look for an alternative route around the muddy, wet mess. I re-routed the two of us around the majority of the water by crossing a couple of downed trees and through some low blackberry bushes. Everything went fine until Beth got her foot caught in a briar, performed a near perfect one-eighty spin and landed right on her skinny little ass. She barked out the eff-bomb as she scrambled to her feet. I couldn't help but laugh. That pissed her off for a minute as I walked over to help her get her backpack straightened out. Then she laughed and said, "I bet that did look funny." I was still laughing when I said, "You'll never know how stupid you looked. Happy Halloween, Beth."

She had her *Bride Left Behind* costume stuffed inside her backpack along with a marker to make phony tears with. She would go into a restroom and change while I scoped around for a good dry box to create my costume. When we met up at the bus station I was busy transforming myself into a television set, complete with rabbit ear antennas. Beth went on ahead of me with her sign and parked her ass on the concrete divider promoting her theme for Halloween. I followed about ten minutes later appearing like a mid-seventies television set. We were sure to at least get as many smiles as laughs.

We had a wonderful time flying the freeway watching all the people look and point and especially enjoyed the remarks made from the people laughing at our creative costumes. We made about thirty five bucks that day, and on the way back someone gave us a half case of beer, rewarding us for making him smile on the rotten day he had. That made my day. Not the beer as much as making his day a little brighter.

We had to go to the mini-mart to let those folks enjoy our ingenious costumes which presented yet another challenge. I had to go sideways through the door because my large twenty-nine inch diagonal screen wouldn't fit going straight in and my rabbit ear antennas had to be collapsed for upper clearance. Beth assisted me on that little detail. All in all, it was a happy Halloween, one we would always remember.

CHAPTER 33

FOR THOSE IN NEED

The time had run out to procrastinate on preparing for the winter season. I didn't get a chance to look up the winter forecast via The Farmer's Almanac, so I figured we should just play it safe and prepare for a harsh winter.

Beth and I sat down and made a list of items that we could and would use by prioritizing from basic to luxury. At the top of the list were items such as proper rain jackets, gloves, and blankets. Those items were the most important. Other items included propane for the heater and better shoes for Beth. Other items came at a lower priority such as more leather treatment for my boots and a new deck of playing cards for those long, wet, cold, and sleepless nights.

I stuffed the list in my shirt pocket as we left McDonald's to go fly sign on the freeway again. I stopped at the bus station to get a newspaper while Beth continued toward the freeway. As I read the local section of the paper which includes local arrests, obituaries, and other things happening in the area, I stumbled onto an article of interest to me.

There was to be a homeless convention at the county fairgrounds free for all people who were in need of clothing, medical, food, and other items and services to prepare people for the winter that had no roof over their heads. The local bus service was offering shuttles to and from the event free of charge throughout the county. There would be doctors of general health, optometrists, hearing specialists, and more.

I took that portion of the paper over to the freeway so I could read it to Beth. Her eyes were getting so bad by then that she could barely see from her right eye, and the left eye wasn't much better. I read the article to her since she couldn't see to read it. The part about the optometrists providing services at the event sparked her interest.

It proved to be a challenge to watch for windows coming down while reading the paper to Beth during a windy day. I managed to hop up and grab two hits during the process though, and still not lose my place in the paper. When I finished reading the article to her, she made the comment, "I think that we should go to that event."

I looked at her and said, "No shit, Sherlock! Why do you think I brought the article over here and read it to you on the freeway in this wind?"

"Quit being a smart ass," she said.

"Oh well, you'll get over it. Besides, it's better to be a smart ass than a dumb ass; how many times to I have to remind you of that?" I responded, knowing that usually when I said that to her it would piss her off. That's why I said it as frequently as I did.

We made a few bucks on the freeway, and since I was the person that held our joint savings account in my wallet, I split the money in half. Half for now as spending money, and half for the savings for items we would need to purchase for the upcoming winter. We decided to wait to purchase anything until we went to the homeless event to see what we would obtain there.

We walked on over to the mini-mart and purchased a couple of brews. I told Beth, "Let's go back to camp. I want to get things out of the tent and stretch stuff out to dry. With this wind and the somewhat warm temperatures, it's perfect for getting it done." She liked that idea so we proceeded towards the McRay River. I wanted to see if I could rebuild the bridge across it since the water level had dropped a bit.

When we reached the McRay, I looked around for a different place to put a makeshift bridge across. I found a more suitable place although it was farther downstream and would require building another detour around the blackberries that protruded both sides of the water. In doing so, I stumbled across another suitable bridge component. It was another pallet, and this time it was made of hardwood and longer in length than the other. I grabbed a hold of that water saturated hardwood pallet, gave it a deep tug, and just about shit my pants. I yelled back to Beth, "Holy hell Beth! You might have to put down your brew and give me a hand with this one. It's a real ball buster."

She walked down to the present job site to lend me a hand. I knew she wasn't all that strong, but just a little help would get the heavy pallet moved and possibly prevent me from blowing a nut. We managed to drag the heavy beast over to the water when I instructed Beth, "Get back unless you want either to get soaking wet or ran over. Once I let go of this thing I'm moving out in a real hurry."

I held the pallet in position standing on end when I yelled, "Fire in the hole!"

I gave the pallet a push on the top and let her fly. I didn't stick around for the show; I had plans to get the hell out of the way from the oncoming splash that no doubt was going to occur. I heard it hit but didn't feel any water hit me. I turned around to see a perfect landing and a new bridge across the McRay River.

I turned to Beth and cracked my beer open. "There," I said. "Now I've accomplished something constructive today." We stepped toward the new bridge admiring the shortcut. I said, "Shall we?" I took the first step.

It was pretty stable but slick as snot on a bumper. I turned to Beth and cautioned her, "Watch it, it's really slippery so be careful." She followed close behind. I figured if she slipped, she would be close enough to grab me and pull us both into the water. I knew how she was thinking.

We made it across the new bridge and then we plowed through some brush, cutting a path to meet up with the main trail. We made it to the tent so I unzipped the door and began dragging some of the wet items out so we could hang them to dry.

The sleeping bags were the most important and also the heaviest so they went up on the highest tree limb where they could receive the most sunlight and wind. Then the blankets were stretched out below the sleeping bags. Everything else I scattered around so the air would get to everything as much as possible. I used ferns and bushes to elevate some of our lighter items from the ground. The tent had screen windows on both sides, and one large window in the back. I tied up the covers an all three windows and then zipped only the screen flap shut on the front leaving an open area for the air to circulate throughout the entire tent.

When we achieved all of the things at camp that needed to be accomplished I asked Beth, "It's almost noon, do you want to go get something to eat now so we can hit the noon crowd?"

"No, let's go have another beer real fast, then go out and fly. We can get something to eat later," she answered.

Against my better judgment, that's what we did. We walked over to the mini-mart and bought a couple beers then went to drink them down behind Burger King. One of the neighbors stopped his GMC Yukon beside us and bullshitted for a while. He was a super nice guy. He told us that he was in a hurry, but he would leave us some cans behind the fence for us. We thanked him as he drove away.

We finally made it out to the freeway to catch the lunch-bunch. We did alright considering how late we actually were getting our asses out there. I was surprised to see that nobody else was out flying sign. Skippy was a fair weather type of guy. He rarely came out when it was raining, but that day it was fairly nice. Danny hadn't been hanging around much and Linda Lou took off to Utah for a while. She said she might go to Montana for a while but only time would tell. For then, it was just me and Beth, which was alright by us.

The day finally came when it was time to catch the bus over to the homeless event at the fairgrounds. We stepped off the bus with about twenty other people to mix in with the hundreds already there. We absolutely could not believe the turnout. It was incredible. I had no idea there were so many homeless people in the area. They seemed to crawl out of the woodwork.

We ran across a familiar face and stopped to chat for a bit. He told us to go check out the lunch that is being served. We walked into the convention hall to see an amazing variety of doctors, dentists, employment specialists and more. There was so much activity going on that we didn't know where to start. I told Beth, "Let's go and eat some of that food that smells so good and then we'll decide where to go from there."

We walked through the line and fixed our own hamburgers as we wanted them. I dumped chili all over mine then smothered it with onions and grated cheese. That took up most of the plate so I grabbed another plate and loaded it with baked beans and cookies. A little farther down the line I grabbed two cartons of milk and a banana then we walked over to a table and sat down to enjoy one hell of a good meal.

I didn't even know it because I was so busy shoveling in the chow, but sitting diagonal from us was a guy which I had known for quite some time from riding the bus to the college. A few years back when I was taking some computer courses at the college, he was taking classes on modern literature at the same time. I didn't recognize him at first because he had always used to be well groomed and clean. He said he had been spending his time on the west side of town in a camp with four other couples. He lost his job due to a layoff, triggering the loss of his apartment, his car, and his girlfriend. That was tough luck for him, losing everything. I sympathized with him and just told him, "Join the crowd man, join the crowd."

We talked for a little while when he told me, "Hey guy, I'll see ya around. I gotta go over there and get my hair cut. There's quite a line."

I shook his hand as I said, "Okay, if you're ever out towards the east side, you'll find me up in the hills just a bit." He took off so I finished eating, put my trash away and waited for Beth to finish.

I spotted the optometrist's table so I grabbed Beth and told her, "Come on, it's time to get those eyes looked at."

She followed me over to the line. Once we made it towards the front, they handed all of us a card to fill out and when her name was called, she could see the doctor. We waited for the half hour they said it would take before asking about it. We were then told another fifteen minutes. Another half hour passed so we asked again. We were then told another half hour. I looked at my watch and told Beth, "I'm starting to feel funny being in here with all these people. Let's go see about getting some goods and get the hell out of here."

We were glad to be within the first group of people standing in line for the supplies that were handed out. There looked to be plenty of hygiene items and most clothing items were in great abundances, but some of the other items were especially limited. Sleeping bags were one of those items. There looked to be only about fifty bags to give out while there were roughly eight-hundred people at the event. Beth and I considered ourselves quite fortunate to be one of the few to leave with each a brand new military sleeping bag.

Walking out the gate was quite a hassle with people asking, "Hey! Where did you get those sleeping bags?" My answer to them was, "Over where they are handing out all the stuff. But you better hurry, they are going fast."

We finally made it to the bus stop and hopped on the first bus towards camp. We were both tired and still had a long walk ahead of us with all of our new equipment and supplies. I actually nodded off to sleep on the way back just listening to the Diesel engine moan from the rear of the bus

CHAPTER 34

VANDALIZED AGAIN

We stepped off the bus at the station at our end of town and walked over to McDonald's to take a leak before going forward to our camp. Just as we left there and started walking, Beth said, "Let's go to the mini-mart and get some beer before heading up to camp."

"Not right now." I said, I'm not carrying all this stuff plus more up there, we'll just have to make a trip back down."

We walked up the trail and crossed the new bridge over the McRay River, then went on to the tent. Everything looked the same, so I unzipped the door flaps and started pitching things inside. Beth wasn't a whole lot of help. She was more involved in rolling her damn cigarette than anything else.

Once I had everything inside, I zipped the flaps back down and picked up all the trash and stuffed it into one of the plastic bags that the sleeping bags came in. "Might as well take down all the trash while we're at it." I explained to Beth, hoping she would contribute some help as she puffed away on her cigarette. We walked down to the mini-mart and I pitched the trash into their dumpster. We then walked inside to make our purchase and bullshit with Kathy for a while. We told her about the turnout at the homeless event and how we couldn't believe how many people were actually there.

Kathy said, "I heard on the radio that next year the head of the thing wants to hold two of them instead of one because of the incredible turnout."

"That's a good idea. That place was packed," I replied to her.

We left there to go up towards camp to enjoy a cold beer. I told Beth, "It's too early to stay up here. Let's finish these and go down to fly sign for a while to kill some time. Then we can get something to eat before calling it a day." She thought that sounded like a good plan so we finished our beers and headed down to find our sign and go out to the freeway.

It started to rain as soon as we made it down to the freeway so we didn't stay very long. We stopped and got some chow at Albertsons like; lunch meat, bread, mustard, Ritz crackers and cheese dip. We walked up to camp to get settled in when it stopped raining.

"Well, I'm not going inside to eat; I'm staying out here since it's not raining," I told Beth.

"I'm not going to eat inside either," Beth responded as she grabbed a dry piece of cardboard and laid it on a log to sit down on. I just stood the whole time enjoying the flavor of smoked turkey and pepper jack cheese on dill rye. We stayed outside and chatted for a while and drank a beer, still not believing the amount of people at the homeless event.

It was starting to get fairly dark so we crawled inside. I was going to read for a while but somehow my book was about the only thing that didn't get dry. Everything else was dry, especially our new sleeping bags that had never been out of the plastic.

It took me a minute to figure the thing out. It didn't work like a sleeping bag that is purchased at the sporting goods section of an everyday department store. These were mummy bags with both zippers and laces. Once I figured out that I was trying to crawl in from the bottom, things made more sense. I flipped the thing around and tried it the other way. That proved to be quite a bit easier. Beth was laughing at me and said, "Having fun over there?"

"Shut up," I responded. "I got it, now leave me alone."

"Diesel Engineer my ass," she mumbled.

"Diesel Mechanic, there is a difference!" I quickly corrected her.

"Whatever, you can't even figure out a sleeping bag."

"Well it's not like I have a whole bunch of room here!"

"I got mine figured out right away."

I gave her the middle finger only visible from a close distance by the illumination of my Maglite as I said, "I just had it turned around backwards dammit. Leave me alone. I got it figured out didn't I?" She let it slide but was still chuckling. I grabbed my headset and a beer and ignored her for a half hour or so.

When I finally decided to take my headset off and talk to her she thought I was actually pissed off at her. I wasn't pissed, I just wanted to listen to my radio and relax for a while. I told her, "I'm stepping out to take a last minute piss then I'm checking out for the night."

"Okay," she said. "I better go and do that too." I crawled back into my sleeping bag and was half asleep by the time she came crawling back in.

I hadn't slept that warm for quite a while. Those sleeping bags were definitely a treat. When morning came, I didn't want to get out but I had to pee. I crawled out to a dreary kind of day. It was cloud covered and looked like it was going to rain.

I told Beth, "You better bring your rain gear with you when you come out, it's going to rain today." When she came out she was coughing up a storm. I knew what that meant. It wasn't too long until she was humped over like a camel on its knees doing the dry heave thing. "God, Beth," I said. "That just ain't right. Normal people don't do that nearly every morning. Are you sure old knuckle head didn't knock you up?" That didn't go over so well; she was thoroughly pissed then, and she didn't talk to me until we reached the bottom of the trail and she wanted a beer and a cigarette.

She got her wish, I had spending money left over and Cabby at the mini-mart gave her a smoke. That made her happy for a while. I thought she forgot about the comment I made about her so-called boyfriend but apparently she didn't. She flew into me like a buzzard on a rotten carcass. I made it worse when I told her, "Well, it's true! Everyone knows it except you. You're in a world of your own with that guy."

She was definitely pissed off again. That really rattled her cage, and she wasn't even in the Betholizer mode yet. I figured I'd better back off before she went into a total tizzy fit.

We finished our snacks and then headed down to hop out on the freeway. Nobody was out there so we went to the island to fly. That would give her a place to sit down. I would stand and grab the hits while she sat there holding the sign. We weren't there but about a half hour or so when I heard a familiar voice from the parking lot across the road. As I turned to look he yelled, "Hey! You guys want some cans?"

All the sudden the day was getting brighter. It was the same guy in the white Chevy four-by-four that saves cans for us and always says, "I hate turning these fricken things in." I told Beth, "Get your ass up! It looks like he has a full load for us again. We won't have to fly sign for the rest of the day." She got up and stashed the sign while we waited for the walk signal to change, then we rushed over to his truck.

Four shopping carts later, we walked out the door about thirty-five bucks richer. That wasn't too bad for an hour's labor, again. As we walked towards the mini-mart I told Beth, "Let's get bus passes and go to the library. You wanted me to check that website to see if I can locate your son and we could also go down to the Salvation Army and have us a hot supper." Now we had plans for the day so we walked over to our spot and drained our beers before walking to Burger King for a couple *Whopper Junior* burgers.

We headed for the bus station and boarded the next bus to the library. Once we were inside I logged onto one of their public computers. I was surprised that my library card hadn't expired; I knew it was getting close. After I checked my e-mail account, I went ahead and executed a search for her son. He had gotten himself into some kind of trouble so I was going attempt to find out where he was lodged.

I struck out finding any information so I decided to grab a book and sit down to read until it was time to head down for a meal that I had been bragging to her about for months. She fell asleep in the library as I read a book, and soon after, so did I.

My alarm went off so that meant it was time to hit the bus to the Salvation Army for a good, hot meal. We finally arrived only to find that somebody messed up and all they had was cold sandwiches and little bags of chips. Of all the damn times for someone to screw up, it had to be that time. The one time I finally talked Beth into going and we end up with cold sandwiches. I was disappointed, of course, but it happens.

We left there and headed to the little store down by the bus station. We went inside and bought a couple beers and I took her down an old alley where I had experience downing a beer on more than one occasion.

Beth was a little bit gun shy, but we made it alright. The alley was not your ordinary run of the mill alley a person sees on television, this was in an area not too far from the police station and surrounded by fenced-in parking lots. It wasn't scummy at all. We drank our beers then put the empty cans back in the sack so we could put them beside a trash can for someone to grab and return them for the money.

We jumped on the bus and headed back to our area. We went to the mini-mart and bought a few rounds then headed to camp. It started raining pretty hard so we picked up the pace. It had rained during the day but nothing like it was about to do. As we approached the tent both of our jaws dropped. Our new sleeping bags were drug out into the mud, our food scattered all over, and the cheese dip dumped all over our tent. Everything inside was now outside and muddy. They didn't destroy the tent but it looked like they tried to take it down. It was a mess. Cheese dip was all over everything. Our new, clean, dry sleeping bags were all wet and muddy. It was just a total disaster. What a disappointing end to an otherwise good day.

It was too late to do anything but shake most of the mud out of our sleeping bags then put them back inside. That task came after we made room inside the tent where everything was scattered about. We used massive amounts of paper towels to mop up the cheese from the tent and the sleeping bags before getting everything situated. The rain continued to fall but it didn't much matter, we were going to have a wet night anyway with our sleeping bags found lying in the mud and water. The only good thing is that whoever did the vandalism didn't tear the tent to shreds. It could have been kids but we knew that we probably would never know.

We made the best of it, the sleeping bags still kept us warm even though they were wet. The next morning, neither one of us wanted to crawl out of the tent. We knew it was going to get really cold really fast with our clothes soaking up the moisture from the sleeping bags. I was the first one out of course, although Beth wasn't too far behind.

We both decided to head on down to Burger King and eat something before heading out to the freeway. Although everything at camp was muddy and wet, there wasn't much we could do about it. The closest laundry mat was a good half hour walk without lugging two wet, heavy sleeping bags, let alone carrying them and any other clothes to wash and dry. It would also cost a small fortune to put them in the extractor first then dry them. It would be an all-day project and who knows, the assholes may just come back and do it all over again. We thought would just make the best of it.

CHAPTER 35

INTRODUCING JERRY

After breakfast Beth headed out to fly sign while I stayed at the bus station to read the newspaper. Right away I saw her get a couple hits and new she would do fairly well out there that morning. One reason was that she didn't have anyone else with her. She was out there by herself. Another reason was that she looked like hell warmed over. Her hair was messed up and she didn't get much sleep so her eyes were all dark underneath.

As I sat there reading the paper and watching her, a guy I knew from riding the bus to the local college came over and started to talk to me. His name was Jerry; he was taking classes in computer basics. He didn't know much about computers, so I'd helped him on several different occasions while he waited for his bus to go home up the river.

We talked for a while before Jerry said he could lose his house on the river at any time. He was upset about the situation and didn't know where he would go or what he would do. I didn't know the details of his situation and it was none of my business anyway. I did mention that if he had to move closer to town and needed someplace to stay other than the mission, he just has to look me up and I would help him out the best I could.

Just as Beth decided to take a break and walk over towards me, Jerry's bus showed up so he ran over and boarded it. I filled Beth in on the situation as we walked over to the mini-mart. Beth gave me that old, "We can't keep bringing people around here."

I told her, "Now look Beth. He might need our help finding a place to stay. There are several places up above us that you don't even know about. They're hard to get to, and I don't think you could even make it." That kind of miffed her a little, but it was the truth. I was talking about the goat trail that Dusty walked up to reach his tent. She'd have a rough time making it up there on a *good* day.

We left the mini-mart and went to our usual spot and drank our beverages while talking about the possibility of Jerry spending some time at our camp until he gets adjusted. He didn't come across as the type who could just jump right out into living in the woods. It's a rough life and if he had to do it, he would definitely need some help and direction from someone that has done it for a while and knows the ropes. That someone would be me although I just didn't know it would be so soon.

The next few days proved to be somewhat boring. Nothing happened that was out of the ordinary until one day Jerry popped up at the bus station while Beth was using the restroom at McDonald's and I was making another new sign.

He sat down with a lost look while he told me, "My family and I got into a dispute and I had to leave my house. I've been at the mission and I'm about to go nuts."

I asked, "What happened? It's none of my business but why did you have to leave so soon?"

"I'll tell you in a minute. I don't suppose you have a dollar that you could lend me do you? I need a beer."

Since Beth wasn't out of the restroom yet so I told him, "Just a second while Beth gets out of the restroom, we'll spring for a round of beers and we can talk about your situation." He acted like he was walking on egg shells as we waited for Beth to get of McDonald's. I knew he had very little self-esteem and would be lost without someone to tag along with.

Finally, Beth returned to the bus station so I introduced her to Jerry and then we walked over to the mini-mart. When we left there we took him up to where we camp at and I showed him around a bit while we drank our beers.

As he nervously kicked a small rock around he explained, "I don't have a tent or anything. All of my stuff is up the river."

"I don't think that will be a problem for a while," I said

"Well, I don't want to impose on anybody."

"We've done it before; it's really no big deal."

"Well, you guys want your privacy don't you?"

I gave him a look and said, "We're not a couple. Some people say we are, but they don't know. Watch this!" He looked at me when I yelled, "Hey Beth. Get over here. Jerry thinks we are a couple and need our privacy together."

"Get real, Jerry!" She yelled.

"Thanks a lot, Beth," I returned.

Jerry just laughed and then took a swig of beer. He then knew that he was welcome and he was not intruding on anything. I made him feel even more comfortable when I told him a few stories.

"Just ask her," I told him as I pointed at Beth. "Every now and then she gets a few beers in her and becomes the Betholizer. She gets really mouthy and starts hitting me. I tell her to shut the hell up and stop it but sometimes she won't listen so I have to up the ante a bit. One time I even nailed her with pepper spray."

"Yeah, it worked real good too, didn't it Kirk? Finish the rest of the story," she said with a shit-eating grin.

"Well, I kind of got the other guy who was staying with us too, by accident of course," I confessed.

We laughed for a while until Jerry got serious again. "I need to go and get my sleeping bag. Will you guys meet me down here tonight when the bus makes the trip back from up the river?" he asked.

Beth responded for me, "Kirk will."

I gave her a look as I said, "Thanks Beth. Yeah Jerry, I'll be down to meet you at the bus station."

We all walked down to the bus station so Jerry could catch the bus going up the river. He had enough time to grab his stuff and catch it on the way back down if he hurried. Beth and I grabbed our sign and headed out to fly. Nimrod was on the island so we flew the south side. We had always done well there, and it's kind of fun watching Nimrod get skunked while we rake in the money. I always wanted to rub that in to him but thought it was best to just let it ride.

It was kind of funny that when Beth saw Nimrod on the freeway flying that she remembered to tell me what she found out a few days back. It was significant, and it sort of pissed me off that she didn't tell me as soon as she found out.

Someone slipped up and told her that Danny offered to pay Nimrod fifty bucks to sucker punch me that day when he said Beth needed my help. That *really* proved my earlier thoughts about Danny that there was something about him that couldn't be trusted. Especially with John out of the picture, Danny just sort of changed his demeanor. John used to keep Danny in line but he wasn't around any longer to do it.

Right then I got to thinking that Danny and I needed to have a little talk. Nothing big, just let him know that I know what a low life he was turning out to be. I just couldn't understand it. I never did anything to Danny to make him turn on me like that. Maybe he just wanted a show. I couldn't figure that one out and I wanted an explanation.

We made a few more bucks out there and we stuck it out longer than Nimrod too. We took off up towards camp to prepare the tent for the incoming company. It wouldn't be much trouble, just move a few things around. Jerry would sleep on one side and me on the other with Beth in the middle.

I was getting a bit on the hungry side. I asked Beth, "I'm going down to get some chow, just lunch meat and the usual, anything you want in particular?"

"Yeah, get some of that honey mustard this time," she requested.

"Okay, Anything else?"

"How about some chips?"

"Do you want the ones in the plastic thingies again?"

"Yeah, that'd be fine," she said.

I walked down to Albertsons and purchased another loaf of dill rye, some honey smoked ham, and of course pepper jack cheese. I also went down the soda isle and grabbed a two liter bottle of cheap store brand soda then slipped over a few isles and grabbed a bottle of honey mustard. I paid for the items and carried it all up to camp.

I arrived at camp just in time to chug a beer and turn right back around to walk down and meet Jerry. It really wasn't a problem going back down there; it was kind of nice knowing there would be someone else to talk with besides Beth. When Jerry got off the bus I stepped forward and grabbed some of his stuff. He didn't have a lot of stuff, but what he did have would be much easier if we both carried it. We walked over to the mini-mart so he could get some beer for himself. He offered to buy me one but I told him, "No thanks, I've got some food and beer up at camp. We can go up and have a sandwich, I bought plenty."

"Sounds good," he said.

We walked on up to the new bridge and I showed him where the other trail starts just in case he gets into a heavy rain situation and the bridge washes out again.

We made it to camp and put his gear inside the tent. Beth already ate a sandwich, which is rare for her to eat anything, Jerry and I sat down and built our sandwiches. We talked and drank beer until the daylight was depleted so we all crawled into the tent for the night. Jerry was pretty quiet; I think he felt kind of out of place. I figured that I would feel the same way if I were in his shoes.

All three of us wakened to a cool, crisp morning. I was the first out with Jerry struggling to get past Beth on his way out. Jerry rolled a smoke and fired it up while Beth made her way out of the tent. She did her morning ritual gag and puke thing while Jerry watched with interest. I told him, "Get used to it, she does this just about every morning. If she didn't do it now, she would after a couple drags from a cigarette."

"Is there something wrong with her?" Jerry whispered.

I explained, "You don't have to whisper, I've been telling her to go to a doctor for several months now. But I think I know what it is. It's from the lack of eating. On top of that she drinks too much, but don't we all. Once she gets a beer in her she'll be fine."

Jerry raised his eyebrows then quickly lowered them as if he hadn't ever seen anything like that before but believed that it could happen.

After Beth finished her morning introduction we gathered up and headed down to see what the day would bring. When we arrived at the bus station, Jerry sat down while Beth and I prepared to hit the freeway. I looked back and yelled at Jerry, "See ya in a few!" He raised his arm once as a wave of acknowledgement then sat back down and rolled another smoke.

Beth and I were out there for almost an hour before we got a hit. I told her, "Well, there's the ice breaker, now we'll do alright."

"Let's go get a beer," she said

"We only got a little over a buck there."

"Well, you still have money left over," she responded.

I stepped over to the crosswalk and pressed the walk signal button. As we walked across, I saw Jerry stand up. "He must have seen us get a hit," I said as we kept walking. As Beth stashed our sign in the bushes I told Jerry of our plans. "That sounds good to me. I'm getting bored over there with nobody to talk to," he said. The three of us walked over and bought four beers then walked over behind the Burger King to visit. Jerry was starting to feel comfortable around us then. He hadn't witnessed us fight and argue yet. He would, there was no doubt that he would, he just had to give it a little more time.

CHAPTER 36

MORE NEWCOMERS

It didn't seem like very long until the hillside where our camp was located became quite an attraction to a lot of people. One more guy moved into the area along with two couples. It became difficult to tell who was coming and who was going. All of their camps were located up the hill a ways from us, so everyone had a little privacy.

One couple moved up near Dusty's camp, although Dusty rarely ever even stayed there anymore. Another couple moved somewhat further to the east. Both of the couples argued constantly, most of the time it was about nothing as far as I could tell. It was annoying at times but it wasn't anything totally unbearable.

I could tell by the way Jerry was acting that he was uncomfortable with all the newcomers moving into the area. He didn't hang around much. He kept to himself when a few of us met up and got into a bullshit session. I figured him as to be somewhat of a loner anyway. There was nothing wrong with that, he just liked to keep to himself.

My parents also got involved with all of the newcomers, especially Jerry, inviting everyone to church and talking with them whenever possible. My parents knew how hard it was on people to be forced to live under those circumstances. In fact every one of them went to church with my folks at one time or another, some of them more than once.

One Sunday while my parents picked people up to head for church, I got into an intense conversation with Beth. Yes, she could get intense once in a while. I said, "There seems to be a stereotype against people who go to church."

"Yeah, and what would that be?" she asked.

It's a stereotype that my parents are helping to prove wrong. Some people think that people who go to church turn their noses up on others that are living under difficult circumstances."

Beth interrupted, "Yeah, but think about it. When was the last time you saw a church that wasn't full of stuck-up people?"

"The point is that most people haven't lived in a situation that leaves them without the luxury of waking up in a warm, dry house with a toilet just a few steps away from the soft bed they slept on. Not to mention being able to take a hot shower and put on nice clean clothes and smear perfume or cologne across their skin to smell nice," I explained.

"Yeah, that's why most church people are snobs. They just don't have a clue of what it's like!"

"But see, that's not the case in most churches," I argued. "Sure there are some fuddy-duddy people that act that way but for the most part, people in a church don't give a rat's ass how you look or how you smell, they care about you as a person, and where you are with God."

She fumbled around thinking about that one for a while before she asked, "How much money you got in your pocket?"

"You mean spending money or saving money?"

"Spending money you moron. I want a beer!"

"Well, I didn't know dammit. I just thought maybe you needed something for camp. You don't have to get pissy about it."

"I'm not, I just want a beer."

"I've got enough, let's go."

I figured I'd better get a beer into her before things really got ugly, so we walked over to the mini-mart and walked inside to find another 'Out of Order' sign on one of the restroom doors.

I asked, "Kathy? When are you just going to put a new toilet in there?"

"That's not the problem this time, somebody went and decorated it with a permanent marker so we have to re-paint it" she said.

"God Kathy! It just never ends does it?"

"Nope."

"Do ya know who did it?"

"I've got an idea."

"Good" I told her, "That's all un-called for!"

Beth already had our items sat out on the counter so I figured I'd better beat cheeks over there and pay before she started whining. I dug out the money and paid for the stuff and then we walked over to the spot where we usually go when I spotted Devin. He was walking over to the field where the trail to our camp was with his son.

He stopped to bullshit for a while so I asked him, "Do you know that guy that lives in that apartment over there?" I asked him as I pointed to a building across the field.

"Yeah. I told him about you being a mechanic."

"Thanks." I told him. "He wants me to change the oil on his Ford Expedition. He didn't know when though. He said he stays pretty busy and doesn't have time to take it somewhere," I explained.

"He does stay busy for sure, what time he doesn't spend working he spends with his family. I've got his number. I'll call him tonight and let him know you're interested. If he's not home, I'll leave a message," Devin replied.

"I would appreciate that, he seems like a nice guy who isn't going to screw me over."

"No, he's not like that at all. You should do okay."

Devin and his son went about their business so Beth and I finished our beers then walked back toward the freeway. As soon as the freeway came into sight, I spotted one of the newcomers, Robby, out flying on the island. "Well, it looks like we are taking this side," I told Beth. Once we moved in a little closer where the view wasn't obstructed, I discovered that Robby's wife, Nancy, was taking up that spot as well.

"Well farts!" I told Beth in disgust. "We're shit out of luck. Nancy has got this side all booked up. Now the two of them have intruded on both sides." Beth got a little pissed. I could tell that the malt liquor was working on her when she said, "I'll just go tell her to leave. They can't take both sides."

"No, you can't do that; just hold on a second," I said.

"Why? There isn't any place for us to fly now."

"I know, let me walk over to the edge of the street so she knows we're here. If she's reasonable, maybe she will let us take this side."

I made it about twenty feet from the edge of the road when Nancy yelled, "Just a few more minutes Kirk, then you guys can have it okay?"

"No problem," I said as I turned around and walked back toward the station. I thought about telling Beth that Nancy told me to *go to hell*. I knew that would have pushed Beth over the edge though and the result would be Nancy knocking the shit out of Beth. I held my tongue and told the truth. Beth was satisfied then. She hadn't had enough of the Betholizer formula in her yet to get her really nasty.

Nancy only stayed out for about ten more minutes so Beth and I walked on out to fly sign for a while. Nancy said she did better than Robby so she wanted to give us a shot at it. I thought that was fair of her. I told Beth on the way out, "I told you she would be reasonable, you were getting your underwear all in a wad over absolutely nothing. She's not Robby, she wouldn't run us off. The least we can do is provide with her the same courtesy."

"Well you can't blame me with all the newcomers moving in all around us now," she said.

We ended up with a few bills and a pocket full of change. Most of the change was quarters as far as I could tell. All I could do was guess at it. We didn't count it while standing there so we counted it after we left.

"We did alright," I told Beth.

"How much did we get?"

"I counted four-eighty in change alone."

"I think there's five dollars in paper here."

I looked at it to discover one of the bills was a five and explained, "You need to get your eyes fixed. One of the bills is a five, and there are four ones. There's nine bucks in paper there!"

"Great, let's go get a beer."

"How about going to get something to eat? I'm about starved."

"Okay," she said, so we headed over to Taco Time and had a couple tacos before heading to the mini-mart. We talked again about all the new faces that had shown up. I told Beth, "It's hard times for people and it's only going to get worse with the economy the way it is." She agreed then we placed our orders then sat down to eat.

We just stepped out of Taco Time when I heard, "Hey man! How you doing?" It was Kerry. I didn't know him all that well, but I have talked to him on various occasions. He was on a bicycle riding in circles, driving his bike with one hand and waving with his other. He was damn near making me dizzy just watching him. I could tell he was already three sheets to the wind. I whispered to Beth, "It's going to be a long afternoon. He always cries when he gets his snoot full."

"How do you know?" she asked.

"I've been around him enough to know. I met him for the first time at the bus stop on down the street years ago. He was drunk and crying when I showed up to catch the bus."

"Oh great. Do you think he will follow us over to the mini-mart then pick up our trail on the way back?"

"Oh yeah," I confirmed, "He'll be back."

Sure enough, he followed us over to the mini-mart and waited outside while Beth and I made our purchases. We met him on the way out the door and he asked, "Where you guys going?"

"Over there a ways," I answered.

"Can you go and buy me some beer? They won't sell me any because they think I'm drunk."

"Well you are aren't ya?"

"Well yeah, but I'm not driving!"

"You're on a bike, plus they have the right to refuse service."

"Please?"

"I'll sell you one of mine if you promise to behave and not create any trouble," I firmly told him.

"I won't, I promise," he responded as he hopped off the bike and began pushing it.

I was glad he chose to not ride it. Me needing to call 9-1-1 to report a drunken idiot that crashed a bicycle and needs an ambulance would shoot my afternoon all to hell. He followed us over to the trail that leads to our camp and I sold him a beer. He wasn't balling his head off then but I figured that if we gave it enough time, he would. I was surprised that we actually had a decent time bullshitting about the day we first met.

I directed my attention towards Beth since I knew she was curious as to how that episode went and filled her in as best as I could recall. They both were smiling then Kerry said, "That sounds like me. Sounds like something I'd do." We continued our conversation long enough to watch most of the day go by then I told Beth, "We better get out there for the late crowd Beth." We said our goodbyes then Beth and I walked back out to the freeway as Kerry attempted to ride his bicycle home.

CHAPTER 37

ANOTHER YEAR GONE

Christmas was just around the corner and the weather was certainly showing it. In the Northwest, we didn't get a white Christmas but other than once in a blue moon, it just didn't happen very often. What we got in the terms of snow was water that wasn't cold enough to freeze. We sometimes got the white stuff around the holiday season but rarely on Christmas day. We usually blessed with just good old fashioned wet rain.

The Christmas tree people set up their stand in the parking lot over in front of McDonald's as usual. That year I decided not to even ask for a job helping. Beth asked me about it and I just flat out told her, "No way! You know what happened last year when I tried that?"

"Yeah, you bitched about it for a week."

"God, Beth, I'm not a spring chicken anymore. That was a lot of trees that I unloaded."

"Yes I know," she sighed and then she dragged it out, "You were sore for days."

"Yeah, and ruined a new pair of gloves. All for twenty bucks, which you didn't mind help spending."

"I told you I would help."

"Beth, most of those trees weigh as much as you do!" I said in a raised voice. "Come on." I lowered my voice as I began walking over to McDonald's. "Let's go get something to eat before we head out."

We sat down after ordering a couple egg McMuffins and watched the cars go by. I really wanted a cup of coffee but the funds were a little low for that. I figured we would make some money fairly quickly out on the freeway judging by the amount of cars going by.

We talked about Jerry, wondering how he was doing. We hadn't seen him for a while. Nimrod hadn't been around for a while either and the last I heard, Skippy was hanging out at his old stomping grounds some forty miles away. I can't say that broke my heart and the same went for Beth. She didn't miss them much either.

I heard through the grapevine that Linda Lou and Randy had been hanging out in near down-town. I thought I knew about where they were but wasn't entirely sure. No matter, the fewer people hanging around in our neck of the woods, the better. Less people meant less attention from Johnny Law. Not that we ever really had any problems with the cops, we just didn't want to push the issue even though flying sign was not illegal. Pan handling was, but not flying a sign.

Beth suddenly said, "I don't want the rest of this. Do you want it?"

"No. Just wrap it back up and put it in your coat pocket for later. If you get hungry before Ted comes around, then you'll have it. What's the big hurry all of the sudden?" I asked her.

"Nothing, but I sure could use a beer to wash that down."

"You are going to have to wait. We don't have any money right now. I'll go check the can rooms while you fly. That usually works out pretty good."

"Okay. I gotta go potty first."

I sighed as I said, "Naturally."

When she finally got done with her business in the restroom, we grabbed the sign and crossed the road. I stopped at the crosswalk and handed the sign to her and told her, "I'll be back in a bit. Hopefully I'll get some cans that Safeway doesn't accept but Albertsons does." She waited for the cross signal to turn green as I walked down to the can room.

I managed to find about three twelve packs of empty imported beer bottles that Albertsons did take. I grabbed them and down the sidewalk I went. I yelled across to Beth alerting her of my find. She stuck her hand up as a signal to go ahead and she would meet me there in the can room at Albertsons.

I already had all the bottles punched through the machines before she arrived. I took the slips up to the customer service desk and exchanged them for cash. That would be enough for a couple brews. We walked out the door towards the mini-mart when Beth informed me, "I think I got a five. You'll have to look. I can't see." God I was getting tired of hearing her say that twenty times a day. "I can't see. I can't see."

I looked and sure enough, she scored a five spot. Naturally, after I walked clear down to the other store, grabbed three boxes of empty bottles that someone had left behind. Then I went and cashed them in for a dollar and eighty cents while she stands there and gets five bucks handed to her. We walked into the mini-mart and bought a couple beers then headed towards camp to drink them and take a break.

She pulled the leftover breakfast sandwich from her coat pocket and began eating it. That made me hungry right away. I hurried up and killed my beer then I told her, "I'm going over to get a hamburger. I'll meet you either back here or on the way over."

After I came out of Burger King I walked to the trail head and didn't see her so I ate my burger while I walked towards the freeway. She was already standing out there as I approached. I figured that since she did so well out there alone before, I would just sit tight where I was and read the rest of the newspaper and bullshit with whoever came by that I might know.

I just sat down and here came Ted. He spotted Beth first, then me. I walked over to his car and talked to him for a while, and of course, he had sack lunches for the both of us.

Ted and his wife had a little daily operation going on, they would get up early in the morning and put together sandwiches, chips, or crackers, a cookie, and a piece of fruit. Usually the fruit was a banana but the sandwiches varied from day to day. Ted, and sometimes his wife, delivered these sack lunches to everyone he knew of that was homeless. He dedicated his time, gas, and effort in driving to the homeless camps around town and making sure that nobody went hungry.

Ted was not a judgmental person in the least. He went to church and received some funding for his project from there. The rest came out of his own pocket without any desire to collect anything from it except his own personal satisfaction that his efforts helped others that were less fortunate than him.

Only a couple times did Ted ask for anything from me. Once he needed to move some heavy items from one storage unit to another. The items were to be sold off at a yard sale to help fund his lunch sack effort and the church. He had a bad back and asked if I could help him with the move. I didn't think twice about it. I jumped in the van and away we went. The other time he needed to retrieve some items from a town on the coast about eighty miles away. There again, no problem on my part; I met him the next morning and away we went. It was the least I could do in return for him doing his good deeds that went unnoticed by most.

I took a lunch for myself and one for Beth while I talked with him for a moment. He usually didn't have a lot of time to visit. He met a person across town daily where a homeless camp is located far up on a hill. He couldn't make it there in his car or his van so this guy met him at the bottom and took food up to everyone at the camp.

After Ted left, I walked on over to the freeway to fly sign with Beth for a while. She made some money but nothing worth bragging about. It looked like it was going to rain but we stood out there for another hour or so until we needed a break.

With Christmas just around the corner I knew things would pick up. Just like the years before, most people are in a giving mood around Christmas. I suppose when people get their bonuses, it puts the Christmas cheer into them.

My parents had already stopped and invited Beth, Jerry, and me to their home for Christmas evening dinner and celebration. Jerry was in kind of a depressed mood at the time but was not the least bit hesitant about going to my parents' house for something different. Beth on the other hand sent out signals that told me that she cared not to go. That didn't surprise me much. She had a really low self-esteem at the time. I thought: *If there is a time to not be alone on a holiday when depression sets in, it's Christmas.*

We had a few days left until the big day, so she could go if she wanted to, even at the last minute. Personally, I couldn't wait to go. I wanted to take a hot shower and trim my beard. I was starting to retain that mountain man look. It kept my face warm, but it was just way to long. Even though I didn't have a house to live in, I still had some pride left. I knew I had to get to my parents' house early enough to shower and trim my beard before my other relatives arrived. I thought: *With clean clothes, a shower, and a beard trim, maybe I wouldn't appear like the total outcast that some were thinking I had become.*

The big day had arrived. It was Christmas morning and the air felt cool and fresh. It looked like it could rain, but it wasn't all dark and gloomy that sometimes accompanies the rain. Everyone was in a bright and cheery mood as far as I could tell. Jerry and I talked about going to my parents' house while Beth cracked a beer. That was the first tell-tale sign that she had no intention of going even though she didn't outright say the words. That wasn't a big deal, if she wanted to miss out, that was her choice.

My mom and dad showed up so Jerry and I climbed in the car and off we went to their home. I jumped in the shower and cleaned up after mowing half the hair off my face. I felt much better being clean with dry, clean clothes on. My brother's family came over so we ate supper and visited. Jerry felt a little out of place which was totally understandable. Everybody knew it and tried to make the best of it. Overall, he did have a good time though. We laughed and told stories while opening gifts and so on until it was time for us to head back to camp.

We got out of the car and told my parents, "Thank you and merry Christmas," as my mom gave both of us a hug and told us the same. Jerry and I then waited for a moment and then headed over to the mini-mart. We were both tired from all the festivities so both Jerry and I wanted a brew or two. We bought one for Beth too but I pretty much figured she'd be pretty well snookered by the time we returned from my parents' house. I was right in figuring that one out. She wasn't quite as pleasant as I hoped she would be. She was about half Beth and half the Betholizer. Jerry knew it too so we stood outside the tent and drank our beers while bullshitting. Basically we just didn't feel like any kind of confrontation at that moment.

Outside the tent the next morning was when Beth finally asked about our experience at our Christmas get together at my folks' house. I told her, "It was alright. Everyone asked about you, I told them you just didn't feel like coming. I said no more and no less. That's the way it was, right?"

"Well yeah. I didn't feel like going in there with a bunch of people that I don't know."

"It's okay, Beth; it's over and no big deal."

Jerry left the camp to go somewhere; he told me where he was going as he walked by me but I didn't catch it. It didn't matter anyway. He could do as he pleased. Besides, I was getting hungry and wanted to go get something hot to eat and a cup of coffee.

As we walked across the field I spotted Craig from Wyoming. He was a contract photographer that had a home in Jackson Hole, Wyoming and a home somewhere in Oregon. He spent a lot of time traveling in his GMC Yukon four-by-four to Alaska so he could photograph wildlife scenery.

He spotted us and invited Beth and I to breakfast at Burger King. We accepted and walked over while he parked his Yukon. We all placed our orders then sat down while Craig said grace. We talked for a while after the meal then he said he had to take care of business before he headed to Alaska for a few months.

I struck up the idea of maybe we could all go to church the following Sunday. Craig thought that was a wonderful idea so we made plans to meet the next Sunday. Beth was in on the deal also. We said our goodbyes and away he went. Beth and I talked of him off and on throughout the rest of the day.

The remainder of the day went as usual with the exception of my taking some Christmas money and going shopping. I didn't go hog wild on things I didn't need; I had other uses for the money later on. I bought new batteries of course, along with some new socks, foot powder, boot grease, and a few other items. Beth was kind of pissed off at me for not just blowing all of it on beer and other unnecessary items but after all, it was my money, not hers.

Sunday came so I woke up telling Beth right away that we had church with Craig that morning. She asked, "What time is it?"

"Ten past seven," I said cautiously.

"It ain't even daylight yet!"

"No shit, Sherlock. It is the middle of winter you know."

"What time do we have to meet Craig?"

"Nine-thirty"

She finally got up and moved around for a few minutes before doing her morning puke and gag thing. We walked down the trail to use the restroom and clean up a bit. I met Beth outside and we started walking across the street when Beth said, "Let's get a beer in us before he gets here."

"Beth, we are going to church in a couple hours."

"It'll be okay, just one so I can get rid of the shakes."

"Okay," I agreed hesitantly, so we stopped at the mini-mart.

Not too long after we left the mini-mart and started walking across the street again, here came Craig. He stopped so we walked over to his rig to talk to him for a while. He offered breakfast so again, we accepted. We went in to Burger King and ate while he asked about our faith in God. I explained my Christianity while Beth pondered her Catholic beliefs. It didn't really matter to him as long as we believed in God. The church we usually attended was a Baptist church simply because it was nearby. It's a little different than what I grew up with but the basics were all pretty much there.

After church Craig invited us to lunch. Again, we accepted. I really think he was kind of lonely being on the road so much. I commented on all the fancy electronic gizmos on the dash of his Yukon. He said, "Well, the radar detector and the scanner are there because sometimes I have a tendency to drive a little bit fast. I put a lot of miles on going back and forth from Jackson Hole to Oregon, Alaska, Reno, and Mexico."

I replied, "Yeah, I bet you do have the urge to stand on it from time to time."

"Yes, but I'm sure I'll get nailed one of these times."

"How many miles are on this thing?"

"Eighty-eight-thousand and its just over a year old."

"Holy crap!" I exclaimed. "I guess you do put the miles on."

"Look in the back. I don't even know what's at the bottom of that pile back there."

I laughed as I turned back around from looking. Yeah, he put some miles on that thing alright. He kept the front part and the outside clean though. It was a pretty nice rig to say the least. It was a nice rig and one hell of a nice guy. He was well mannered and just an all-around good guy. Beth and I enjoyed his company very much.

After he left, Beth and I couldn't help but talk of him again and what an interesting lifestyle he must live. I told her, "It's weird how some people have money flowing out their ass and won't even acknowledge your existence but then someone like Craig just treats you like family." She didn't say anything. She just nodded her head in agreement.

The next couple of days just blew by then it was New Year's Eve. I told Beth, "I'm not standing out on the freeway after four o'clock this afternoon. Some people will be having a few drinks when they leave the office and I don't feel like being a statistic today."

Beth agreed with me so we made an early day of it. We hit the freeway at about eight that morning and only took about five breaks until four o'clock. We made a substantial amount of money out there so it was time for our own celebration. I was glad we did well flying sign. We ate at Taco Time and had a quiet celebration up until the fireworks crackled from the skies. "Happy new year!" I shouted. "May this one will be far better than the last."

"Amen!" Beth yelled excitedly.

We both climbed into the tent and went to sleep on a new calendar year.

CHAPTER 38

RELIEF FROM THE COLD

The new year started out cold on the very first day. Beth and I crawled out of the tent on New Year's morning after staying up late listening to all the yelling and fireworks exploding from all directions. Needless to say, we both were tired and cold. Neither one of us wanted to climb out of our sleeping bags which were just then beginning to dry out but our bladders told us differently. We crawled out of the tent to meet the cold, brisk air of the winter morning to get the day started.

After taking the first morning yeller piss, I walked back and zipped the tent flap down before we walked over to get a cup of hot coffee. It was definitely a coffee morning, the steaming hot liquid felt excellent when it hit the back of my throat. After we sipped some coffee we grabbed the sign and headed out to the freeway. There wasn't much traffic that morning; I figured most people stayed up late for the New Year celebration and then slept in. It didn't matter much; within the first five cars that went by we got a "Happy New Year! Here you go!" yell from some guy who looked like he was still about half sloshed from the night before or he never quit all night long. Either way, he gave us a ten dollar bill. That put a smile on Beth's face. We walked over to the mini-mart as usual but I stopped at the bus station and got a newspaper to read.

It was the Thursday paper and on the front page said something to the effect of *Warming center open through weekend for the homeless.* That caught my attention so I turned to section that contained the article and read it while walking through the parking lot.

The warming center was to take place at the Armory across town. The bus ride would be free to anyone in need and bus tokens would be given out upon exit for a return trip.

After Beth came out of the mini-mart, I filled here in on the details. She was a bit leery about the whole idea but I told her, "We might as well try it out; it's worth a shot."

We discussed it for a while and decided to give it a try. It had to be more comfortable than a tent, and it couldn't be any worse than the mission. The newspaper said the center would be open form seven pm to seven am. Everyone must be ready to leave by seven o'clock. They were to have some kind of small meal during the evening for those who wanted it and a pastry and coffee or orange juice in the morning. Showers were provided although numbers were limited on how many would be able to use that benefit.

We flew sign for the rest of the day taking an occasional break then went over to camp to check things out before we left. Then we hopped on the bus at about five thirty and headed for the Armory. When we arrived we could not believe the turnout. Beth and I managed to acquire folding cots to sleep on but some were not so fortunate. Some people were forced to sleep in different rooms on the floor with nothing but a blanket. It was warm though, the temperature was supposed to drop into the low teens the next four nights. When a person is exposed to that kind of cold, it can lead to death very rapidly. In fact, one homeless person did lose his life that year from hypothermia because he couldn't make it to the only warming center that was in operation.

The shelter from the cold didn't get quiet all night long. I knew there were some people there who had enough meth pumping through their veins to power up a train engine and those people rarely ever sleep. It did quiet down enough around one o'clock to finally get some much needed sleep though.

It seemed like six thirty came around early for some reason. I told Beth, "Well, we did stay up late the night before, and we couldn't sleep very well last night due to the tweekers bouncing around."

"Yeah, I know," she said. "Where is there a store around here?"

"A Store?" I asked. I don't know, probably a convenience store around here somewhere, I suppose, why, or should I even ask?"

She didn't answer but I knew what she was getting at. We packed up all of our stuff and walked to the exit line. There they took our names and gave us bus tokens and information on other services around town to make life a little easier for homeless people. We thanked the lady and out the door we went.

We walked around for about twenty minutes looking for some kind of a small market. It seems like wherever you go, you always see some kind of little *get-n-go* market unless you are looking for one. We walked our frozen asses off when I finally spotted a little piss-ant mom and pop store. We walked in and bought a couple beers and some beef jerky. It wasn't the most inexpensive store in the world but we didn't have much of a choice.

We couldn't find an inconspicuous place to drink them, so we ended up walking almost all the way back to the bus stop at the Armory before I spotted a little trail leading into some tall trees. We walked down the trail, chewing on jerky while we froze our asses off even more.

We went down the trail about thirty yards to a place in the trees that looked to be fairly secluded from anyone driving down the main road and cracked our brews. I told Beth, "Make it quick, I want to get the hell out of here. I don't know this area at all."

"Okay, I'll do the best I can," she said as she tipped her can up for another pull.

We finished up our little task there then walked back to the main road to catch the next bus. We only had to wait for about five minutes but then Beth was complaining that she had to piss. I told her, "Well you are just going to have to tough this one out. There are no restrooms around here. You can go when we change busses at the station."

The bus arrived so we hopped on. There wasn't much room on the bus at the time, so we had to sit in separate seats with other people. I knew it was only a matter of time before she started to squirm. She did that when she was on the verge of pissing her pants.

I watched her as the bus putted along all the way to the station. I think the bus stopped at every stoplight and every bus stop on the way there. Beth would lift one ass-cheek off the seat for a while, then roll over a bit and lift the other cheek for a while. It was so funny I wanted to bust a gut laughing but I knew people would think I just escaped from the nut-house. I did keep my composure, I don't know how, but I somehow managed to hold it in.

As soon as the door opened on the bus, Beth hopped off and ran to the ladies room while I sat down and waited for her and the bus that would take us back to our neck of the woods. I saw the bus round the corner but Beth was still in the pisser. As the bus came to a stop and people began boarding she finally came waltzing over.

I told her, "Jeeze, Beth, you about made us miss the bus and its fifteen minutes till the next one."

"I told you I had to go!"

"I know, let's get on. I'm curious to see if anyone messed with our shit while we were gone."

We got on the bus and took our seats. Even that bus was busier than it usually is. I figured that people took a four day weekend for the holiday or something along those lines.

We got off the bus and headed for our camp to see if everything was alright, stopping first at the mini-mart first of course. When we arrived, we found everything just as we left it. We were only gone over night but you never knew what might happen.

We went out and flew sign all day and left again just like we did before. We made it to the Armory and found that the people who were forced to sleep on the floor the last night got smart and arrived a little earlier. Beth and I still managed to get fold up cots but in separate rooms. That was okay; some kind lady helped Beth around because she was having a hard time seeing where she was going. I needed a little break from her anyway.

As we approached the exit the next morning, two idiots got into a fight. One guy threw a chair at another guy and they were both yelling at the top of their lungs.

I turned to Beth and said, "Well, I hope you enjoyed the last two nights because I bet these two idiots just shot the whole thing all to hell."

We received our bus tokens and watched the city police come racing through the door. I just shook my head as we walked away and told Beth again, "This was it, no more I bet. It only takes one or two assholes to ruin it for everybody. Fricken tweekers!"

We got on the bus and headed towards camp again only to find that someone had indeed decided to take advantage of our absence and stole our military sleeping bags. Now we were stuck. I told Beth, "Of all the damn things to happen, I'll bet they close the center so we won't be able to stay in there tonight. We better go make some money, we need sleeping bags now."

"That just pisses me off! I'm getting pretty fricken sick of people taking our stuff all the time. Now we don't have anything, again," Beth said

"I know, I know, but at least they didn't trash our tent. We still have that."

"Let's hope the Armory is still open tonight."

"Yeah, no shit, it's going to be another cold one."

We headed over to the cardboard bin and retrieved a suitable piece to write a new sign stating that we needed sleeping bags. We thought maybe someone would have some spare ones they use for camping or something. "You never know Beth, we might as well try it," I told her as I popped the cap off of my permanent marker.

We stood out there for no longer than an hour when some guy yelled; "Meet me over there in a half hour!" as he pointed towards McDonald's. We went ahead and walked over to the bus station to keep an eye out for him. He came pulling in with two brand new sleeping bags from the department store across the street. I thanked him several times as he was getting in his car. He then handed me a ten dollar bill and said, "Here, you two, go get something hot to eat."

I told Beth, "Problem solved, and these are going with us to the Armory tonight." We went to the mini-mart then took the new bags up to the tent. After that we went and got a couple of hamburgers at Burger King before going back out to fly sign for a little while longer.

It became time for us to go get our new bags and catch the bus so we stashed the sign and headed to our tent to get ready. We grabbed our bags from the tent, zipped it down, and walked to the station, stopping again at the mini-mart to get a couple beers just in case. "Might as well get them here in case the warming center is closed, I don't want to carry these things all the way to that little store down there do you?" She shook her head.

As we rode the bus to the Armory we heard people talking about the place being shut down for the lack of personnel. The driver even acknowledged that as he partially turned his head and said, "I heard the same thing."

We rode the whole way there anyway just to see for ourselves. Sure enough, they were turning people away. Some people were walking down towards those trees where we had walked to before. Others were getting back on the bus. One of the ladies spotted us and called us over explaining what had happened. They had some sandwiches and things handing them away out of the back of a Jeep Grand Cherokee. People were upset about the deal but the people who were upset the most were the people who were donating their time for such a cause just to see it shut down.

It wasn't good all the way across the board. We walked down that trail to the trees. I told Beth, "You know, we have our bags with us, we could go follow everybody if we wanted to."

"No," she said. "Let's just go back to our camp."

"I agree, I just was saying we could if we wanted to. Let's get these down and head back," I said.

We were upset, of course, but there wasn't anything anyone could do about it. We walked to the bus stop and entered the next bus going towards a more familiar place and our own tent, hoping it was still there.

CHAPTER 39

GOING TO WORK

What remained of a bitter winter was gently evolving into an early spring. That didn't bother us one bit. After the warming center shut down, we were lucky not to have all that many cold spells. It was wet at times, of course, but we were used to that, living in the Pacific Northwest.

Something in the spring air made me think that this year things were going to change for the better. I don't know if it was the contentment of knowing we made it through another winter even with the odds against us several times, or just that knowing that things couldn't get a whole lot worse. I just thought that the summer would bring better things into my life.

The sun was warm but the wind let me know that it was not quite summer yet. Beth and I walked to the freeway to spend the day cold and shivering like so many other days in the past. We were just about to go take a break when a silver Dodge van, kind of a new one, pulled off the side of the freeway and the driver rolled down the window. He asked, "You want to go to work? Meet me over at McDonald's." I jumped on that like a fly on shit.

I hustled over to see what this fellow had to offer and to make sure it wasn't some kind of stupid joke. A person had to be careful about that kind of stuff; some people have a morbid sense of humor when it comes to homeless people. He introduced himself as Lenny and asked if I would like a hot apple pie. I said, "Sure that sounds good!"

We sat down inside McDonald's and ate our pies while he explained who he was and what he was doing. It turns out that at one time, he was in building custom vans until the market fell out. He then traveled for a while until he met a special lady and decided to stick around and do light construction work. He asked, "Are you interested in making some money under the table?"

"Music to my ears," I replied.

"Good. Do you have any experience?"

"In construction I am limited, I am sorry to say. However, I am a good mechanic if that helps," I answered

"Are you a hard worker?"

"Yes, and I can do whatever I set my mind to. I'll tell you right now that construction is not my specialty but I'll give a whirl. If I don't cut it, just let me go."

"Meet me tomorrow morning right here at eight o'clock."

"I'll be here at eight tomorrow."

Lenny walked out the door and drove off in his van as I watched out the window walking towards the restroom. As I was standing there watering the urinal, I could not wait to tell my mom and dad that I actually landed a job in that economy and didn't even ask for it. I knew then that it was going to be a good summer. I walked over and explained the situation to Beth. She was excited almost as much as I was. I knew that I would have some definite income at least. The money would be spent at my discretion of course, and she understood that.

When it became time to pack it up for the day I walked over to the hardware store and bought a pair of gloves. I had no idea what Lenny would have me do but judging by his age, he more than likely needed a grunt for the rough stuff. That was alright by me; I had never been afraid of hard work as long as I got paid fairly for it.

I couldn't sleep that night. I tossed and turned all night long. As soon as I dosed off into a deep sleep, Beth woke me up by crawling over my feet to get out of the tent. She had to piss. I couldn't get mad at her for that. It's just that of all the times I really needed a good night's rest and I didn't get it.

When morning came I crawled out and couldn't wait for eight o'clock to come. We walked down to the freeway to fly and by half past seven I found myself sitting at the bus station staring at McDonald's parking lot waiting for a silver Dodge van to pull in. *A watched pot won't boil*, I kept telling myself as I checked the time about every five minutes.

Finally Lenny pulled into the parking lot. I quickly walked over and met him as he got out of his van. He said, "Good morning, Kirk."

"Good morning, Lenny," I returned

"I have to use the restroom before we leave. You want a McMuffin or something?"

"Sure. If you're going to work me hard, I guess I better have some energy food."

"Good Idea," he said. "I'll be right back."

He came out with a bag in his hand and his travel mug filled with coffee. He climbed into the van and handed me a McMuffin and a hash brown. We ate those as he drove us up the road towards the river. He handed me his hash brown and told me, "You want this? I really don't even like them but it came with the meal and I substituted your coffee in order to fill this." I smiled at him as he pointed towards his travel mug. I could tell that we were going to get along just fine.

We pulled up a steep side road then into a driveway that led to a medium two-story house with a detached garage about fifty feet downhill from the house with a large Douglas fir tree in between the two. The house looked as if it needed paint and the porch had definitely seen better days. The driveway was gravel as well as the sidewalk leading from the garage area to the house. The lawn was nothing but one giant mole hill with a thick crab grass blanket. The place needed help to say the least but that's why we were there.

Lenny started out by telling me about the place and showing me around. He said, "The guy that owns this place is going to sell it. He works twelve hour shifts and works four days on and four off. We don't work on his days off because he likes to entertain the ladies, if you know what I mean. I think he mostly entertains himself if you ask me. Anyway, this porch is going. We're going to build a complete new one. The walkway is going to be made of large flat stone, inset into the ground. The garage needs a new side door and frame. I hope you like to paint because the whole place needs painted, garage included. The lawn is a mess, but we aren't going to do anything with that."

We walked back to the van and he opened up the side door exposing a large selection of hand tools, an air compressor, and nail guns. He walked me down to the garage and retrieved two ladders. He carried one and I carried the other to the porch. "Let's tear it down," he said as he handed me a hammer and a large pry bar.

"Are we saving anything?" I asked.

"Nope," he answered. "Just the house."

"Alright, that means go," I said

We ripped and tore for about an hour on the porch when he stopped me and said, "You're going to have to slow down. You are making me look bad; I'm an old man you know." I laughed as he dropped his hammer and sat down. "Take a break. I'm anything but a slave driver," he explained. From that moment on I knew that I hit it lucky meeting this guy. He drank his coffee and told me about more jobs he had for the nice weather. He made it very clear that he did *not* work in the rain.

We worked about four hours before he called it quits. He told me he didn't like to work the whole day because it didn't leave enough time to goof off before his lady friend got home from work. I didn't laugh at that moment but after he dropped me off and I was telling Beth about him, it came out. I started laughing and couldn't quit. I told her, "This guy I really like. He is so easy going it's unbelievable. He works steady, but he certainly doesn't over exert himself and he doesn't want me to either." Beth got a chuckle out of that.

I asked how her day went as we sat down for a cold one. Nimrod came prancing by to throw a wrench in the works.

"You owe me a beer," he said

I told him, "I owe you nothing. You told me that if I was flying, you were buying. That means we're even."

Beth could tell that I wasn't going to put up with anymore of his shit and if he were to start something, I would finish it. Nimrod turned and walked away when Beth yelled something at him that I don't recall.

He turned to me and yelled, "You better control your woman!"

I yelled back, "She's not my woman. She will say what she wants." He kept walking which was a good thing. The less I saw of that asshole the better.

After Nimrod left, we waited for a few minutes and then we went over to Taco Time and I treated us both to a good supper before heading back to camp for the night. When we crawled inside I turned on my Walkman to check the weather forecast. It didn't sound good. Rain was in the forecast starting around noon. "Well Beth that pretty much shoots my day all to hell tomorrow. Lenny won't work in the rain," I reminded her.

"Is he going to pick you up tomorrow?"

"He said to meet him at McDonald's at eight."

"Are you going to meet him?"

"Beth, don't be stupid. Of course I will, we'll be down there anyway right?"

"Well, yeah."

"If he doesn't show up, that means he thinks it would be a wasted trip. He lives on the other side of town."

I told her goodnight and tried to make myself as comfortable as possible. I knew I was out of shape, but didn't realize I was that much of a wimp. I knew right then that I was going to be one sore hombre when morning came. I rolled over and went into a deep sleep. I was beat.

The morning rolled around as soon as I closed my eyes, it seemed. I crawled out of the tent and it was already sprinkling.

I said, "Get your ass up, Beth, no work for me today. It's raining already. We might as well head on down to the freeway and claim a spot before Nimrod shows up." I heard her yawn as I walked over to water the bushes. Beth finally made her way out of the tent and did the same.

We were walking across to the freeway when this short, white-haired lady came up and asked if I knew anything about lawnmowers. I told her, "Yes. As a matter of fact, I'm a former Diesel Mechanic so I'm sure I can repair a lawnmower."

"I live right over there. I've seen you before but just never asked. Are you interested in fixing it and mowing my yard when it dries out?"

"Sure, just tell me when."

"You can come over in an hour to work on it if you want to. I'll be home then. Just knock on the door. I'm Paula by the way. What's your name?"

"Mine is Kirk, this is Beth here."

"Hi, Paula," said Beth

"I'll see you in about an hour then," I said

"Alright," said Paula as she walked towards Albertsons.

I turned to Beth and said, "This is turning out alright; the work is finding me for a switch." I was pretty happy at the moment. I actually had some real work to do. It put a little self-esteem back into my otherwise dismal life.

The clock never moved slower as I anticipated the repair work I was facing on Paula's lawn mower. It started to sprinkle again so I knew I was not going to be able to cut her grass. When it finally became time to knock on her door, she swung it open before my knuckles could make contact with it. "I'll get the key," she said as I walked onto the already shin high grass that made up her lawn.

I could tell right as she showed me to the shed and the lawnmower that she definitely had her own way of doing things. I made a mental note of where everything was and how it was arranged. I knew how older folks could be kind of funny that way.

Not that it's a bad thing really; I just had to make sure everything was put back in the same place as I found it.

She took a brick off of a piece of automotive floor mat that covered her lawnmower exposing a new looking bicycle lock. She had the key on a special key ring designated only for the lock on the mower. I took amusement on the procedure of just getting the mower out to where I could even work on it. Once I had the mower out in the open, I discovered that it was a fairly new mower. It wasn't the best mower made by any means but new enough that it shouldn't take much to get it going.

The first thing I did was check the gas and oil. The levels were adequate and the gas didn't smell like a dirty old sock, so I gave the start rope a tug. Nothing happened but the sound of an engine that was not going to start. That is when she laid it on me, "My son came over and tried to fix it but he couldn't get it going either."

I think she knew what I was thinking when I turned to her and asked, "What did he do to it already." I used words as carefully as I could. I tried not to let her know that most the time when this sort of thing happens, some moron tries to fix something and screws it up even worse than it was in the first place.

I asked if she had a socket set with a spark plug wrench. She said, "I just bought a wrench. I'll go get it." Here she came a few minutes later with a slightly used spark plug wrench placed back in the package with a piece of masking tape marked *lawnmower spark plug tool.* I silently laughed at the excessively proper labeling and then proceeded to remove the spark plug. It didn't take much effort to remove the spark plug because the threads came with it. Not knowing her son, I pictured a football linebacker whose mechanical skills are about as sharp as a tractor tire.

The job suddenly became larger than it should have. I told her, "The head has to come off so I can get a heli-coil put into it."

She looked at me, then the mower, then back at me and said, "Let's go buy a new one then, I guess."

"You don't need a new mower, I can fix it. All I need to do is take the head off and take it to a machine shop. It won't take that much," I explained to her.

"Well, alright," she said before going inside.

I took the head off of the small *Briggs and Stratton* engine and we jumped in her car and headed to the machine shop. Ten bucks later at the shop and we were back in business. The lawnmower was running like a top and I walked away with twenty bucks in my pocket.

That cheered me up, for sure. I was kind of down about the weather preventing me from working with Lenny, but it worked out better in the long run because I scored on another summer job as well. Now I had a job working construction and another job taking care of Paula's lawn. Both jobs were under the table so nothing could be garnished for child support either. Things were looking up for me.

CHAPTER 40

BUSY SUMMER

The next morning, I informed Beth that I needed to take care of some business downtown and asked if she wanted to ride along. She didn't have much to do downtown so she decided not to join me. One of my stops was to renew my library card since it was outdated. Another stop was to visit the employment department to see if there were any full time jobs available. On top of that, I wanted to stop at Goodwill to see if they had a backpack for a decent price.

I needed to complete all of my business that day because the weather was supposed to turn off hot and I would no doubt be working for Lenny. Paula's lawn was alright for the time being, so that wasn't a concern. My first stop was the public library. I sat down at one of the computers to check my e-mail and sure enough, the system wouldn't let me log on. My card had indeed expired.

I originally got my card when I was living with a friend on the outskirts of town. The street we lived on weaved in and out of the county and city limits. The woman at the customer service desk retrieved a city map showing these boundary lines and informed me that I was not within the city limits. I told her, "I got this card when I lived at that address."

The bitch grabbed my card, used scissors and cut my library card into pieces right in front of me. I couldn't believe my eyes. She cut up my fricken card that I had for five years. Needless to say, I was thoroughly pissed at her so-called customer service.

I wanted to rip her a new asshole but instead decided to maintain discipline. The security guard standing about fifteen feet away influenced that decision. I furiously marched out the door and walked toward the bus stop thinking: *I'll just check my e-mail at the employment office. All those people know me in there anyway. Piss on the library, and piss on that bitch that works there.*

Once I got on the bus I was calm and quiet. I departed from the bus at the Employment Department and went to the back room to log onto one of the computers there. I finished there and then boarded the bus again and headed towards Goodwill. They didn't have what I wanted so I hopped back on the bus and headed towards camp.

As soon as I got off the bus, I saw Beth heading over to the mini-mart. I hurried and ripped on over there to join her. She was in the restroom when I showed up so I bullshitted with Kathy for a while until Beth walked out. We purchases a couple brews and walked over to our usual spot.

The first thing she asked was, "Did you find my son on the computer?" It was like throwing salt on an open wound. I filled her in on my heart warming experience with the bitch at the library. I said, "You know, that just chaps my ass; and there ain't anything worse than having a chapped ass!" Beth was blowing beer out her nose from laughing so hard. I continued, "You know, it would have been okay but that bitch cut my card up right in my face. I wanted to slap the piss out of her!"

Poor Beth then developed a bad case of the hiccups and had a hard time finishing her beer. I was glad someone thought it was funny, I was furious at that bitch. I went at her again, "That kind of action is all uncalled for in a public place. It wasn't like a license to drive; it was a fricken library card for crying out loud! Does the bitch want a brownie button or something?" At this time Beth's laughter got me to laughing. It's like the saying goes, *Laughter is the best medicine.*

Beth finally got over her hiccups so we walked out to the freeway. She knew I had money but didn't want to see it all go without saving it for something useful. We only stayed out for about an hour or so then headed for camp. I stopped and purchased some sliced smoked turkey meat for sandwiches and then met up with Beth at camp.

We were only there about ten minutes until Dusty showed up to visit for a while. I always enjoyed bullshitting with him; we had a lot in common. He was someone I could talk to about welding and not be overwhelmed with pure bullshit. He knew what he was talking about. We yakked for a bit and then he left. It was time for me to hit the hay anyway, because the next day I was to work with Lenny.

I slept pretty well considering I still had that bitch at the library on my mind. It was funny how something like that pissed me off to the point of wanting to just slap the shit out of her. When I woke up, Beth was already out and walking around. I crawled out and did my morning ritual things then we got together and went down the trail. It was already seven o'clock so I only had an hour before Lenny would show up. I went into McDonald's and used the restroom to clean up a bit then joined Beth on the freeway and flew sign while waiting for my ride to work.

Lenny didn't show until a few minutes after eight. By that time I was beginning to wonder if he would show up or not. He had no way of getting in touch with me and I didn't have his cellular number. I caught up with him when he went in to get a cup of coffee.

When we arrived at the jobsite he asked me if I knew anyone else that would be a good worker. Confused, I asked, "Am I not working out for you?"

"No no," he answered. "I need to get some more done on this project. The weather slowed things down, and the owner wants to put it on the market."

With relief I said, "Oh, okay, yes I do know a guy I bet would work out just fine. He's a friend of mine; I can ask him tonight if you want."

"Sure, just have him come with you tomorrow morning if he's interested."

"Okay, I'll ask him tonight. I'm sure he'll be happy about this."

"Tell him what he will get paid, ten an hour, cash."

"I don't get a raise? I have seniority," I joked.

"Not today, besides, I have a special project for you."

"Special project? I don't know if I feel happy or scared."

"It's nothing really; you don't have to go if you don't want to. I need to go down towards the border and do a project that also requires mechanic skills that I don't have. But you do," he grinned as he explained.

"I'm listening."

"It may require spending the night in a motel. It depends on how long it takes us to do."

"That doesn't bother me any. What kind of work is involved?"

"Mainly cleanup, some light woodwork, and get an old Jeep running."

"Sounds like fun, I'm in!"

We carried our equipment up to the house and went to work. Lenny worked on the new porch while I carried the flat stones from the van, up the hill, and laid them on the grass. The stoned were going to be used for the sidewalk. I dug into the ground to inset the stones then positioned them so they all fit together like a jigsaw puzzle. It was quite challenging but fun at the same time.

Lenny came over to see what I had done so far and told me it was time for a break. He asked, "Do you want to do something else for a switch? That's hard work setting those rocks in there."

"What did you have in mind?"

"Well, I need all that lower trim that's rotten knocked off so we can replace it. After that, we've got to go get some sand and lumber for tomorrow," he said pointing at the house.

"Well okay, I'll clean up this mess for the time being."

I didn't mind at all doing something a requiring a little less effort. Pushing that wheelbarrow up the hill loaded with flat stones tuckered me out. I went ahead and cleaned up the work area where I was then started stripping all the rotten trim off the bottom of the siding.

I was almost done when Lenny yelled over at me, "Let's go back to town and get the lumber and some sand and bring it back. After we get in unloaded, we'll call it a day."

"That won't hurt my feelings one bit but how are we going to haul sand in your van?"

"Five gallon buckets, one by one. No, we aren't quite done yet; we still will have to carry the sand up here from the van."

"Now I know why you gave me an easy job for a while. So I would have energy left for the sand."

"You catch on quick," he said as he carried equipment down and put it into the van. I grabbed some stuff and carried it down as well. A couple of trips and we were ready to hit the road.

On the way down the driveway the owner was coming up the drive. He stopped to talk to Lenny for a while; I just sat tight trying not to eavesdrop on the conversation. Apparently he was going to take a long five day weekend and didn't want Lenny and me working up there while he was taking his time off. Lenny didn't seem to mind but it meant I wouldn't have any work for at least five days. Paula's lawn was good until the next week, and if I can't work for Lenny, I wouldn't have any work to do.

Lenny informed me, "Well, that puts everything to a halt. Now we can't even go get sand because I don't want to carry it around for five days. Let's go get your money and we'll call it quits until next week."

"What about the job down south?" I asked excitedly.

"That's right! I'm getting old and my memory is going. That's why I have you around," he said jokingly.

We made plans to go to the other job the following day. It wouldn't take much for me to get things ready. After Lenny paid me and dropped me off at McDonald's I went to Albertsons and bought stuff for lunch. That's pretty much all I had to do except set my alarm for five thirty so I could meet him at six.

I took my lunch stuff up to camp and stuck it inside the tent. Then I took off towards the freeway to find Beth and fly sign for a while. Lenny gave me an extra ten bucks for the lost time and short day, which was nice but I still went out to fly sign with Beth for a while.

On the way down my mom pulled up and stopped me. I walked over to her car to shoot the shit with her for a while. I filled her in on the plan to go to an out-of-town job the next day to work. She was excited about it. She was digging in her purse and pulled out a twenty dollar bill and said, "Here, take this."

"No mom, that's okay. Lenny is paying for all expenses."

"No, take it," she said. "You can't go all the way there without any money."

If there is one thing you didn't do to my mother, its refuse something from her when she offers. She would keep it up until I did accept it. I accepted the money and told her, "Thank you. I don't know for sure if we will stay the night, but I think it will be good for me to get away from this place for a while."

Mom left so I walked out to Beth and told her, "You're on your own tomorrow. I'm headed to a job out of town early in the morning for possibly two days." She didn't seem to mind, she probably needed a break from me as well. She had been out there flying for about two hours and wanted to go and sit in the shade.

I was standing there with Beth observing that Skippy was back from the town where his wife lives. I told Beth, "He's going to get busted laying on the grass like that you know. If a cop drives by and sees that, it's not going to be good."

"Yeah." said Beth. "You know where he's been, and what he does when he's there. He's coming down you know."

"Yeah, I know. I'm kind of hungry. Do you want me to go over and get something?"

"Sure, what are we going to have?"

"How about those sandwiches that look like a burrito and come with chips and a cookie?" I asked.

"Sounds good," she answered, so I walked over to the store to get a couple meals. On the way there I saw a woman in the parking lot screaming holy terror at some guy and then the cops showed up. I was glad I was getting away for a day or two.

When I came out I walked by the freeway and yelled for Beth to come over by the trees in the shade so we could eat lunch. She followed, so we sat down. I tore open the small bag of chips that come in the lunch and was dumping them into the lid of the container when someone kicked me from behind in the back of my head. I folded forward, dumping some of my chips and wondering what the hell was going on.

I turned to see Skippy standing above me on the hill holding a three foot steel pipe like a baseball bat. He had a weird look on his face like he was on some other planet. Luckily, Dusty was there also. Dusty jumped up and told Skippy, "Put the pipe down. Put it down *right now!*"

Skippy dropped the pipe. I got up and told everyone there, "I don't know what the hell the deal is here but I'll have no part of it." I walked off and Beth followed. I thought that was the best thing to do. From the looks of Skippy, any rationalization with him was long gone. I didn't know what he was thinking and apparently neither did he.

Beth and I walked over to the freeway where we finished our sandwich thingies while we talked about what happened. I asked Beth, "What the hell did I do? I never did anything to him to make him fly off the deep end like that!"

"He's coming down off of meth. They get that way," she reminded me.

"Fricken tweekers anyway," I muttered. "You just don't know what they are going to pull off. I never held much trust in him but what little trust I did have just went bye-bye."

"Well it's not his fault," she said.

"Not his fault, how? Did someone hold him down and shoot that shit in his veins or make him snort it? I don't think so. Don't give me that bullshit!" I yelled.

I then could then tell that I was starting to get a little pissed, so I needed to change the conversation before I got really mad and did something stupid. I had to get up early and go to work, so I wouldn't even drink a beer that night.

When we got back to camp I got everything I needed all gathered up just in case Lenny and I did end up spending the night. It wasn't much but I didn't want go there totally unprepared. By the time I was done, I was ready to sleep.

I woke up the next morning before my alarm clock even went off. I was excited about the trip down there but still managed to get a good night's rest in. That helped tremendously. As soon as I crawled out of the tent my alarm went off signaling that it was almost time to head down to McDonald's to meet up with Lenny.

As I grabbed my lunch sack, I whispered to Beth, "See you later. Have fun with Nimrod and Skippy!"

"Shut up. I wish I was going too."

"Well, you can't. See ya!"

Off I went with a grin on my face and walked down the trail leading from camp. It looked to be a nice, clear day although I knew that it might not be that way where Lenny and I were headed. It was about a three hour drive if you stood on the gas pedal.

I met up with Lenny and we headed towards new jobsite, stopping only twice. Once for gas and a piss break and the other to latch onto a U-Haul trailer to haul some garbage that Lenny had mentioned. Judging by the size of the enclosed trailer that he rented, I knew then that we had our work cut out for us. That was only part of the job too. I still had no Idea what was wrong with the Jeep that I was chosen to repair.

We stopped in town to get some lunch. Lenny bought lunch for both of us like he said he would. I ordered the same thing he did except the hot apple pie. He gave me a funny look then told the guy taking the order, "I'll take his apple pie too. Just put it in my bag." Lenny did enjoy his hot apple pies.

When we left McDonald's and headed for the jobsite, I had the distinct feeling Lenny didn't have a clue as to where we were supposed to go. Judging by the look on his face as he read the directions on the hand scribbled map, we were definitely lost. Somehow I had assumed that he knew where he was going. After all, it's a relative of his lady friend's house.

I started looking around for distinct landmarks in case we started to backtrack in circles when I asked Lenny, "Why don't you just call the guy and get directions?"

Lenny looked at me and said, "Because he's pushing up flowers."

"Well, that's not going to do us much good is it?"

"Nope. I can always call home and ask, but after the conversation me and her had last night, I really don't want to do that."

"Well Lenny, you do have an address. We could stop and ask someone instead of dragging this trailer all over town."

"I'll pull in here; you go ask," he said

It didn't bother me a bit to go ask directions. The gal working the counter was kind of cute. Not that I would ever see her again but it gave me a chance to talk to a pretty girl. That was more than Lenny got to do on that trip.

I walked back out with directions and told Lenny where to take us while he was choking down the other now cold apple pie. He reached over the steering column with his left hand and placed the shifter in drive being extra careful not to drop any of the pie held in his right hand. Off we went like a herd of turtles.

We finally found the place and not a minute too soon. After viewing the place and the work that needed to be done, I knew that we were going to have to work really hard to get it done. Unless we spent the night we would really need to concentrate. I didn't really think Lenny wanted to spend the night there. I sort of did however; a chance to take a hot shower, and watch cable TV at a motel room; that sounded pretty good to me. I hadn't seen a television since I was released from the Community Corrections Center nearly a year before.

Lenny showed me the Jeep that was to be my main project. Wow, was I impressed. This old boy was quite a backwoodsman. He had that Jeep prepped for the worst possible situations. He had Military MREs for nutrition, a CB radio, jacks, chains, pretty much everything a person could think of for an excursion into the deep woods.

Lenny explained, "The old fart would pay all of his bills in advance, have his mail held, hire someone to take care of his lawn, and then take off. He would go deep into the woods with nothing but his Jeep and be gone for weeks at a time, not letting a soul know where he was going."

I thought to myself how neat that would be just to be all alone, nobody to explain anything to except you and the wildlife. With the Jeep prepped the way it was, you'd have transportation, food, and a tent, everything you'd need.

He even had spare parts for the jeep like belts, hoses, u-joints, and more. This guy was prepared to the hilt.

I managed to get the Jeep running; it was no big deal really. It just sat for a while and the gas in the carburetor was gummed up. I was able to get it apart and back together without messing up the gaskets so we were in business.

Lenny was almost done loading the trailer except for the really heavy stuff that required my help. About three hours later we were at the dump and ready to drop off the U-Haul then head north. It would be dark by the time we got back but that wasn't a problem. We only stopped once at a Casino because Lenny said he had to piss. My ass, it doesn't take forty minutes to take a piss while I sat in the van. He put some money on the tables. He didn't fess up to it, but he did; I know he did. No problem though, we were on our way again.

When he dropped me off at McDonald's he paid me for the services rendered and five dollars an hour traveling wages. I told him it wasn't necessary but he insisted. What a guy. He told me, "Remember, no work tomorrow."

"Okay by me, when do you want to hit it again?"

"Tuesday morning?"

"Sounds good enough." I said as Lenny pulled away. I walked over to the mini-mart to get myself a couple beverages then headed up to camp. Beth was already inside so I talked to her from outside the tent. Then she came crawling out asking, "Are you going to share?"

"I guess. We'll have to go back down to the mini-mart though. I figured you already brought some up for yourself."

"No, everybody was taking turns out there today. Skippy, Nimrod, and even some new guy that I have never seen before."

"Oh great, not another one." I remarked, somewhat disgustedly before telling her, "I don't have any work until Tuesday now, Lenny doesn't have anything until we can work on the house."

We finished those two then we both moseyed on down to the mini-mart for the final round. I sat there and talked with Beth while my eyelids gained about two pounds. I crawled in the tent and didn't even crack another beer. I was too exhausted. I crawled in my sleeping bag and started wondering how long working with Lenny was going to last, and how much more grass was I going to be able to cut for Paula. I wanted the work to be steady all summer long. I closed my eyes and drifted off to dreamland.

CHAPTER 41

BEGINNING TO
AN END

The work with Lenny was dwindling off at a faster pace than I expected. We had hoped we had much more to do but the owner accepted an offer on the house we were working on so everything we had planned to do didn't take place. All the work left for us to do was just finish what we had started.

Lenny had some work for me at his own house to do so I spent a couple days there. It was mostly grunt work such as moving some concrete blocks around and hauling rock into the garden area with a wheelbarrow. It wasn't very interesting work, it was just things that he couldn't really do anymore, but it was work all the same.

Knowing that Lenny didn't have any more work scheduled for the summer, none the less work on my side of town really bothered me. I guess it was good while it lasted. That's how I had to look at it anyway. Finishing out the summer with some money saved up would have been really nice. Heading into winter without a decent amount of money saved back is not a good feeling.

The grass wasn't greener on the other side of the fence either. At Paula's house the grass was all dry from the hot weather we were having so there wasn't any yard work going on there at all. Basically I had to go out and fly sign with Beth unless something else came up. I would jump on the opportunity to do just about any kind of work that came along, but it was getting late in the season and most people had completed their summer projects. It appeared as though the summer work was over and it was time to stretch pennies.

As Beth and I headed out to the freeway, we ran into a guy we knew but not all that well. He informed us that Linda Lou had suffered a massive intracranial hemorrhage and passed away. I later read in the obituaries that she died of cancer. Knowing Linda, I knew she would have told me if it were cancer or something along those lines. I didn't know which cause of death to believe, it didn't matter anyway. The important thing was she was no longer with us here on Earth. That news didn't start the day off very well, let alone the rest of the summer. I didn't know of any memorial service planned for her; the paper didn't announce one and I didn't know who to contact to find out if there even was a service.

It was a sad thing to think that someone can just disappear from the face of the Earth and not even receive a decent farewell simply because the person didn't make a mark in the proper places. Linda Lou was missed by all that knew her though and she will not be forgotten.

The rest of the day we spent flying sign and thinking of the memories and good and not so good times we had with her. They were mostly good times for me, especially locking her up with Billy and Randy multiple times in the portable toilet. Also I remembered her damn hair that was always near perfect. She was a good person deep inside. She lived a rough life but always made the best of it. *She will be missed.* I kept thinking.

After we left the freeway we walked back to camp with some food and beer for the bullshit session we were no doubt going to have about Linda. It lasted until dark then we crawled in for the night. It had been a rough day finding out about the lack of upcoming work and Linda's death. I didn't think things could get much worse.

Beth and I woke up the next morning to the sounds of machinery up on the hill. We were informed by fellow representing the local park and recreation district that the entire hill including the area where we were camped at was just donated for a new park project. We couldn't be around there any longer.

Their plans were to build a trail and put a recreation facility on the top of the hill including a golf course for elderly citizens. Now that probably looked really good on paper and sounded awesome to the person who thought up the idea since that person would surely win brownie points and sustain his or her position within the district.

I held my tongue when I listened to all that bullshit knowing all the time it was a load of crap. After that fellow left, I asked Beth, "When was the last time you saw a group of senior citizens having the physical ability to climb a hill as steep as that?"

"I don't know; that's pretty steep. I can't even make it up that hill," she responded.

"I mean, it's a really nice gesture, but come on. There ain't any way in hell some eighty year old lady with a hip replacement would even make it past the bottom of the hill, let alone climb it to the top."

"I know, I know, calm down," she said trying to extinguish my flaming temper.

Beth could tell my crock pot was about to boil when I continued, "My God, the fricken idiots actually said they were going to put a golf course up there. Where? I know that hill like the back of my hand. The whole thing is one giant blackberry bush. You know how hard it is to kill those things? Where are they planning to punch a road in? It's all private land where you could gain access to it!"

"I know. I know," she said wishing I would shut up.

I vented a few minutes longer and then decided to focus my attention on the problem at hand. We had to move. Not far though, just down the hill, close to the McRay River that had dried out for the summer.

What we would do for the upcoming winter was beyond me. We would figure that out in due time. As for the time being we would move just past the downed barbed wire fence that we believed separated the donated land from city property.

I left to go and scout some possibilities for another camp while Beth stayed behind and began to tear down. Somewhere between the time I looked for another spot and the time it took for me to get back to the gate on the other side of the road, the local police got their noses involved in the newly developed situation.

They caught me while I was on my way to the former campsite but not on the property. They caught Beth on the property tearing down our camp and wrote her a citation her for criminal trespass. The officer could only give me a warning because I wasn't on the property. The officer told me to go and help her move her stuff. The asshole didn't have to write Beth a citation; Beth was obviously attempting to move from the area. The officer was out of line giving her that citation.

Beth was pissed, so I came at her with one of my standing funnies, "He was probably just in a pissy mood because he missed out on the fresh donuts." She laughed a little bit even though she was still mad. I thought maybe I could play with her temper just a little bit.

We stashed all of our stuff inside some bushes, hidden for a while until the area calmed down. Then I asked Beth, "Ready for a beer yet?" She just looked at me with fire in her eyes.

"He didn't have to give us tickets!" she exclaimed.

"I didn't get a ticket. I got a warning."

"What? How come I got a ticket and you only got a warning?" she yelled.

"Tricks of the trade my dear. Tricks of the trade," I smugly told her.

I knew that would piss her off even more, and again, that's why I said it that way. She didn't talk to me all the way to the mini-mart. She slacked off the ignoring thing a bit though when I asked *Tadpole* for a box of tobacco for her. I only did it to keep the peace. I had money that I wanted to save but this was well worth it, I thought. She had been through enough for one day I figured. Besides, I'd played with her mind enough for a while.

We set up our sleep spot for the night when it was getting late in the afternoon. By that time, all the excitement would be over with and there wouldn't be anyone around to pick at us. We had a few beers while we set things up while thinking all the time that we had better be quiet here since we were fairly close to an apartment complex. Sound really travels during the night, so Beth couldn't start yelling at me in the middle of the night like she so frequently did.

We had to make camp easy and quick to pick up so it didn't look as if we had long term plans to stay there. All we had was a couple tarps and two sleeping bags. That would keep us off the ground and warm but nothing like the camp that we had before. That camp was quite functional with a tent and a place to sit down.

We didn't have any plans at all. The only thing I could think of is back behind the ponds where we were a couple of years back. I had looked it over while I was scouting around. It looked grown up quite a bit, but if worse came to worse it would be our only option. Not a very good one because of the kids with the pellet guns knowing about that spot. The other hill down the road where we had set up before wasn't an option because it was being developed while I was doing time for the child support. That left us right where we were at until something else happened.

"You know Beth, it's the shits being homeless," I said to her.

"Tell me about it. What are we going to do?"

"There's always the mission!"

"You know where you can stick that idea?" she asked in disgust.

"I know the general vicinity," I told her with a smile. "I use it daily."

"Always a smart ass. Wait! Better to be a smart ass than a dumb ass. I beat you to it this time, huh?"

"Oh just drink your beer and smoke a cancer stick. Everything will work out, it always does doesn't it?"

"Yeah, I guess so," she replied in a sad, low voice.

"Well just look at it this way. We've been through some rough shit before, a lot rougher than this. Remember the time when we went to the mini-mart one morning and it was so cold I had icicles hanging on the brim my hat and ice in my beard? Come on, this ain't all that bad. You just got a ticket, no biggie," I explained to her while trying to sugar coat our situation.

"I remember that cold morning but at least we had a place to go. What are we supposed to do now? Just disappear off the planet?"

"This is where the rubber meets the road, Beth," I told her.

We went down and got a bite to eat before turning in for the night. When we turned in, it was like it wasn't time to sleep or something. Neither one of us could fall asleep. It's funny how a person has a hard time sleeping in a new spot even when it's just a few yards away from the old place. We slept alright though, considering what had happened that day. The stress level was up for the both of us. Naturally the stress was a little too high for me and I slipped right into another seizure the next morning. That wasn't anything new to Beth; she knew exactly what to do. When I came out of it I had no idea where I was. It didn't sink in for about a half hour or so.

We got around and headed down to fly sign on the island before Nimrod or Skippy showed up. I was sore from the seizure but at least it wasn't a big one. I was able to move around alright, and I didn't piss my pants that time. I did bite my tongue again, but thank God, I didn't wet my jeans.

We made it to the island and put out the sign. Beth asked if I was alright. I nodded my head at her. After a while Beth suggested I go fly the other side while she stayed where she was. That sounded good to me so I walked to the other side to fly my own sign that read the same words as the one Beth was flying.

It wasn't too much later when a city cop pulled up beside me and asked how I was doing. Wondering why he even asked was puzzling me so I laid it on about as thick as I could lay it on. I told him, "Well, not too good yet, but I'll have enough money for a McMuffin pretty quick I hope."

He replied, "Well you better be gone by the time I come back through."

That was the first time I had ever been jacked around by Johnny Law. As a matter of fact, I hadn't ever even heard of anyone getting jacked by them for flying a sign. It wasn't illegal what we were doing. We did not impede traffic or step out into the road. I thought I'd better split anyway though. I yelled over at Beth and waved at her to meet me at the bus station.

When she walked up to me I filled her in on the cop situation. She wasn't even aware of what happened. She didn't even see it. I told her, "Well Beth, things are changing around here. I don't think it's for the better either."

"Yeah, I know it. What'll we do? We don't have any place to go."

"I don't know, Beth. I-just-don't-know," I told her in a most serious voice.

We walked over to the mini-mart to get a couple beers and kill some time. I was thinking that maybe that cop would have made his way back by the freeway before we went back out to fly sign again. We stood and talked of our situation some more as we finished our brews. I was sure he had passed by that time so we went ahead and walked over to fly sign some more.

We had stayed there long enough to be tired of it so we packed up our signs and headed out. We went to get a bite to eat and a couple beers and headed for the spot where we would spend the night. We were both just about exhausted, me from the seizure and her from all the shit going on.

Beth and I rose the next morning to what looked to be another nice day. It was late August so we were still in for more sunny days. We hoped for an Indian summer because we had not yet figured out where we were going to move to. If it started raining for the season, the McRay River would soon be giving us an unwelcome bath in the middle of the night.

We walked down towards the freeway to fly sign and bumped into Barb and Rick on the way. Barb used to have a fifth-wheel trailer up the river that she had lived in for several years with her husband Rick. Beth had spent some time with the couple in the past so she already knew Rick. I only knew Barb, so an introduction was necessary for Rick and me.

Apparently the two ran into some problems living at the trailer park where they were living, so they sold the fifth-wheel and moved to town. They didn't have any place to stay. They only rented a storage unit for their belongings but that was all.

We talked for a while when Beth mentioned that they could sleep where we did. There wasn't a tent but the weather was supposed to hold out for a while. They took us up on the offer and decided to stay where we were staying.

Beth taught Barb the so-called proper way to create and fly a sign, so now Barb was in on the deal. She didn't fly sign very often; she received a check each month from Social Security. I didn't know what Rick's story was, and what put him there but it was none of my business anyway.

We flew sign periodically throughout the day when it was time to head to our so-called camp and get ready for the night. We stayed up and bullshitted until it was good and dark then turned in.

All four of us were deep in sleep when we awakened quickly to a police officer with a K9 standing over me and Beth asking for identification. I crawled out of my sleeping bag and dug out my identification and handed it to the officer while Beth told him that she didn't have any but they had her on record.

The dog then discovered Barb and Rick about ten feet behind us, so the cop rousted them around for identification. By that time another officer had showed up. I just knew someone was going for a ride. I glanced at my watch and it was about ten after four in the morning. It was pitch black and the only light offered was the illumination from their flashlights. I wanted to grab my Maglite so I could see better, but I decided that wouldn't be the smartest thing to do at the moment; the cops and their dog might take the small move the wrong way and I'd have a nine-millimeter pistol shoved up my nose.

After he called all four of us in, out came the notice to appear book. All four of us received a citation for criminal trespass 2 and also stating that we must appear in court in a few weeks. What a way to start the day. None of us got a free ride to the county motel though, that was the only good thing about it.

Rick spoke up after reading his citation and asked if we could wait until daylight to move out. They said that would be okay but be gone and don't come back. They said they would come back in a few hours to check.

After they left, none of us were going back to sleep. No way would anybody sleep. I told Beth, "I'm out of here. I'm out of here *right now*." I picked up my stuff and headed down the trail with Beth, Barb, and Rick not too far behind me.

Barb and Rick went their own way so Beth and I just sat down and waited for a while. We talked about our now critical situation some more. I was running out of ideas. I told her, "If you have any ideas or brainstorms, now is the time to let me in on them."

"I have nothing, except maybe up by the ponds again."

"Do you know how risky that is? We would just get attacked by those punk teens again."

"I know, but where else can we go?"

"I don't know. There is always up the river again but it's a long ways away and the only store around charges an arm and a leg for everything."

"What about that place Ted always talks about?" she asked.

"We don't know those people and don't know what they're like. I think that's a dangerous proposition."

"Yeah, I suppose so," she concluded.

"It's almost six, let's go down and fly sign for a while then we can walk down to the little store and get some biscuits and gravy. I always think better with something in my stomach," I said as we started walking.

Flying sign that morning proved to be a real challenge; it wasn't fun at all. I didn't want to even look for something interesting to watch in the traffic. Usually we saw at least one dumb-shit run a red light or cause an accident or both but that morning, I wasn't even paying attention. The mood just wasn't there. I was too involved in wondering where we would sleep the upcoming night and beyond.

That night Beth and I were both unclear as what the next day would bring except for a lot of unanswered questions. I knew we couldn't go back on the property to sleep though, so we would have to accept the challenge and find somewhere else.

That's when the way out of this mess really came about. Somehow or another, and I don't remember how, I ended up the next morning with my foot caught in some tree roots or something. I couldn't get unstuck and Beth was of no help so she ended up calling for some help. A police officer came along and gave it his best shot and failed as well. He told Beth that he needed to call in the troops on this one.

A few minutes later the paramedics showed up and proceeded to get me out of the mess I was in. Little did they or I know that they were getting me out of a much larger mess than just getting my foot unstuck. They reefed and tugged on my ass until they got me out, then looked at my leg.

I had no idea that it was in that bad of shape when they told me, "We are going to take you in and get that leg looked at."

I don't think anyone realized, including me, that I was not only going with them to the hospital but I was also going with them to start a new life as well. I just didn't know it as I was shoved into the ambulance and delivered to the hospital.

CHAPTER 42

A WAY OUT

Being in the hospital is no fun for anyone. I had spent my fair share of time in hospitals and was hell bent on not staying that time. I called my parents to inform them that I was in the hospital when I was placed in the intensive care unit instead of the emergency room. When they put me into intensive care I knew that something was really wrong with me.

All the times in recent past that I had the pleasure of being in the hospital, it was whenever I had experienced a seizure and it freaked people out. Most people don't know what to do when a person having a seizure, so they call the paramedics and I ended up in the hospital. That was not the case this time though.

The doctor told me I had a sprained ankle, possibly a hairline fracture on my foot, and a serious infection on my leg where the scrape was. I had no idea it was that bad and they couldn't figure out how the infection became that bad so quickly. It wasn't like I took a shower daily or had the opportunity to do self-examination on a regular basis. Hell, I didn't even have a mirror to look into except when I went to use the restroom at a local business.

My parents were there at the hospital every day with me as I laid there using a portable bedside toilet having everything measured and weighed constantly. I had more hoses and wires connected to me than a modern automobile engine. It was not a pleasant experience by any means. I didn't sleep much, a person rarely does while hospitalized, partly because every time you sneeze someone needs to check you out.

While I was lying in the bed with nowhere to go I spent a lot of time thinking about what had happened to me over the last four and a half years. I tried to figure out how it all came about. I concluded that it was a series of events, not just one thing that happened to put me where I was.

I'm sure there had been a lot of talk within family, friends, co-workers and such but that's only normal. It wasn't my responsibility to change anyone's mind either. I only know what I know to be true. I will never be the same after the incident that lasted for what seemed to be an eternity.

I had met many new people; some of the best there is, and some not quite so pleasant. I found out what happened to them, where they would like to be, and what or if they could have changed things. I remember the ones as well that didn't make it through the journey. I thank God for walking me as far as he did and allowing me to take his hand while he guides me onward through the rest of my life.

As I continued to lie in that hospital, I thought also of the changes that took place deep inside me during the experience. The changes in my attitudes and the feelings I have towards people. The attitudes and feelings that I never knew before even existed within me. It took a hard solid knock to get me to the point of not being judgmental or jumping to conclusions about people on the corner holding the signs that read anything starting from, *Homeless* . . . to *Why lie* . . . I used to drive by those people in my loaded GMC Jimmy or my nice Ford Diesel pickup and tell my wife, "Look at that those freeloaders. Why don't they get off their lazy asses and get a job like everyone else?" Then I would drive home to a nice warm bed, clean clothes, and the luxuries that most people in an industrialized nation take for granted. Most days I would get up and go to my more than adequate career job saving money for an even better lifestyle.

I was finally released from the hospital and began a new life of recovery from the past; mentally, spiritually, and physically. I was in the hospital for ten days and had months of recovery left before my leg would heal. It may never be totally healed but at least I still have it. There was talk of me spending the rest of my life as an amputee. I thank God for the healing of my leg. Now he's working on my heart. Not the heart that beats, the other one.

While sitting in a comfortable chair at the beginning of the rainy season, I watched a story unfold on the nightly news. A transient, (I despise that word), who's name had not yet been released, was struck and killed by a westbound vehicle at the intersection of Main Street and the freeway. My heart stopped beating for a moment as I wondered who it might have been. Only until the news broadcast mentioned that it was a male did I realize that it couldn't have been Beth, so it must have been either Skippy or Nimrod.

The news stated, "Alcohol may have been a factor, but toxicology tests will be performed." Automatically, people who also saw the news assumed that the person must have been drunk since he was a transient. Later that night as I caught the late night news, I discovered that it was indeed Nimrod that had gotten killed, and alcohol was *not* a factor.

Even though I didn't care much for the guy, it still hit me fairly hard. Nobody deserves to leave this world without a mark of some sort. It then got me to thinking. Of all of the persons I have met that were living a difficult life without a home; I wonder what would have happened to them if they were still alive when the pendulum on the clock of life stopped and suddenly swung the other way for them. It made me think of Billy, Linda Lou, and even Nimrod. Everyone has good qualities deep inside them somewhere; sometimes it just doesn't appear on the outside very well.

Looking even deeper after the loss of Nimrod and while realizing that there are a lot of phonies out there as well as there are drug problems, alcohol problems, and people running from the law, I also realized something else. I realized that just because a person might appear to have certain problems that are on the surface and noticeable, it doesn't necessarily mean it is the only problem that person has. It may not even be a problem at all. It may be more of a symptom than a sickness. A scar that runs far beneath the surface that is only visible to people who have gotten to know that person right down to the core.

When I dig around in those memories, I find that after years of being on the top of that society mountain and slipping clear down to the very bottom, the experience will be something I will use for the rest of my life. I gained knowledge that is only obtainable through living the life. I don't think a person or even a group of people could put it into words what actually happens to a person who find themself at that bottom.

I can speak for myself when I say that when I was down to the very bottom it was dog eat dog. To the person that is at the bottom, it's like nobody cares. It doesn't matter if someone says, "I care about you!" It may strike a nerve for a moment but if the person is down so low that he or she just doesn't give a shit anymore, then that's it. That person just doesn't give a damn about him or herself, period. Therefore it is impossible for that person to give a shit about anybody else's feelings or what anyone else thinks.

When I was down that low, the only place to turn was to God. Sure, I drank the booze, and I have often thought of what I would say when someone asked why most homeless people drink. I would have to answer; *When it's twenty five degrees at three in the afternoon, and you are looking forward to a night with the low temperatures dipping in to the single digits, catching a little buzz makes things a little more bearable. That probably sounds awful. If it does sound awful, try sleeping on and under nothing but cardboard for a week in that kind of weather. You'll get it.*

These days I don't have to resort back to those ways. Fortunately, I have a home and a caring family and God has provided me with the sanity and the skills to improve life for myself and others in a way that never before seemed possible. I look at things now with a whole new perspective on life in general. Not just for me, but the ones that are out there now and will be there in the future.

It is a sad thing when a person gets into such a mess that there seems to be no way out. It is a delicate situation that cannot be ignored. It can't be blamed on anyone either. That includes the person who lives that life. There needs to be more attention and less blaming for these persons. Sure, there are the ones that won't get off the streets for whatever reason. But for those of us who are living a more comfortable life and not just simply surviving, let us remember that we don't know what happened in the lives of the ones who appear dirty and grubby or the true stories of the ones who we scowl at as we walk or drive by on the streets. What about the ones who may have a heart of gold and you'd never know it? How about the ones who would give the shirt off their back to you or the ones who cry at night because they can't sleep due to loneliness, hunger, or bitter cold? What about the ones who are so depressed that they just don't care anymore and silently cry out for the help that cannot be explained with a marker? Let us examine ourselves and then take a deep look inside those persons living one miserable day at a time, one long hour to the next and simply existing *Behind the Signs.*

The End

Made in the USA
Middletown, DE
01 September 2022

72803936R10187